DEC 0 9 2015

# MOTIVATION

## AN ATM CARD FOR SUCCESS

# MOTIVATION

## An ATM Card for Success

**Sharon Lund O'Neil, Ph.D.**

University of Houston

JOB SKILLS

NETEFFECT SERIES

Prentice
Hall

*Upper Saddle River, NJ 07458*

Library of Congress Cataloging-in-Publication Data

O'Neil, Sharon Lund.
    Motivation : an ATM card for success / Sharon Lund O'Neil.
        p.   cm.
    Includes bibliographical references and index.
    ISBN 0-13-017086-0
    1. Motivation (Psychology).    I. Title.

BF503 .O54 2002
153.8—dc21                                         2002017079

**Publisher:** *Steve Helba*
**Executive Editor:** *Elizabeth Sugg*
**Director of Production and Manufacturing:** *Bruce Johnson*
**Managing Editor:** *Mary Carnis*
**Manufacturing Buyer:** *Cathleen Petersen*
**Production Liaison:** *Brian Hyland*
**Design Director:** *Cheryl Asherman*
**Senior Design Coordinator:** *Christopher Weigand*
**Full Service Production/Formatting:** *BookMasters, Inc.*
**Editorial Assistant:** *Anita Rhodes*
**Printing and Binding:** *Von Hoffman, Owensville*
**Cover Printer:** *Coral Graphics*

Pearson Education LTD.
Pearson Education Australia PTY, Limited
Pearson Education Singapore, Pte. Ltd
Pearson Education North Asia Ltd
Pearson Education Canada, Ltd.
Pearson Educatión de Mexico, S.A. de C.V.
Pearson Education—Japan
Pearson Education Malaysia, Pte. Ltd
Pearson Education, Upper Saddle River, New Jersey

Prentice
Hall

10  9  8  7  6  5  4  3  2  1
ISBN 0-13-017086-0

# Dedication

In memory of my wonderful parents who taught me I could accomplish all of my dreams and who exemplified the best support team any person could be so fortunate to have;

To my hard-working brother, Harold, whose love, protection, and guidance I've always felt;

To my loving husband, Roger, who is definitely the most caring, supportive, and wonderful person in the whole universe;

And, to my greatly admired editor, Elizabeth Sugg, who is an exemplary role model and the true creative motivational influence behind this book—

I love you all dearly.

# Contents

# Preface

## ABOUT THE BOOK

Motivation—who needs it? Motivation is what gives meaning to life. It is what helps you get up in the morning and gives you a good feeling that you've done your best for the day you've just completed. It is what picks you up when you are discouraged and gives you the boost to go on—to succeed.

Motivation comes in all shapes and sizes. Motivation can be found in obvious and obscure places—it is free and abundant. But, to be useful; *you* must discover it; and *you* must activate it. So, who needs motivation? Everyone does, of course. And most people can't have too much of it!

Because motivation is essential for everyone, the purpose of *Motivation: An ATM Card for Success* is to help you:

a) identify, understand, and activate your motivators,

b) better understand yourself and your actions,

c) understand and appreciate the actions of others (and help them to do the same), and

d) maximize how you contribute to your own (and others') motivation for a more fulfilling life.

*Motivation: An ATM Card for Success* stresses how motivation is personal. That is, motivation is a choice each person makes—no one does it for anyone else. You as an individual, manager/leader, parent/family member, teacher/facilitator, or colleague/friend have a responsibility of being a contributing citizen of life. Thus, helping others improve their motivation is possible and highly desired for enhancing your own life as well as the lives of the people around you.

# ORGANIZATION OF THE BOOK

*Motivation: An ATM Card for Success* is an interactive book with 12 chapters organized into four sections: I: Creating the Right Motivational Atmosphere, II: Valuing the Elements of Motivation, III: Mobilizing Your Motivational Portfolio, and IV: Maximizing Strategies for Motivation. Each of the 12 chapters is independent of the other; however, Chapter 1 sets the stage for the rest of the book.

The approach taken with *Motivation: An ATM Card for Success* was to incorporate a potpourri of concepts, elements, and ideas that have significance for identifying, understanding, and applying motivation to everyday activities. The premises of motivation are reinforced and expanded throughout the book to help the reader think about their importance. To further reinforce the concepts, the reader is encouraged to get "involved" with the book by completing (and revisiting) the interactive activities and exercises. Also, instructors, facilitators, leaders, supervisors, and managers will find the book to be one that, because it is focused on the reader, can be used and applied in many diverse settings.

Many of the captions and side headings of the book are intentionally trite and nonsensical in nature, so that the reader might question and find deeper meaning in what are sometimes subtleties and absurdities of everyday life. The captions may also stimulate the reader to consider and internalize the frequently difficult and emotional topics. Additionally, the captions may help the reader remember the ideas of a section more readily because they are somewhat "nontraditional" and even "gimmicky" in their approach to the upcoming topic.

Some of the chapter components of *Motivation: An ATM Card for Success* include:

**Who's Motivated?:** Two or more short vignettes entitled "Who's Motivated?" are included in each chapter. Each one is introduced by a small ATM Card icon. These scenarios depict situations that can be considered by the reader, discussed by a group, or both. The four or five questions for each vignette are meant to get the reader involved in considering insights, values, and outcomes which are important to and affect motivation. Suggested solutions for the Who's Motivated? vignettes are provided in the back of the book.

**Value-Added Motivator:** Each chapter contains several interactive value-added motivator (VAM) activities for the reader to complete. The reader will find it very worthwhile toward maximizing motivation to give considerable thought and attention to the VAMs. In addition to taking the time to complete (and revisit) the VAMs, the reader can further enhance learning by working with another person or a group to explore the VAMs.

**Adjustments Toward Motivation:** Each chapter ends with an adjustment toward motivation (ATM), a thought-stimulating statement or saying depicted in an ATM Card box. The ATMs are included to give the reader additional thoughts to ponder for exploring and increasing motivational staying power. Suggestion: Select an ATM saying and memorize it (or post it in a prominent place) at the start of each weekend (or another specific day/time). Consider, apply, or practice the essence of the ATM saying, in as many ways as possible, over the next week.

**Motivational Reinforcement:** At the end of each chapter, 10 to 12 short answer questions are provided to reinforce the chapter narrative. While most questions usually require only a brief answer, the reader is encouraged to respond to the questions as a review of the chapter ideas, elements, and concepts. Also, because the questions sequentially follow the chapter narrative, the reader is encouraged to refer back to the chapter to check her or his responses. Suggestion: Answer all questions on the first reading of the chapter. Then take an alternating approach to the questions as a chapter is revisited in subsequent reviews: a) answer the odd numbered questions for the first review, then b) respond to the even numbered questions when the chapter is reviewed again.

## USING THE BOOK

*Motivation: An ATM Card for Success* is a multipurpose, interactive book that is appropriate for all types of people in many diverse settings. The book can offer much food for thought to individuals as well as groups. It can be very meaningful to the reader who is seeking personal improvement. It may be quite interesting to the casual reader who wants to expand his or her perspective. Also, managers and trainers will find the book extremely useful to help foster motivation and to promote better working relationships among individuals and groups. In large or small group settings, the book can be used successfully as a classroom text supplement, training tool, seminar guide, workshop supplement, and so on. The book works well as a stand-alone text supplement for a nearly endless list of courses, a topics seminar or workshop, or an add-on companion for situations where a specific focus is needed. Chapters can be selected at random; however, it is recommended that the Preface and Chapter 1 be read first.

Because the book is based on using **The Card** presented in Chapter 1, as well as having many interactive activities to which readers need to respond, anyone using the book will find it beneficial to own her or his personal copy of the book. **The Card** is intended to be a very personal, tangible icon of motivation. Leaders, teachers, facilitators, coordinators, or anyone else using the book will find many ways to apply **The Card** even if they elect to randomly select chapters or activities from the book. A leader's Guide further expands the book.

While the book can be read casually, *Motivation: An ATM Card for Success* is not intended for only a single reading. The reader is strongly encouraged to take whatever time is needed to complete the interactive parts of the book. Stopping to ponder questions is desirable. Also, the reader who revisits all or selected parts of the book and repeats the activities and exercises from time to time will, no doubt, reap additional benefits from such reviews. Motivation is not, and cannot be, a one-time event. Thus, the author hopes every reader of *Motivation: An ATM Card for Success* will also find the book to be an ongoing and enjoyable endeavor toward adding more satisfaction into his or her life and the lives of others.

## LEADER'S GUIDE

A separate publication, but an important and useful accompaniment to *Motivation: An ATM Card for Success*, is the Leader's Guide. The Leader's Guide was designed for readers to help others apply the book's premises to further expand their motivational horizons. The guide, when used in conjunction with the book, helps the reader apply and reinforce the elements and concepts of motivation.

Additionally, trainers, managers, supervisors, and leaders of motivational satisfaction will find the guide useful in many different environments including classroom, training, seminar, independent study, and workshop settings. The focus of the guide is to help the facilitator maximize her or his role by:

a) getting people to assess how they view themselves and others,

b) expanding the book's ideas via group discussions,

c) role playing to focus on ways to view things from different perspectives, and

d) exploring the book's concepts, exercises, and scenarios to seek a deeper understanding of self, others, and the environment.

The Leader's Guide is a helpful instructional tool for motivational development and offers a compilation of additional exercises and activities to augment *Motivation: An ATM Card for Success*. The Guide also can be used as a tool and an idea bank for training teachers, facilitators, supervisors, managers, and coordinators to work with individuals and groups. Any facilitator whose goal is to assist others with their personal and professional improvement will find The Guide to be a valuable supplement to *Motivation: An ATM Card for Success*.

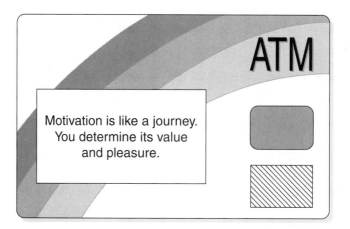

Motivation is like a journey.
You determine its value
and pleasure.

## ACKNOWLEDGMENTS

The author thanks the many special people who read parts or all of the manuscript and who offered comments and suggestions for improving the book. In particular, the author appreciated the thoughtful reviews by Kenneth Davis, Ph.D., Villanova University; Joe Meredith, Ph.D., Virginia Tech Corporate Center; and Jeffrey G. Reed, Ph.D., Marian College.

# About the Author

Sharon Lund O'Neil, author of *Motivation: An ATM Card for Success*, is a widely published author. Her human relations cases, based on the corporate work environment, are popular with both trainers and educators. With a common-sense approach to problem solving, she has led national professional and educational organizations and has been the recipient of many teaching awards. She holds a doctorate from the University of Illinois and is currently a professor at the University of Houston.

# MOTIVATION

An ATM Card for Success

# SECTION I

# Creating the Right Motivational Atmosphere

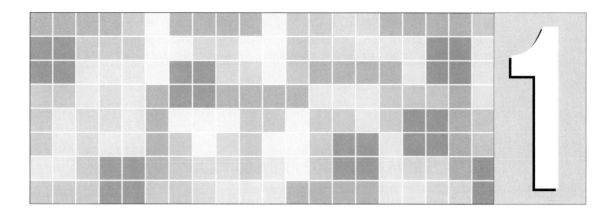

# The Exceptional Value of Owning the Card

## A MOTIVATIONAL ATM CARD?

Who me?

You're thinking, "You're kidding, right? Why would I want or need a personal Motivational ATM Card? What can I do with a Motivational ATM Card?" Frankly, owning the Card may be one of the best things you can do for yourself. Why? Because the Card is an important icon, specifically designed to give you the frame of mind or incentive for the motivation you need—when you need it the most. And, depending on how you use the Card (which, obviously, is the focus of this book), you will find there are considerable rewards and immeasurable benefits from using it. Even if you may be somewhat skeptical about owning your own personal Motivational ATM Card, you'll soon find in the chapters ahead how important the Card can be to you and those around you. It's a fairly sure bet that you'll quickly join the ranks of those who have and depend on the Card. Once you do, you'll wonder how you were able to get along without one!

What motivates you? Why? When are you motivated? Do you have the motivation you need for those really trying times? Regardless of your answers, motivation is what gives true meaning to life. Motivation is what helps you attack each day with enthusiasm, to work toward the goals you value, to "keep on keeping on" when the going gets rough, and to look back on what you've done and be happy with the result. Motivation is essential to your well being; and the more you know about motivation and how it can work for you, the more you will find enjoyment in the added pleasure it gives to you.

With your own personal Motivational ATM Card, you have a ready reminder that you can maximize your motivation toward enjoying life more fully. Your own personal Motivational ATM Card carries with it many privileges and benefits that you may never have considered. And, if the Card is used frequently on a daily basis (and it should be), the benefits can be rather astounding and quite far reaching. But, before we get too far into why and how a Motivational ATM Card can be so vital to you, it is necessary to identify what makes carrying the Card so important. (If you haven't done so, you may wish to refer to the Preface for an overview and components of the book. The Preface also points out ways to use the interactive parts of the book to your best advantage.)

## THE FREEDOM OF CHOICE AND RECIPROCITY

There is nothing like having the freedom to do nearly anything you want to do—to live and work where you want; to have as many friends as you wish; to eat, shop, and travel where you want; to wear the clothes and buy the things you like; to conduct business and form friendships via e-mail and over the Internet; and to talk and communicate with anyone you desire—just to name a few. Freedom is an important state or way of life for many people in the free world. It is a state, however, that most of us take for granted. Freedom to do what we want—when, where, how, and with whom—is a privilege, as long as we use discretion in the way we apply acceptable practices (rules and laws) that govern the situation. Take Valerie, for example:

### Who's Motivated?

Valerie recently became a night guard at a major downtown bank. Previously she worked nights at a local convenience store just around the corner from where she lives. Her parents live next door, but they don't see her very often. Valerie's parents are rather upset about her career move because they are concerned for her safety—she now wears a security uniform, carries a weapon, and parks in the bank's underground parking garage. Even though Valerie has assured her parents that the bank has never had any type of criminal incident, they cannot believe she left her job of four years to put herself in such danger. Valerie believes she has made an ideal career choice, in spite of the risks, because she now works shorter hours. Also, she has a good excuse to continue going to the firing range for target practice, a sport she learned from her dad. And, she reasons, what a great way to spend more time with her dad doing things they both really like to do.

1.  As Valerie takes on the authority and responsibility of her new job, what consequences could be associated with her possible actions and choices?

2.  Do you believe Valerie has made a good career choice? Why or why not?

3.  Do Valerie's parents have good reason to be concerned about her new job? Why or why not? How did they possibly contribute to her decision?

4.  What are the pros and cons for Valerie and her parents in comparing Valerie's previous job with the one she now has?

Because Valerie really likes her new job and wants to spend more time with her dad, she's confident her parents will warm up to the job choice she has made.

In turn, she and her parents can enjoy the reciprocity of doing things together. Freedom to choose what you want to do, when you want to do it, and with whom is based on reciprocity. That is, you cannot expect to receive if you don't give.

Alternatively, you know you will wear out your welcome if you sit on the doorstep of someone who doesn't want you there. If you can't find a way to establish reciprocity, you may need to look for other avenues to find enjoyment. So, go away and get a life! Find another place to channel your energies—a place where you are appreciated, a place that gives you enjoyment and satisfaction, a place that is rewarding and is based on reciprocity.

Reciprocity applies to nearly everything you do in life; that is, if you are nice to someone, the other person probably will be nice to you. If you treat someone badly, you, too, may reap some adverse behavior. Reciprocity is based on consequences; and frequently there are consequences associated with getting up too late, eating too much, shopping too often, driving too fast, . . . the list goes on and on.

In the case of your finances, reciprocity has special meaning since the process of spending carries certain assumptions, responsibilities, limitations, and outcomes. One underlying principle of finance reciprocity is that you have to have money in the bank or a credit account if you expect your checks and charges to be covered. The freedom we enjoy of writing checks and of using a charge or debit card is based on an honor system of reciprocity: being certain not to extend your credit any further than your worth.

This reciprocity concept of mutual dependence also can be applied to nearly everything—even to personal attributes such as emotions. If you consider how the reciprocity of your emotional state relates to your emotional bank account, you probably know when your emotional bank is full—you are happy. Others around you can see the effect of your full emotional bank as your happiness may be projected as friendliness and helpfulness—and they enjoy being around you. Your happiness makes you feel good. Happiness is a good reward. It is the reciprocity of keeping a positive attitude. Further, your attitude is extended to those around you. Your freedom to project your happiness is shared by others who, too, have the freedom to accept or reject your emotional state. If they choose to reap the benefits of reciprocity, the yield can translate into mutual rewards for everyone. Thus, as long as certain rules are followed, we can fully enjoy many freedoms—freedoms that include privileges of expression, projecting a positive attitude, and enjoying life.

## YOUR OWN PERSONAL MOTIVATIONAL ATM CARD

There is probably no better example of full reciprocity than having a Motivational ATM Card. Owning and using your own personal Motivational ATM Card gives you freedom because it provides rewards both for you and for others. As you use the Card, it gives you pleasure, satisfaction, and peace of mind. And when the Card is used frequently, the rewards are also more frequent and satisfying.

So why doesn't everyone have a Motivational ATM Card? The answer is simple: Most people don't know they need one! What is worse, many of the people who need the Card most are the last to see they really need it. Let's look at what a Motivational ATM Card is and what it can do for you.

A personal Motivational ATM Card represents a wealth of motivators that are present in your surroundings—motivators that are out there just for the taking! The Card is the icon that suggests you should strive to find pleasure or enjoyment in everything you do. This is not to say there may not be negative moments, but the Card provides a great opportunity for you to enjoy life more by giving you the freedom to choose the things that make you happy. And the Card increases in its value every time you use it because the more you use it, the greater its value and personal satisfaction.

The Card is convenient and it's easy to use. It can be used 24 hours a day, 7 days a week. Unlike a conventional ATM card, there is no application fee, no approval, no interest to pay, and no monthly payments with your Card. There are no penalties or negatives for using the Card. And what is even more remarkable, the Card is more than affordable to everyone—it is *free*! You can have the Card right now and begin using it immediately to enjoy its benefits. The many benefits of the Card and how to maximize your Card, for yourself and others, is the focus of the rest of this book.

With no risk whatsoever, you can't afford not to at least *try* the Card. To make it easy to get started, here's your own personal Motivational ATM Card. Take the Card out of the back of this book and give it a whirl! Read further to find out how to discover and capitalize on the enjoyment and satisfaction you can derive from being a Card holder.

I, _____, control my destiny. It is up to me to enjoy life and help others do the same. By understanding myself and learning why others do as they do, I can assist them to make the most out of their lives and, in turn, I will find more enjoyment and satisfaction for myself.

**ATM**

☐ I will keep my attitude positive and guard it as my most prized possession.

☐ I will take quick action to replace my negative thoughts with positive ones.

☐ I will turn up the air-conditioning before my emotions overheat.

☐ I will learn more about myself to channel my actions in positive directions.

☐ I will continuously work on my weaknesses to mold them into strengths.

If you haven't already done so, remove the Card. Read the fine print—the conditions—on the Card. Now reread the Card and make a commitment to the conditions of it. To activate the Card and begin enjoying its benefits, you need to sign it. Do it now!

Can you feel the power of the Card? If so, you're on your way to reaching greater satisfaction for yourself! If, however, right now, you can't feel the Card's power, you will be pleasantly surprised how easy it is to make progress toward making the Card work for you. Of course, the greater the effort on your part, the more you will see the benefits of the Card. In fact, the effort you expend to seek out and find enjoyment and satisfaction will be proportionately significant to the Card's rewards.

In the chapters ahead, you will find many ways to control your destiny toward getting more enjoyment and satisfaction out of the things you do every day. Most of the ideas presented in the chapters can be applied to all types of situations to help you find the motivation you desire and need. As a manager or supervisor, you'll find benefits of the Card for your work group. As a student, you'll find value in using the Card for career success. The Card is for you at whatever stage in life you are—no matter your age, ethnicity, status, position, or affiliation. Motivation is for everyone and everyone needs it. When you're motivated, it is reflected to those around you. And when relationships with your family members, work associates, and friends are enhanced by your motivation, everyone benefits.

Finally, using the Card is probably the easiest thing you will ever do. Making a commitment to discover how the Card can work for you may be the best reward you have ever given yourself. The Card can help you through difficulties and it can give you a lift when you need it. Best of all, you can share your Card with others—and let them benefit from your having the Card (and you can tell them how they can get their own Card, too). As others around you also use the Card, you truly get bonus rewards for yourself. So, if you have not picked up the Card and signed it, *do it right now*. Sign your personal Card and carry it with you. Remember, once you learn how to use your Card, you'll find the more you use it the more you benefit from its value. Can you think of anything else in life that comes with such promising benefits?

## YOUR NO-RISK INVESTMENT

If you applied for a credit or debit card that may have been sent to you in the mail, you assume considerable responsibility. You must be careful not to go over your credit limit and you must pay your account when it is due. You may also find that with certain cards there are only a select few ATM locations where you can access your account. You may have limited ability to make withdrawals or debits from your account. While you have been given the authority to use your card, you have considerable responsibility and accountability for its use.

In a similar way, you have responsibility and accountability for your Motivational ATM Card. The responsibility and accountability, however, come with a no-risk, nothing-to-lose investment. With the Card, you have nothing to lose—only to gain. By accepting the Card, you accept the idea that you want happiness by staying motivated. You accept the premise that it is important to improve yourself, and to help those around you, even though it may be very difficult to do.

*FREE!*
*NO RISK!*

Your desire for self-improvement is what life is all about—to be the best you can be, to be the keeper of your own destiny. And that's why managers and leaders, especially, can expand their influence via the Card.

Using the Card will make your daily life more fulfilling. It will give you the motivation to go on when the going is tough. It will give you the stamina to go the extra mile when it's needed. And the Card will make you a winner—with no risk—to enjoy the rewards of your efforts.

## COMMITMENT DEPOSITS

Although there is no risk to the Card, it does require commitment. The commitment does not need to be great, but, as already noted, the rewards are directly proportional to your commitment. Thus, if your commitment deposit to your Card account is significant, you can expect significant returns on your investment. There is still no risk, but you need to be responsible for your actions. That is, you will need to make commitment deposits on a regular basis for your Card account to remain open and active.

What does commitment mean to you? Do you feel you can benefit from helping others? Can you help someone if you know there is nothing in it for you? Do you see an exciting challenge in most everything you do? Commitment, just as many things in life, has various meanings to people. Frequently the meaning of commitment may change depending upon how involved you may be in the situation in which commitment is a factor. To assess your feelings about commitment, take the following quiz to determine your commitment quotient.

| **Value-Added Motivator** | MY COMMITMENT QUOTIENT |
| --- | --- |

Circle the best answer for each item. It may be difficult to select only one answer for each item; however, try not to linger too long in selecting the one choice that best describes how you feel.

1. If my friends were to describe me, they'd say I am
    a. compassionate
    b. honest
    c. smart

2. For my flower garden to be beautiful, the most important thing for me to do is to
    a. water and fertilize it
    b. weed it
    c. plant flowers that compliment each other

3. Computers, with temperaments of their own, need operators who
    a. find the tool useful
    b. have patience
    c. enjoy exploring

4. Taking a busy route to work, school, or to the store
   a. may be avoided if I choose the time of day I travel
   b. is usually the best route
   c. is usually very slow

5. If given my choice for a vacation to do anything I want, I would choose
   a. a cruise or safari
   b. just to be left alone
   c. a shopping spree

6. Spending a day in the hospital visiting a friend who is ill is
   a. a satisfying experience
   b. depressing
   c. my duty

7. Given my choice of getting any wish, I would
   a. carefully consider my first priority
   b. ask for money
   c. not worry about the answer since it's not going to happen

8. The ideal friend is someone who
   a. cares about me
   b. takes the brunt of my mistakes
   c. has lots of charisma and charm

9. If you fill a glass with water to the half-way mark, the glass
   a. is half full
   b. is half empty
   c. has water in it, but the volume cannot be determined

10. I enjoy the weekends mostly because I can
    a. take a break from my job
    b. have a total change of pace
    c. reenergize myself

SCORING: Give yourself 10 points for each "A" answer; 8 points for each "B" answer; and 6 points for each "C" answer. If you scored 90 or above, you probably have a very strong commitment factor. If you scored between 75 and 89, you are someone who can be counted on "most of the time" if you are interested in the task at hand. Any score below 75 suggests you may frequently question making a commitment. In Chapter 2 you'll have the opportunity to identify your motivators. Throughout the book you will be able to identify new motivators and reinforce your existing motivators. As you do, you'll be able to apply the significant factors and elements needed to make satisfying commitments.

While the results of "My Commitment Quotient," may not have scientific merit, it does tell you something about your feelings. You may find it easy to make a commitment under some circumstances, yet extremely difficult to make a commitment under certain other circumstances. In the latter case, learning more about what motivates you can help you to more fully appreciate the type, nature, extent, and value of your commitments. You will also be more cognizant of how others perceive your commitments and how you can enjoy increasing your commitment quotient.

In actuality, your commitment quotient can be increased with the use of the Card. That is, as you use your Card, you actually make commitment deposits. The size of each deposit is dependent on the significance of the type and value of your commitment. If your commitment wanes, you may find a fee or interest associated with your Card account. The "fee," in essence, becomes the price you must pay (or added effort you need to take) when you slack off on your commitment. Thus, if you fall back on your commitment, you may need to pay a fee (expend more effort) or even be assessed "interest" (expend an even greater effort if you've let time slip away) to regain your momentum.

While owning your Card truly is a no-risk investment, the lack of significant gains may cost you in the end if you don't make a commitment to your Card. Using your Card toward achieving your desired goals is the best way to assure your Card can offer significant and rewarding benefits. And, along the way, there will be many alternatives provided to enhance the Card's benefits. You'll no doubt want to share your successes with others who could also benefit from knowing about some of the positive benefits of the Card.

## NO MONEY DOWN TO THOSE WITH POSITIVE ATTITUDES

The Card is designed to provide the benefits to anyone who wants to have a more enjoyable and rewarding life. Its ultimate value comes when its owner has a positive attitude. In fact, the Card's commitment deposit, to even the most doubting, can become automatic as one becomes more positive, and assuming a positive attitude expends much less energy than being negative. For example, a positive person will look at a problem as a challenge rather than as a roadblock. An "it can be done" approach is one way to move toward reaping benefits of the Card. Once a problem, obstacle, or situation is viewed as a challenge, it is possible to think more positively about how to meet that challenge. And using a positive approach to problem solving is a commitment to being positive. In subsequent chapters of the book, you'll find a variety of ways, ideas, and activities to foster a more positive attitude. For example, here's an activity for becoming more aware of the ways a more positive attitude can be developed.

| **Value-Added Motivator** | "I CAN" BE MORE POSITIVE |
|---|---|

For each of the following items, complete the statement by adding an action verb and what steps you can take to be more positive. As you complete each of the items, consider the steps you can take immediately as well as long term.

1. I can be a better friend by

    _____

    _____

2. In my work or school relationships, I will

    _____

    _____

3. Around my family members I can

    _____

    _____

4. Over the weekend I will

    _____

    _____

5. Today, the first day of the rest of my life, I will

    _____

    _____

Review and modify each statement as necessary to reflect action that you can take immediately. Can you start now to put your action statements into practice? If you don't think so, consider what it will take to get you started to take action now, even if your action starts with and is incremented in rather small steps.

As you accomplish some part or all of one of your "I Can" items, ask yourself, "How do I feel about my accomplishment?" If you don't feel good about what you did, refocus the item until you find an action that makes you feel good. Note: You may not be excited about what you *need* to do, about what you *should* do, or even about what you *want* to do. But what you *have done*—your accomplishment—has been worth the effort. By focusing on the end result, you may be able to initiate action much more readily.

Even when each action you take becomes a routine accomplishment, continue to review and modify your "I Can" action statements. Make each one more and more challenging toward becoming more and more positive in all aspects of your life. As you do, you are using your Card to help you be positive. Remember: At first, not everyone may react to you in a positive way. But, over time, your positive attitude will be catching and it will help others to be more positive too.

## KEEPING YOUR CARD ACTIVATED

Carrying your Motivational ATM Card is a privilege. Using the Card enhances the privilege. That is, if you use the Card regularly, you will increase the value of the Card because you extend the Card's privilege beyond your immediate sphere. As others see you as a motivated, positive person, most people cannot help becoming more motivated and positive too.

The way the Card is used is truly up to you—and it is the purpose of this book to give you lots of ideas for keeping your Card activated. But the ultimate decision as to how you use the Card depends on your finding ways that work for you to maximize the Card's benefits. It is up to you. Part of your challenge is to maximize your Card for yourself; another more far-reaching challenge is in getting others to respond to you in ways so that both of you become more motivated to do positive things.

Maximizing the benefits of the Card depends on how well you can keep the Card activated. Keeping the Card activated may seem difficult, but it is really quite easy—all you need to do is use the Card on a regular and frequent basis. Thus, it is as easy as making a commitment to do something you enjoy. And because having and using the Card is a privilege, it is wise to periodically renew your commitment to value it. Renewing your commitment to the Card may take frequent and conscious efforts on your part. But, if you let yourself take the Card for granted, you have lessened its benefits and need to quickly renew your commitment to using it. Yes, it bears repeating: The more you use the Card, the more you benefit from its use; and others around you will benefit, too.

## ELECTRONIC TRANSACTIONS AND SECURITY FEATURES

Most everything you do in life carries some risks, cautions, and consequences with it. For example, if you cook with the stove element turned on high, you may risk burning your food. If you drive on a newly paved street, your car may get spattered with oil. If you leave your wallet in a public place, you may lose your valuables to someone who may claim your possessions as their own.

Your Card, and what it stands for, also needs to be protected and treated with care. Just as you protect the things you value, you need to place a value on your Card. The more you value it, the more you will take precautions to protect it from abuse. If you think of your Card as a prized possession, you will treat it as such. You would never leave your valuables unsecured, even for a period of time, if you knew the risk was high for losing them. Treat your Card the same way and the motivation it provides to you can work for you throughout your entire life. In the chapters that follow, you'll be provided with a number of ideas and ways to help you care for and protect your Card.

# BECOMING A CITIZEN OF MOTIVATION

The Card should be viewed as a convenient means of giving you a lift when you need it. In essence it is a debit card—except you don't need to find an ATM location to use it. As a debit card, it needs your attention. That is, the more you pay into it, the more you can use it. To pay into your Card, you know that all you have to do is make a commitment to yourself that your Card is important. If you trust in the importance of your Card, it will be easy to make a commitment. Thus, paying into your Card is as simple as anything you do frequently. For you to maximize your Card's benefits, making a commitment to your Card must become an important part of things you do on a routine basis.

Routine matters and tasks sometime get forgotten because they are taken for granted. If you find yourself forgetting to pay into your Card, you doubt the worth of the Card and you may begin to lose your motivation to be positive. Others around you will probably quickly sense your negativism, or at least your lack of positivism. As a result, you could lose interest in a lot of things. Consider Bob, for example:

## Who's Motivated?

Bob, an instructor in the state community college system, cannot understand why his students are so unreceptive to him. He is always prepared, has content-rich lectures, and presents the material in a sequential manner. Furthermore, the subject matter on networking communications is really exciting, interesting, and needed by everyone today. Bob doesn't understand why some students come to class late—if at all. And frequently others neither have their projects completed on time nor seem to take pride in their work. Bob doesn't have time to meet with his students outside of class; however, he has told the class, time and time again, they must be more responsible. He has cautioned them that probably 50 percent of the class will be unhappy with their final grades, but he stands firm on his policy of not discussing grades.

1. What are some of the reasons Bob's students seem so disinterested in a class that has such relevant subject matter?

2. Could Bob, as well as his students, lack a commitment to the class? Why or why not? Discuss the rationale for your answer.

3. What suggestions do you have for Bob's students to improve their interest and enthusiasm for the class?

4. How could Bob contribute to his own motivation as well as to that of the class?

5. What do you speculate will be the end result (for the class/for Bob) if nothing changes?

Everyone gets discouraged once in a while, but you cannot stay in a negative state of mind very long before it affects your whole life and others around you. You can "visit" discouragement as a tourist, but don't let yourself become a citizen of it. If you think of the Card as a debit card to which you will give your commitment to be positive, you can avoid becoming a citizen of negativism. Your commitment to be positive is the first step in becoming more positive—a commitment to become a positive permanent citizen of motivation.

## THE TOP 20 BEST SELLER LIST

What are the factors or elements that contribute to your positive attitude? You probably can think of several right now. But do you know that most of them also are or can be turned into motivators? What are the powerful motivators that make you want to wake up and start a new day, to seek out new challenges, and to find ways to reach your potential? While you'll be given an opportunity to identify your motivators in subsequent chapters, here's a listing of what are considered the 20 most powerful motivators. Circle the items on the list that you feel are good motivators for you.

| TOP 20 MOTIVATORS | | | |
|---|---|---|---|
| loving/being loved | expertise | working hard | family |
| expressing values | happiness | helping others | politics |
| accomplishment | leadership | competition | religion |
| humor/laughter | challenge | satisfaction | money |
| positive attitude | creativity | praise/honor | exercise |

Obviously this is not an exhaustive list. But you may be able to easily identify with some items while totally rejecting others. Why do some of the items on the list pop out as important to you and others don't?

Let's look at how this listing can be turned into benefits of your Card. First, cross out any of the motivators on the list you feel are not important to you and exchange the rejected items for others you consider more important. Write your substitution next to the crossed-out item.

What conclusion can you draw from your final listing of 20 items? With each item on your list, can you associate a specific activity that is a real motivator for you—an action that you do or can do; an action that gives you pleasure and sustains your positiveness into another activity? List three such activities here:

1. _____

2. _____

3. _____

If you can compare your listing with those of three or four other persons, do it. Discuss the items to determine a) if you want to further modify your list and

b) if the group can come to a consensus on at least 15 important motivators. What do you believe can be gained (or what can be learned) from such a discussion and comparison?

It shouldn't be too difficult to conclude from this exercise that you probably have learned something about yourself (as well as something about some of your friends or coworkers). Your Card now has meaning; it has been initialized with the magnetic strip of motivators that you believe are important to you. You can use the Card—immediately—especially if you employ an action associated with one of your motivators. While you may not have the same motivators tomorrow as you identified today, the important thing is that you've started to identify the value and benefits of owning the Card.

## MY INVESTMENT IN THE CARD'S BENEFITS

When it comes right down to it, it is nearly impossible to list or identify all the benefits of the Card. Why? Because some of the Card's benefits are a direct result of how and when you use your Card. That is, if you go ahead and complete a task you don't really want to do, but know you must get done, you have accomplished something. You probably feel good that you completed the task. You are pleased with the result and like what you've done even though it may have been drudgery while you were doing it. The end result, however, or the satisfaction of a project completed, may be a strong motivator for you to dive into yet another project.

The satisfaction you get from an accomplishment, no matter how small, is a motivator in itself. The accomplishment serves as a boost to your expectations. By raising your expectations through a sense of accomplishment, you have raised your level of motivation. There is nothing like feeling you have succeeded. And one success breeds another success. What has happened with your success is that you have positioned yourself to tackle another project with more enthusiasm. And your good feeling and positive attitude are projected to those with whom you have contact. Again, everyone benefits.

Throughout this book you will have many opportunities to maximize your motivation. The ideas, activities, and exercises are offered for you to ponder and to apply as you wish; that is, it is up to *you* to decide what to do about and with them. If you approach the activities and exercises with vigor and a positive attitude, you'll find equally satisfying benefits. Muster as much energy as you can to complete the activities and projects that are interspersed throughout the chapters. Expand the concepts and exercises by entering into discussion and debate with others. As you do, take advantage of the exceptional value of your Motivational ATM Card to be positive in your thinking and actions.

Finally, each time you encounter a roadblock in life, take out your Card and use it as a positive motivator to find the detours that give you encouragement and satisfaction to reach your fullest potential. No doubt you'll find many, many benefits of owning the Card. As you do, you'll be the ultimate winner. Good luck.

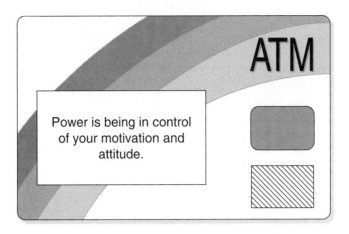

## CHAPTER 1: MOTIVATIONAL REINFORCEMENT

Reinforce your understanding of the chapter by responding to the following items.

1. What is a personal Motivational ATM Card and who can get one?

2. Explain the importance of the statement, "the freedom to choose is based on reciprocity."

3. Why is the significance of owning a personal Motivational ATM Card so important?

4. Describe how your motivation can affect others around you.

5. What makes the Card different from other cards?

6. Why is making a commitment (especially to the Card) so important?

7. Discuss how problems are viewed by positive people.

8. Describe how the value of the Card truly is determined.

9. Why is it important to identify your motivators?

10. How is accomplishment associated with motivation?

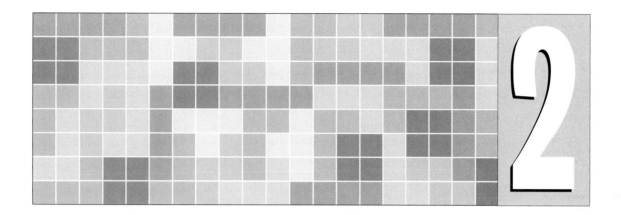

# Sugar and Spice and Everything Nice: What Motivates *You*?

## MY PERSONAL HELP DESK

Having your own Motivational ATM Card is like having your own personal help desk—a place to get the assistance you need when you need it the most. As with a help desk, the Card is there to give you support; it provides many benefits that should not be underestimated. How is it possible that your Motivational ATM Card can do this? As you read further, you will find the Card is truly a powerful personal tool that gives you assistance, and even reminders and incentives, to help motivate you to action.

Motivation is a state of mind that is influenced by your environment. When the surroundings are positive, it is easy for most people to be positive and supportive. But when the environment gets negative, it is more difficult to stay on track. If the environment stays negative for a period of time, it will be even harder to become motivated to positive action. Especially if you are a supervisor or manager, it is important to get the negative environment turned around quickly because your influence to help others become motivated to positive action may be critical to the welfare of a great number of people—on and off the job. Your Card, as you begin to understand its potential and power, acts as a positive influence for enhancing your total environment.

Motivation, to be long term and truly beneficial, must come from a source that is constant and controlled. The best way to keep motivation continuous is to understand what motivates you so you can control your motivation. You need to know when to "turn up" your motivation to stay positive (and help others do the same). As you experience ups and downs of life, it is the counteraction to each event that suggests when (and what type of) motivation needs to be increased. That is, the peaks and valleys you have and the extent to which you have them determines the degree to which you need motivation. Because you are the one who determines when, how, and where you are motivated, you are the best person to meet the challenges that may cause your motivation to fluctuate.

Once you recognize your fluctuations and how they affect you, you can control the fluctuations and help yourself to meet the challenges that require different degrees of motivation. Your Motivational ATM Card becomes the reminder to help you determine what motivators are best for the situation as well as the timing and proper balance of the motivators.

## ORCHIDS AND ONIONS

In some situations a motivator may become a demotivator or a negative motivator which you should adamantly avoid. A good example of a motivator that can become a demotivator is a food you enjoy. Chocolate, for example, is enjoyed by many people. It can be a good motivator, especially if a special chocolate dessert is your reward for something you have accomplished or is your special pick-me-up. However, if you are on a diet where chocolate is to be avoided, you actually may feel depressed if you know you should not reward yourself with the chocolate dessert. And if you eat the dessert (and possibly overindulge in it), deviating from your diet, you may become even further depressed. In this case, chocolate has become a demotivator, and you may feel worse than when you felt you needed a chocolate boost.

| Value-Added Motivator | MY FAVORITE MOTIVATOR |
|---|---|

At this point, see if you can identify one thing that motivates you. Complete this sentence: "Frequently I can be motivated by

_____

_____."

What you have just done is identify something that makes you feel good, gives you a boost, or spurs you to action. In general, a motivator is something positive—or at least is viewed as positive for you. How is the motivator you described positive for you? Complete this sentence: "The motivator I described above is positive for me because

_____

_____."

On the other hand, a demotivator usually is negative. Can you determine whether or not the motivator you just identified can be a negative for you? If so, describe how your motivator can also be a demotivator for you. Complete this sentence: "The motivator I just described can be a demotivator to me when

_____

_____."

Taken one step further, you probably can see that motivators are not the same for everyone. A motivator for you may even be a demotivator for someone else. That is, what motivates you may not motivate someone else and may even be so negative for the other person that it is a demotivator.

Can you see how the motivator you described can be a demotivator for someone else? Complete this sentence: "The motivator I just described may be a demotivator to someone else because

_____

_____."

A motivator that you value may be viewed by you as an orchid, whereas someone else may see it as an onion. You think the orchid is pretty, smells nice, and gives you a lift. The other person views the motivator as harsh, pungent, and possibly distasteful. The onion may even cause the other person to shed some tears. Keep in mind, however, that both motivators and demotivators change for most people. There are many contributing factors as to why this happens. Consider the following scenario:

## Who's Motivated?

Jack and Charlie met in the park where both had brought their children to play. As their children ran off to the swings, Jack said to Charlie, "I came here to have some quality time with my kids and look—all they want to do is go off and play on the swings." Charlie smiled at Jack, but did not respond.

1. Why was Jack so disappointed his children wanted to play on the swings?

2. How do you believe his children feel about a) going to the park and b) their father taking them to the park?

3. What was Charlie probably thinking when he smiled at Jack?

4. If Jack could reflect on the benefits of taking his children to the park, how might he feel about the experience as well as about himself?

5. Consider the elements related to the park experience and draw at least three conclusions from this scenario.

_____

_____

_____

Reflecting on the experience of Jack and Charlie, you can see how your expectations influence your motivation. Frequently your expectations involve three of the most important factors of motivation: timing, balance, and saturation. But, before we discuss these and other factors that contribute to motivation, let's consider some of the ways you can meet (and possibly exceed) your expectations.

## PROPELLED BY HIGH OCTANE FUEL

What makes you tick? How much effort can you give to an activity without giving up? What constitutes your motivators? The answers are dependent on what it takes to keep you on track and focused in the right direction. For example, if you drive a vehicle that requires high octane fuel, you know you will not get the desired results from your car or truck unless you fill the tank with the right fuel. If your car requires premium gas, you wouldn't think of filling your tank with regular. Why? Because you know the end result probably will be less than you expect—your car ends up sputtering or possibly not running at all. Does a manager-leader need to be concerned about how this analogy may be applied to all the employees in a work setting? Of course; because a good manager will provide the leadership to influence others to want to produce significant results.

The same is true for reaching various levels of motivation. Pump in just a little low grade fuel (effort), and you'll get—at best—just a bit of energy (motivation) to move you on your way. But pump in the right octane that matches your expectations, and you'll be propelled. The key is finding the motivators that propel you into positive action. Can you identify what propels you to a more positive you—a person who is motivated to action? As a starter to answering this question, complete the following exercise.

| **Value-Added Motivator** | **WHAT PROPELS ME?** |
| --- | --- |

For each of the following items, indicate by a rating of 1 (lowest) to 10 (highest) how much you enjoy or are motivated by the activity. Enter your rating in the blank to the left of each item.

_____   1. Taking a day off (vacation day, weekend, etc.) is important for me to get back into my routine with more interest.

_____   2. If I can participate in or be a spectator at a sports activity (golf, tennis, soccer, basketball, running, etc.), I get reenergized for other things.

_____   3. Listening to music helps me to relax and enjoy my surroundings more.

_____   4. Completing a project before or by the expected deadline (self- or otherwise imposed) gives me great satisfaction.

_____   5. Competing in a contest with a friend or colleague (watching or playing a competitive game) gives me self-assurance and confidence.

_____   6. After spending some time with people I enjoy being around, I usually feel better than I did before we got together.

_____ 7. Talking on the phone with a friend, writing a note to a relative, or communicating with someone I like is enjoyable and stress reducing.

_____ 8. Reading a book, gardening, cooking, jogging, resting, or _____ gives me an inner peace of mind.

_____ 9. Daydreaming about things I enjoy or brainstorming ways to do something better helps me to approach things in a more vigorous way.

_____ 10. After time away from my present surroundings (even for a work-related seminar or workshop), I am more appreciative of what I have.

_____ 11. Doing something nice for someone makes me feel good inside and lessens some of the tension I have.

_____ 12. Exercising is enjoyable and gives me a lift because I know I am doing something that is good for me.

_____ 13. Being creative is one of the most enjoyable things I can do to make my environment pleasant.

Even if you feel some of the above items need to be "split" or changed for you to give an unqualified answer, don't be concerned about the details at this point. Give yourself some leeway and take the most positive approach you can to respond to each of the items. Review your answers.

How many of the 13 items did you rate high? If you rated at least half of the items as a 9 or 10, you probably can be motivated by a wide variety of activities. If you rated most of the items with a 6 to 8, you probably can find enjoyment in many things, but need to make a little more effort to find your niche. If your ratings were 5 or below on most items, you cannot afford to let your Motivational ATM Card out of your sight—even for a minute! Regardless of your ratings, you most assuredly will benefit from learning how to use your Card effectively by finding significant ways to let your Card enhance your life.

## LUCKY IS WHAT LUCKY DOES

Frequently, the more effort you put into something, the more you get out of it. Motivation usually falls into this category—output yields more than the input. It's like the saying, "Luck is what you get when you work hard." Your propensity for being motivated depends on how interested you are in the activity, what action you take, how quickly you commence that action, and how satisfying the results are.

Success is satisfaction; and usually there are progressive steps to reach the ultimate satisfaction. Successful supervisors and managers, for example, know that if a team starts out too aggressively on a complicated project, some members of the team may soon lose interest because the project may be too big to accomplish according to the prescribed standards (time, effort, and so on). The same principle can be applied to everything you do. That is, if you attack a project or activity step by step, you will probably find you can succeed with just a little effort.

And each success is the motivation you need to be willing to take the next step toward what initially may have been an impossible goal. You have succeeded with many steps or mini-goals that have given you the motivation to take the next step toward the overall goal. You'll now be more successful because you are focused on success and you are motivated to succeed. You have the confidence and the frame of mind to move forward.

## GRIND THE PEPPERCORNS FOR PALATABILITY

Success and motivation, as you know, are firmly rooted in your state of mind. If you are tired, lethargic, anxious, depressed, under stress, or experiencing a variety of other such things—some of which you may not even be aware—your state of mind may stand in the way of your being motivated. That is, motivation is your "will to action" and it takes some effort on your part. Your environment—a situation which usually includes timing, balance, and saturation of several other elements—comes into play to provide the stimulus for action. If you *feel* you cannot exert the needed effort, your state of mind has influenced your effort or lack of it—the very reason you may want to dissect each project or activity into smaller tasks or mini-goals.

By identifying small tasks of a large project, you are more apt to see there really is a light at the end of the tunnel that cuts through the darkness. Frequently it is just a little flicker of light that may be all that is needed to motivate you to some type of action. A little action can lead to bigger and bigger actions. What is needed for the activity to continue? Is it to determine the importance and significance of the action? The size or extent of the action is not as important as taking the initiative to begin an activity. Getting started may be very difficult at any stage of an activity—even for the smallest job—because of the effort required.

For motivation to occur at any level, each of the action tasks, steps, or mini-goals should require some effort to reach. If you skip any one of the incremental steps, take steps that are too large, or do them in a random order, there is risk that the overall goal may not be attainable. That is, your overall goal may not be realistic or realized if you don't make the effort to accomplish sequential and incremental stages along the way. Consider a recipe that requires pepper for balanced seasoning. Whole peppercorns may look great, but grinding the peppercorns to disperse the flavor may make all the difference in the world. A few whole peppercorns could actually spoil the recipe. By grinding the pepper into smaller parts, you can add the seasoning at the appropriate place and time to maximize flavor. The ground pepper can be properly mixed and blended with the other ingredients. If a gourmet dish can be enhanced in appearance (and taste) by freshly ground pepper on top, it doesn't make sense to take this step earlier than at its prime time. Thus, when added at the most desirable time and in proper amounts, the presentation and palatability of the end result can be delightfully successful.

## Who's Motivated?

Marshall wants to move up in his career. He is a licensed physician's assistant, but really wants to be a physician. He feels he knows just about as much as the doctors do about the patients in his care. Furthermore, he certainly has a lot more charisma than most of the doctors he knows. However, he has been reprimanded time and again by his supervisor for "playing doctor." Now his career is in jeopardy because he continually goes beyond his medical expertise.

1. If Marshall is motivated to become a physician, why hasn't he taken some action to be one?

2. Do you believe he may have a realistic goal? Why or why not?

3. What are some of the ways his supervisor can be helpful to him?

4. What advice would you offer to Marshall to ensure he will be more successful at whatever career he chooses?

A goal must be something you can actually attain or believe you can accomplish. While some goals may be easily attained, it is obvious that others may be more difficult. Goals that are most successfully attained are those that take a certain amount of effort to reach. Goals that are within easy reach can be motivators to reach higher level goals or goals that are more difficult to reach. The point is: Unless you make an effort to attain something, your level of satisfaction is not as great as it could be had you worked for the end result. That is, a motivator that comes too easily will not sustain your interest or momentum until you make some type of effort that gives you satisfaction. Whether you are a student, an employee, or a head of a company, becoming good at reaching goals usually depends on becoming quite astute to your total surroundings. Paying attention to your own needs, level of interest, and momentum—as well as being alert to the same attributes of others—is not an easy task. The satisfaction of accomplishing your own goals and contributing to goals of others can be very rewarding, strong motivators.

The truly satisfying motivators are those that spur you to action. And usually the most satisfying motivators come from the good feelings you have within yourself (intrinsic satisfaction). Intrinsic satisfaction is the satisfaction you feel "inside your gut." It usually contributes to the best motivators you can have. External or extrinsic satisfaction frequently comes in the form of honors, awards, and rewards given to you by someone else. While internal and external satisfaction will be discussed in more detail later in the book, it is important to find motivators that are satisfying. The more satisfying a motivator is, the stronger it is toward helping you take action. What are your strongest motivators? How many motivators do you have? Which ones are short term and which ones long term? Can you identify the motivators that really move you in a positive direction? The following exercise should help you begin to answer some of these questions.

| Value-Added Motivator | MY PRIMARY MOTIVATORS |
|---|---|

Complete the sentence below by naming 10 things you really like to do. The things you describe in each of the items may be simple and quick activities or may be sustained activities that take a longer period of time. They also may be things you do frequently or possibly those you don't do at all. (If you need to go back to your previous listing for ideas, feel free to do so.) Be as specific as you can with each item. For example, you may like to read a mystery novel that has high suspense.

For the present, ignore the parentheses at the right of each item.

I really like to:

1. _____ ( )
2. _____ ( )
3. _____ ( )
4. _____ ( )
5. _____ ( )
6. _____ ( )
7. _____ ( )
8. _____ ( )
9. _____ ( )
10. _____ ( )

Now, go back and read your list. If some of the items need to be modified or changed to reflect your real interests and desires, make the needed modifications. If you haven't been as specific as you could be, try to reword items to be more descriptive of your likes and the pleasurable activities you enjoy.

If you can assign a rank order to the items you listed, give a 1 to the activity you enjoy doing the most, a 2 to the second most enjoyable item, etc., in the parentheses at the right of each item. If you have difficulty ranking some of the items, don't be overly concerned about the rank order since the order of the items may depend on a variety of factors you feel need some clarification. While your listing may reflect that you get enjoyment from a lot of activities—even from those activities you cannot do as frequently as you wish—the rank order will, however, help you to identify your preferences.

Now, for each motivator you listed, especially for those priority items you ranked high, indicate how often you are exposed to that motivating activity by adding one of the four frequency indicators to the left of each item as follows: F=frequently; O=occasionally; S=seldom; and N=never.

Which of the items on your list fall into each of the four categories? Are there similar activities in a category? That is, do you have mostly outdoor activities in your "Frequently" category? Does a category have a common pattern—such as activities which involve other people, or items which are sports oriented or physical in nature? Are your activities diversified or do they cluster in a small sphere if you measure them against activities that other people like to do? Do your activities depend upon your being entertained rather than on entertaining or engaging yourself? Are your motivators within reach, do they require some effort, and do they give you (and maybe others) satisfaction?

Based on your responses to these and other questions about your motivators, draw some conclusions about your list. Be sure to consider in your answer how often you actually do each of the motivational activities you identified (or why your list may contain an activity you never do). Also, are any items included on your list that are virtually impossible to do because of factors that are beyond your control? In the space below, summarize your thoughts on the points suggested:

_____

_____

_____

_____

Does your list (or summary) suggest that you have highly ranked motivators you don't do often or you find impossible to do? If so, these motivators may be things that a) you need to do more often, b) are unrealistic for you, or c) may be pseudo-motivators (activities you think motivate you or are actions that you believe should motivate you without your really knowing for sure).

If your identified motivators are not realistic, they are not your true motivators. For example, if you indicated on "My Primary Motivators" that money motivates you but you neither have wealth nor have a plan to get it, it is not a very realistic motivator for you. In fact, even if you know the money is available but you can't access it, it probably will become a demotivator for you. Money is a good example of an external or extrinsic reward—a reward that provides some external satisfaction. External rewards, as compared to intrinsic rewards, frequently diminish in value and provide much less long-term satisfaction than your accomplishments. While money is important to many people, employees and managers alike know that monetary rewards usually are not a motivator for higher productivity. Motivators that will be most beneficial to you (regardless of your position or status) will be those that will give you the most internal satisfaction—and they must be within a realistic realm. They must be within reach or attainable as well as be something you can do or experience to make you feel good—things that take some effort and things that give you a lift.

Your motivators, then, must be activities, actions, or things that are important and meaningful to you. They should not and cannot be things that others want you to do if you don't want to do them (although it would be good to keep an open mind to try new things, especially when a situation calls for a specified outcome). Doing what motivates you may, however, be enhanced by doing what motivates others if you can find enjoyment in the activity, too. Developing some motivators based on others' likes and interests is to your advantage. That is, you will frequently find increased satisfaction in motivators that make you happy as well as give enjoyment to others.

Complete the following exercise to identify the motivators that give pleasure both to you and to those around you.

| Value-Added Motivator | EXPANDING WHAT MOTIVATES ME |
|---|---|

List five things that you like to do, that are within your reach to do, and that you feel give meaning to your life *as well as* give satisfaction to people around you. Be as specific as you can about your activities. (You may want to go back to your previous listing for specific items to transfer or combine into this listing.) Also, be realistic!

1. _____
2. _____
3. _____
4. _____
5. _____

How does this listing mesh with the 10 motivators you identified earlier? If you have focused your new list around a particular group of people (friends, for example), how can you expand it to others such as coworkers, superiors or subordinates, family members, etc.? If you don't know what motivates your friends, family, and associates, it's time to find out!

List below what you believe to be two things a friend, family member, or associate really enjoy doing—two things that motivate them and make them feel happier and more satisfied. If you have difficulty identifying two things for each person (or want to make sure you're on the right track), ask each of them to identify two activities or things they especially enjoy doing.

Motivators of a Friend: (Name _____)

1. _____
2. _____

Motivators of a Family Member: (Name _____)

1. _____
2. _____

Motivators of a Coworker, Boss, or Subordinate: (Name _____)

1. _____
2. _____

Are any of the motivators from your friend, family member, or associate also on your expanded list above? Do any of their motivators come close to yours? Are some of their motivators things you may enjoy doing, but haven't considered? You may be surprised to find compatibility you never thought was possible. You may also discover another important fact: You may have been pushing some panic buttons of your friends, family, or associates that need to be avoided in the future.

Expanding your motivators to include others is one of the best ways to find motivators that may have been overlooked. It is also a good way to enhance your motivators because of the value you gain from becoming aware of interactions with other people. Interpersonal relationships can only be strengthened as people are willing to interact with each other—to respond to and be concerned about the feelings, likes, dislikes, and values of others. The important thing to keep in mind is that as you understand yourself more, you will also get better at understanding others. Be alert, don't take things for granted, and keep others' needs in mind as you work on identifying and practicing your motivators.

## A SATISFYING FORTUNE COOKIE

There are many very powerful motivators. As you know, what motivates one person may not necessarily motivate another. However, two of the most important motivators to the vast majority of working people are the answers to the question: "Why work?" What two reasons would you give to the question when applied specifically to you: Why do you work?

1. _____     2. _____

Do you consider the reasons you listed to be motivators? If not, you possibly need to reassess your answers.

According to many different surveys, the two main reasons most people work are a) for money (to provide clothing, shelter, food, basic needs, and things that make us comfortable) and b) for satisfaction (to be around people, to contribute to society, and to make a difference). It is interesting to note that many people change jobs based on finding satisfaction versus better pay. Here's a case in point:

## Who's Motivated?

Jason and Peter, experienced lumbermen, were hired to conduct an experiment to determine who could be motivated the longest. Jason was given a blunt-edged ax that could not possibly be used to fell a tree, but was given an hourly salary five times greater than Peter's. While Peter was not terribly excited about his salary (although it was reasonable), he was given a sharp ax. As both men went to work, Jason was much more enthusiastic about his job than was Peter. However, before the end of the day, Jason became quite discouraged, especially after seeing Peter's progress—the impressive stack of trees Peter had felled.

1. Why do you think the enthusiasm and motivational levels of the two men changed dramatically?

2. Assuming Jason and Peter assessed the experiment, speculate as to what conversation they had at the end of the day.

3. How do you think Jason's and Peter's initial perceptions changed? Will the outcome influence things they do in the future? Why or why not?

4. What analogy can you draw about this situation which relates to your own motivation?

From this experiment (and many similar experiments that may be just as absurd), it is easy to see that satisfaction from progress in doing a job well—a job that requires effort—can be an extremely good motivator. However, effort (even with a significant reward that is anticipated and expected) that also is coupled with enthusiasm may not be sustained for any length of time if it is merely based on money. Effort, enthusiasm, and satisfaction go hand in hand and are classified as rewarding motivators. This is not to imply that workers who do menial labor cannot be satisfied or that creative people will always be excited about their work. You know there are many factors that influence your lifestyle; the significant thing is to find out *what* drives you to reach the goals you believe are important.

## RING OUT THE OLD, RING IN THE NEW

As suggested earlier, probably the most important single element that contributes to motivation is getting into the right mind-set to take action. You have heard people say, "No problem! I can do that . . . " or "As soon as I get enough money, I plan to . . . " or "When the time is right, I will . . . " but nothing ever comes of anything you hear from them. Frequently talk is cheap; certainly much easier than action. Big plans and dreams are good to have. But it's important to take action steps—no matter how small—toward implementation of a goal. And action needs to be frequent and regular along the way if progress is to be made toward the ultimate goal.

Growing up happens in more than a few days; learning a skill takes practice; gaining expertise comes with experience; and motivation becomes greater with each new challenge that is accepted. Visit the past only long enough to learn from it. Then move on to begin a new endeavor. You can begin something new as often as you wish—it is the starting point that becomes important. Thinking about beginning an activity will usually increase your adrenaline and give you an incentive for embarking on it. Motivation to get started is essential. When your energy, enthusiasm, and drive wane along the way, motivation also is essential to get restarted.

Your motivation to action may require that you take a "begin again" approach at the point of lagging interest. That is, starting anew at one of the activity's measured steps can be as important (and sometimes even more so) as actually completing the task. Since starting a new task is motivating for most people, it may be beneficial to set a realistic timeline for completing the task or a portion of it. The timeline can and should include rewards or perks along the way. For example, it may be that you can plan a sports activity for the weekend that will be a good reward for making progress on a work task you've been doing. The reward also may serve as the motivating factor to get back to your project with more enthusiasm. Interspersing motivating activities within a project timeline is an excellent way to make progress toward reaching a desired goal. The key to knowing what activities motivate you as well as when and how to engage in them will start to come automatically as you really become to understand yourself—a definite benefit of the Card.

Another way to get old or inactive projects completed, in addition to the establishment of timelines, is to give priority to a new project. Then attach "conditions" to start it—management may call this "an incentive." That is, the priority for starting a new or fun project may be to first complete an existing project that is hanging over your head. Prioritizing jobs with timelines for completion, along with enough rewards interspersed at critical intervals, may become the powerful motivator you need for providing the desired accomplishment.

Remember, too, the motivational head game is very real. You are the only one who can get satisfaction from the game. It's up to *you* how you will play the game toward achieving the end result. You can experience satisfaction by using your Card as an incentive to action and to remind you of the rewards you can receive by completing a task. The Card can help you put the past behind you and forge ahead into the challenges that lie ahead.

## DON'T SWEAT THE SMALL STUFF

Do you sometimes dwell on the minutiae and miss the whole point? Or vice versa? Do you know people who think totally opposite from the way you do? Most people like to give their point of view and state their opinions about things in which they strongly believe. If you are one who states your point of view, good! If you go further to think or say "And I'm right" you may not be considering the fact there are others who feel just as strongly as you do that their point of view is correct. Usually there are lots of alternatives to most situations; expand your horizons by listening and considering others' ideas.

Watering the bits of clover in the grass at the expense of caring for the whole lawn can be just as critical as skimming over the details that are needed for the whole picture. If people think you are too detailed, you may not be taken as seriously as you'd like to be. Alternatively, if you are a person who always comes up with the grandiose ideas, but the ideas are never implemented, you may be viewed as a dreamer who cannot get things done.

While you may not be terribly concerned about what others think of you, you would do well to consider why it is to your advantage to understand your mode of operation. For example, if your style or manner of communication does not achieve the results you desire, you should ask yourself why it doesn't.

| Value-Added Motivator | MY MODE OF OPERATION |
|---|---|

Consider the following three questions: 1. Do you think people you know or work with are too critical or petty? 2. Do they take you seriously and value your opinion? 3. Do others like to be around you? Having answered these questions with a yes or no, now ask yourself, "Why or why not" to each of the questions. Write your assessment of each question in the following spaces:

1. _____

_____

2. _____

_____

3. _____

_____

Now ask at least two close friends, colleagues, or family members to assess you on the same three questions. If your answers mesh closely with those of their responses, you probably have a good assessment of yourself as well as how others see you. If there are significant differences, you should ask yourself why and analyze (maybe with the assistance of others) where and how discrepancies can be narrowed.

This simple exercise does not provide any profound insights into your behavior, but it should make you more aware of your feelings. It's a starting point for considering new directions and an indicator to help you to understand yourself better. It will have achieved its purpose if you get an indication of whether or not you're "sweating the small stuff" at the expense of the bigger issues (or vice versa). It is important to first understand yourself before identifying if and what changes need to be made and how you can make such changes, no matter how small.

Most of us can benefit from periodic self-assessment to identify what makes us tick. If you find you are leaning in a direction that is not totally acceptable to you, you may want to consider how you might change. Change might include finding and doing more things that give you satisfaction. Satisfaction usually follows from a positive attitude—doing positive things, speaking positive words, thinking positive thoughts, and so on. No matter how positive you may be, make a concerted effort to be even more positive. Finding satisfaction in what you do every day, including your routine activities, is a good way to become more positive. It will also help to bring more balance into your life.

## GROCERY LISTS AND OTHER MUNDANE CHORES

No doubt you have found that all people have a certain amount of routine in their lives—routine that may be mundane, uninteresting, and even distasteful. Getting through those undesirable chores and work tasks will be easier if you let your personal Motivational ATM Card work for you. How? Use your Card as a reminder to ask yourself: "How can I make my day more interesting and fun?"

"What can I do to create more time for the things I really like to do?" "How have I enhanced someone else's life today?"

Frequently many people find that if they set realistic time frames for activities—work and leisure included—they enjoy their lives more fully. Setting realistic timelines that you meet can give you the satisfaction of accomplishment. For example, if you determine how much time it really takes you to get to work, park, and get settled in your office after greeting a few people along the way, you may be able to avoid rushing to your first appointment (and you'll reduce some stress too). If you can avoid hurrying from place to place, you may find you are more relaxed because you were really honest with yourself about what you can and cannot do. You may be able to accept yourself as you are and, as you do, you begin to understand yourself better. You may also find that the more you accept your behavior and understand yourself, the easier it is to make positive changes.

Wanting to change for the better can be motivating. Doing it *is* motivating. Even small changes can enhance your life. Giving yourself reminders can help you make the changes on a regular basis. For example, write a note that says, "I'm going to smile at the first person I see." Post the note in an obvious place—on the bathroom mirror or console of your car—to act as a reminder for enjoying your day. Find sayings such as "Today is the first day of the rest of my life . . . and I will enjoy it to the fullest" or, "I will do something nice for myself today by being nice to someone else" or, "Just for today, I will . . . ."

Alternatively, attach a "happy face" to your calendar—every time you see it, you're sure to smile. Smile at yourself and laugh at yourself—don't take yourself too seriously. Smiling and laughing are good for the soul and can be very strong motivators. And these motivators, should they be seen by others, are definitely catching. You know that if you smile at someone, you'll probably get a smile back. That's reciprocity. You've made two people happy! And you've made your Card work for both of you.

In addition to reminders in obvious places, keep focused on the task at hand when a focus is really needed. For example, if you're going to the grocery store, take a list of the things you need to assure you will get the things you need so you will not have to make another trip for one or two items you need at a critical time. Incremental accomplishments, including a simple check mark beside an item on your calendar, can be very motivating. For more detailed or complicated activities that may take considerable time to complete, you may want to have a checklist to finalize the fact you've completed a stage of the project. You may even want to put up a chart that you (and possibly others) see on a frequent basis. Your chart could even motivate others to take action they may have been avoiding.

## HAVING YOUR CAKE AND EATING IT TOO

Keep in mind, there will be those days that won't turn out anywhere near to what you have planned. But you can avoid further frustration, and actually be motivated, if you do a few of those easy, small, or quick things—maybe make a telephone call or write a check to pay a bill. It may seem to be a small matter to record an accomplishment for the day, but it can be vitally important to your mind-set to complete something. If you let your Card demonstrate how little things can add up, you may be pleasantly surprised.

Don't be discouraged if your greatest accomplishment for the day has been to give a little happiness to someone else—maybe a smile or kind word to a colleague. Just think of the impact of your deed if everyone around you were to do a similar thing on the same day—which means your Card really is working! The bottom line is if you do nothing, you'll get nothing. Success is the direct result and product of hard work—it always has been and always will be. Don't depend on others to guide your life unless you want to accept the norm. You can raise the standard with your personal Motivational ATM Card; and, if you do something for yourself or others, you're bound to get others involved too!

# CHAPTER 2: MOTIVATIONAL REINFORCEMENT

Reinforce your understanding of the chapter by responding to the following items.

1. Describe some ways a personal Motivational ATM Card enhances your environment.

2. What is a demotivator and how can a motivator become a demotivator?

3. How much motivation is needed to achieve a desired result or goal?

4. What is the meaning of "lucky is what lucky does?"

5. Why is it important to take incremental steps to complete a large endeavor?

6. Describe the difference between intrinsic and extrinsic satisfaction.

7. Name three things that contribute to or form motivational patterns or clusters.

8. What is the value of finding out what motivates your friends and associates?

9. How does "visit the past only long enough to learn from it" relate to motivation?

10. If the motivational "head game" is real, who controls it and why?

11. Describe why it is important to understand yourself as well as the behavior of others.

12. What is the significance of setting timelines, making lists, posting reminders, etc.?

# SECTION II
# Valuing the Elements of Motivation

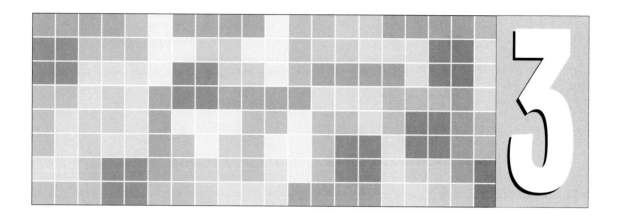

# The Care and Feeding of Your Motivational ATM Card

## YOUR CARD NEEDS CARE

While it's true that your Motivational ATM Card carries a "no-risk" guarantee with it, that doesn't mean it will take care of itself. Your Card needs to be protected and cared for just as you take care of other things you value in your life. The fact is your attitude belongs to you and you alone. Similarly, *you*, too, are the only one who can care for your personal Motivational ATM Card. You also need to be alert to the signs that point to your Card being abused by others.

So how do you care for your Card and recognize the signs that your Card may be headed for abuse? The simple answer is: in much the same way you protect your attitude and guard against letting other people damage it. Let's look at some of the ways you can protect and successfully nurture your Card and thereby increase its value.

## A PRESCRIPTION FOR A HEALTHY CARD

Most people with positive attitudes make a conscious effort to be positive. Their positivism comes from looking at things in a positive light. It is their desire or will to find what is good and pleasant in life rather than finding the faults, negatives, or what is bad in a situation. Positive people believe and act in a positive manner; they are those you like to be around. Frequently they are the doers. And because of their positive deeds, the fruits of their labor are reflected in other people's happiness. Positive people also tend to be creative; they are people oriented, and seek out and find pleasure in life as well as help others do the same. Many times they are people who avoid negativism at all costs—a factor which can get them into trouble if they aren't realistic about things.

No matter how positive a person may be, it may be rather easy to fall into a negative mood or slump. If you look around you, there are many things in our environment that tend to capitalize on less than positive things—things that can, if you let them, drag you down. For example, can you name one thing in a news broadcast that gets the attention of most people? Is it always the most newsworthy event?

Let's be more specific. Which one of the following two news items gets your attention: 1) a local school system achieving high test scores or 2) a robbery at a local bank? The school news may not be as exciting to you (or to the general public for that matter) as hearing about, or seeing the action of, a robbery at a local bank. Why?

We have been conditioned for wanting to be entertained. And for entertainment to be really entertaining it needs to be interesting, exciting, and stimulating. In a nutshell, sensational events get noticed. Consider further the example of the school test results and the bank robbery. One is positive; the other is negative. One has taken a long period of time to achieve; the other is a fleeting event.

Most sensational news and events not only involve something that is negative, but also something that happens quickly and within a short time frame. Because sensationalism tends to be short term—a quick event that gets our attention—we need more and more sensational stimuli to be entertained to ensure our interest doesn't diminish. That is, the more sensationalism we experience, the more we want. In a way, motivation is similar, even though the analogy is not parallel since the goal of motivation is to become positive and productive over the long term.

So how do you get into the frame of mind for really wanting to be motivated? What can give you motivational satisfaction that lasts? Finding motivation that is sustained over a period of time can be compared to finding the perfect prescription for treating a nagging ailment. Sometimes a prescription needs to be taken in large doses and other times small ones achieve good results. It's always a good idea to learn about and consider plausible alternatives because it is sometimes advantageous to change to another type of prescription altogether.

## THE PERFECT MOTIVATIONAL PILL

There is one very important active ingredient that is essential in any prescription for increasing motivation: a positive attitude. Developing and maintaining a good positive attitude always must be first and foremost for you to motivated. A good motivational attitude doesn't just happen; it depends on your dedicated effort to make it happen. You must *want* to be motivated, to find ways to achieve your goals, and to take action for progress to be made.

*If* a perfect cure-all "pill" could be packaged and sold, motivation would be it. In a way, a motivational pill can be compared to taking a multivitamin or complete dietary supplement. It needs to be taken on a regular basis in the proper dosage to be effective. A complete dietary supplement usually provides you with many different types of vitamins and minerals, but it does not take the place of a healthy diet.

If you compare this analogy to the school test scores example above, there are many similarities. That is, the school test scores didn't get changed in a day, week, or month. It probably took a year or more to achieve the newsworthy result. Also, there were many factors which influenced the end result—factors such as teacher competencies, books and materials, student study habits, support (moral support, financial resources) from a variety of sources, as well as encouragement, incentives, and rewards along the way. Similarly, a dietary supplement and your personal Motivational ATM Card are most beneficial to you if used on a long-term basis.

Motivation is made up of a plethora of motivational elements and factors. And what motivates you today may not motivate you tomorrow—let alone be of any motivational value to your friends, colleagues, or family members. Motivation is what helps you stay on track, enabling you to reach your long-term goals. It is what sustains you and gives you the momentum to focus on the long-term goals you value most—goals that are the most rewarding and satisfying. To see how this works, complete the following exercise:

| **Value-Added Motivator** | **WHAT MOTIVATES ME?** |
|---|---|

Do you exercise on a regular basis? If so, why? If not, why not?

_____

_____

If you answered yes, you may have listed reasons for exercising as: you want to look good, you know it's good for your health, you feel better and have more energy when you exercise, and similar things. If you answered no, you may have explained that you don't enjoy exercising, you don't have time or are too tired to do it, or you don't see any real value in it. While these are probably only a few of the reasons exercise may or may not be important to you, consider for a moment a further explanation. That is, ask yourself how you may be able to relate to the following scenario about exercising (and then a suggestion is given as to how this scenario is linked to your motivation).

Read the following three descriptions. Determine which of the three descriptions comes closest to your feelings.

1. Don't get in my way (All Pumped Up). Exercise is very important to me. In fact, I view it as a priority above many other things I do on a daily basis. I may not always really enjoy exercising, but I always feel better after an exercise session. Exercise is a way of life for me. It is a regular activity that is vital to my well-being, especially to my mental attitude. In fact, my exercise program is a permanent fixture on my daily calendar. I would rather miss other things during the day than to slight my exercise routine. Without a doubt, it is exercise that makes me feel "all pumped up" for meeting the challenges of life.

2. The balancing act (Ready, Set, Go): It is important for me to maintain a good balance in my life, especially as it relates to a proper diet, sleep, and exercise. I have developed a good exercise program that works for me. The key to keeping a proper perspective in my life is to identify a schedule that works for balancing all my activities. I look at my overall well-being as a good balance of healthy eating, proper rest and sleep, and regular exercise. My balanced approach to life works well and keeps me in a "ready, set, go" frame of mind to approach every day with my best foot forward.

3. Classic couch potato (Down, But Not Out): It is terribly difficult for me to exercise or to even consider exercising, let alone doing it as a regular day-to-day activity. What many consider as "proper" exercise is not attractive to me at all. Perhaps I should be exercising regularly, but I really don't enjoy even thinking about it. I believe I've even heard that if you don't enjoy exercising, it really doesn't do you any good. Even if that statement isn't true, I have resigned myself that I don't really need to exercise (though my friends say I would feel better and have more energy if I did). I have so many other things that I enjoy doing more, it doesn't make any sense at all to waste my life on things I really don't like doing. Please leave me alone; I like being a couch potato and don't want to feel dejected or depressed because of it. I may be "down, but not out."

Which of the three scenarios *best* describes you? (Select the one that comes closest to your feelings about exercise.) Why? Write your answer below:

_____

_____

Was it difficult to select just one of the three scenarios? Why or why not?

_____

_____

If you said that one or more of the statements within a scenario did not describe you, you are not alone. It is possible that you may have strong positive feelings about one or two of the statements, but totally reject others. For at least one statement from Scenario #1 that you either rejected or feel did not describe you, give the reason why.

_____

_____

What can be learned from what you have just described? If you described something you hadn't considered before, is it possible you might give some consideration to the merit of the idea? Why or why not?

_____

_____

Whether you exercise regularly, some of the time, or not at all, what do you believe are two real benefits of exercising?

1. _____

2. _____

Do you believe you are reaping the benefits you just described? Why or why not?

_____

_____

What conclusions can you draw from completing this activity? Write your summary here:

_____

_____

_____

If you can compare your results about the exercise with those of at least two friends or coworkers, do it now. What differences of opinion appear to surface? Do each of you feel as strongly about your opinion as the others, even though opinions are diverse? What argument can you (as a friend, family member, colleague, or leader-manager) give to someone for that person to consider a lifestyle change? That is, if a person's focus doesn't include a long-term goal or if a person feels strongly against doing something, what can you do to change that person's mind? Do you believe you could influence someone else to think more like you do? Do you have an open mind to others' ideas and are you willing to at least consider their opinions? Can you possibly be persuaded by someone else to find enjoyment in something you don't presently believe is possible? The answers to these questions should give you some insight into whether or not you need to seriously contemplate expanding your horizons and, at the very least, be aware of some of the alternatives that others believe are important. Undoubtedly, the astute supervisor or manager must be cognizant of the significance of identifying the likes and dislikes of the work team toward making that team more effective.

As a special note for the wise person, regular exercise is an important factor to your total well-being. It will contribute to your motivation for completing everyday activities. Exercise, in fact, may be a good motivator for you to reduce stress, clear your mind, and help you sweat out (figuratively and maybe even literally) the small stuff. If you don't engage in physical exercise, you may want to find a way to add some exercise to your lifestyle. In addition to an exercise program and active sports, you may want to consider gardening or house cleaning— you may even reap some satisfaction from the results that such activities provide, in addition to the exercise.

## MOTIVATED FOR MOTIVATION

The questions relating to the exercise, "What Motivates Me," can be applied to nearly anything you do—reading, participating in sports, cooking, shopping, listening to music, and, yes, even to cleaning and doing routine, mundane chores. As you apply and test your activities via an introspective analysis similar to the way you considered the exercise questions, you will find the results are firmly grounded in what may be termed your motivational philosophy. That is, your philosophy is what you believe. It is what drives your actions. Because

motivation frequently is associated with enjoyment and with achieving a desired result, you should continuously seek out ways to nurture your motivational "drivers" and let them become an integral part of your motivational philosophy.

Also, keep in mind that whatever drives your motivation toward achieving desired results is usually represented by varying degrees and duration. A desired result may be a delayed gratification (long-term goal) such as if you exercise regularly (even though it isn't particularly enjoyable), you will be healthier and probably enjoy a better physique. A delayed gratification is possible if you are highly motivated and disciplined to continue an activity even though you don't get instant results. Most people need both kinds of motivation—immediate and long term. And you have learned that both need care and feeding.

It is not the intent to prolong or belabor the point, but the following example should provide additional considerations of merit, especially with respect to the significance you need to place on determining how important a priority really is to you.

## Who's Motivated?

 Fred, who is overweight, wants to look like Stephen who is slim and trim. Fred really wants to diet. In fact, he probably has more books on the topic than are in the local bookstore. Other than reading and talking about diets and dieting, Fred never does anything about his weight because he enjoys eating so much. He, however, always vows to diet *after* a meal. Stephen can't believe Fred doesn't have the drive to do something about his weight when all Fred seems to talk about is how much weight he has gained. A little tired of Fred's complaining, Stephen finally said to Fred, "Where's your priority—eating or dieting?"

1. Why is it so hard for Fred to diet? Is he being honest with himself about his priorities?

2. Is eating a motivator for Fred? Why or why not? How could eating become an advantage to Fred? Or can it?

3. Is it possible that Stephen can help Fred to either achieve his desire or get him to change his thinking about himself so he can enjoy his life more? Why or why not?

4. What advice could Stephen give Fred? What advice and action do you think would be best for Fred?

 While dieting for many people is one of the hardest goals in life, it brings home an important point: Sustained motivation can be very difficult. That is why smaller steps need to be taken when undertaking a truly big endeavor. Starting out slowly and building in incremental steps, with rewards and incentives along the way, may be your best approach to developing and maintaining your motivational stamina for successfully meeting your most challenging hurdles.

Can you think of some difficult hurdles, like Fred's, that are present in your life?

---

| **Value-Added Motivator** | **HURDLES TO MASTER** |
|---|---|

Name at least one hurdle you'd like to master relating to your a) work, b) friends or family, c) personal gratification.

Work hurdle: _____

_____

Friend/Family hurdle: _____

_____

Personal hurdle: _____

_____

    To tackle each of the hurdles, follow these steps. First, decide if you can do something to overcome the hurdle. Then, identify the components of each hurdle (if possible, identifying logical steps to master it). Identify several possible solutions that might be feasible to achieve desired results. Identify what motivation (activities you enjoy or rewards and incentives you can give to yourself) that you believe you need. Determine how much and at what intervals you believe your motivators are needed to attack the hurdle. In the space provided, outline your plan for at least one of the hurdles you identified above.

_____

_____

_____

_____

---

    If needed, expand your outline into a more detailed plan, but don't set it aside. Put your plan into action—not next week, not tomorrow, but today. There is no time like the present to get started.

    If at first you don't succeed to your desired degree of satisfaction, try another avenue of attack. Assess your progress; if you have made some progress, you've been rewarded (by a good motivator) and will be spurred on to the next level of success. Let your Card be the constant reminder that you can be motivated; you just need to know how, when, and how much.

    Motivation comes with "feeding" your Card; that is, motivation is developed with the effort you make based on the value you place on it. And it usually takes time and patience to find the right motivators for the right situation (but it does get easier each time you make progress and are successful). Remember, too, that motivation comes in varying degrees and at varying times for most people. What worked yesterday may not work today, but it may be the ideal for tomorrow.

## EVALUATING YOUR CARD'S DAILY REGIMEN

Hurdle jumping is usually more successful if it is based on a decision-making model such as the procedure of steps that was just described. That is, you need to make certain decisions before you can proceed to the next and subsequent steps. Each decision, no matter how small, becomes important to the next decision to arrive at a destination. Thus, the decisions you make, whether or not you realize you are formally following a procedure, help you make progress to the desired end result.

Making decisions can be motivators in themselves. How? Each time you make a decision, you take a step toward some action even if you haven't embarked upon an activity. For example, you may make a decision that it is necessary to do something such as clean off your desk (possibly because you must find a letter that needs to be answered). Your next decision may be deciding when, where, and even how to proceed. Each action, based on a decision, is a motivator. If you are successful in accomplishing your task, you have experienced satisfaction in the fact that you have completed what you set out to do.

Let's say, however, that as you are cleaning off your desk and looking for the buried letter, you find other things on your desk that need to be done. You may deviate from your original mission of finding the letter and possibly make a phone call relating to a message you found promising you would make the call yesterday. Each of these deviations requires a decision. You must decide what is most important to do at the moment—to clean your desk, to find the letter, or to make the call. Let's say you decide to make the call and you do it. Having made the call, you either have made progress associated with it (even if you had to leave a voice message) or have some closure on that task. Completing a task, even if it deviates from your original plan, can give you satisfaction—you are motivated because you've found closure and gratification from deciding to change your course of action.

Skipping from one activity to another can be very frustrating and demotivating; thus, always give consideration to the merits of completing an activity. Even if it is a small task, and especially if it is important or needed, there is motivational gratification. If you complete the task, it no longer is one that is hanging over your head. The satisfaction of accomplishment cannot be overemphasized—even the satisfaction derived from the fact you did the job in a timely manner and completed it successfully. If, while completing a task or jumping a major hurdle, you have provided yourself with some rewards and incentives at intervals along the way (maybe the relief from seeing your clean desk), you probably have reaped some additional benefits and found certain pleasure in the whole activity. Thus, by identifying ways you may experience enjoyment—immediate or delayed—from completing a task, you have found a way (or ways) to motivate yourself to action. Satisfaction in itself is a strong motivator that comes with your mind-set.

## CONFIDENCE FEEDS EXPERTISE

Would you consider traveling to another continent or country for a vacation when you know it is totally unsafe to do so? If you enjoy taking risks (including those that might be life threatening), your answer may be yes. However, your answer probably is no, unless you have a compelling reason to make the trip. Similarly, you wouldn't expect to set out on an extended sailing trip if you didn't have the confidence that your sail could effectively move you at the speed and in the direction you want to go. A large billowy sail is reassuring. It augments your navigation skills and capitalizes on the good sailing weather. The sail gives you peace of mind for your trip and it biases the chance you will successfully reach your destination. The sail helps you feel well prepared for the task at hand and gives you confidence to make the journey.

Like the sail, motivation is what gives you confidence to move forward. If you can depend on a reward, and it comes through for you, you believe in that reward. The reward is a motivator and probably will be one that you'll tap into again. The reward, especially if you have enjoyed it repeatedly, will give you the confidence to move into more uncharted territory. The reward is a motivator.

Several things happen as you are motivated to take action and move forward. First, you gain more and more confidence with the activity in which you are engaged. You are exposed to a better understanding of yourself and to whatever it is that gives you confidence. As a result of increasing your confidence level, you may find a comfort zone with the experience. The experience may, in fact, contribute to your expertise as well as to your satisfaction.

Expertise can be a very powerful and strong motivator. Expertise, as a motivator, is based on having the satisfaction you know you are good at what you do. Your expertise is established and you know it. Your expertise, as a motivator, can also be expanded if others respect you for your expertise and seek you out because of your abilities. You help them solve their problems and both of you feel good. Both of you are rewarded and, as a result, your motivation has expanded beyond your own sphere.

---

| Value-Added Motivator | MY MOTIVATIONAL EXPERTISE |
| --- | --- |

Can you identify an area of expertise (an asset, strength, or something at which you excel)? Describe it.

_____

_____

Does your response also serve as a motivator for you (or others)? Why or why not?

_____

_____

Ask a friend or colleague what that person believes to be your expertise or major strengths (Or, alternatively, write down what you think others would say are your strengths.)

1. _____

2. _____

3. _____

Which of these three things are (and are not) motivators for you? Why or why not?

_____

_____

If the three items from others did not include the item you identified as your area of expertise, why do you think your identified item was missing?

_____

_____

Why do others sometimes perceive your strengths very differently than you do?

_____

_____

From this exercise, summarize what you have learned about yourself and your motivation.

_____

_____

It may not be clear to you why others perceive you differently than you perceive yourself. Your perception of yourself in terms of your expertise, strengths, assets, or abilities should be a motivator for you. The degree of motivation depends on how strong your feelings are about your abilities. If you feel you cannot contribute because of any reason, you would do well to assess your strengths. You also need to assess your weaknesses and determine whether or not and how you can turn some of them into assets. The exercise that follows will help you identify your strengths, weaknesses, expertise, assets, and liabilities toward learning more about your motivators and understanding yourself.

| Value-Added Motivator | MY STRENGTHS AND WEAKNESSES |
| --- | --- |

In the space provided, identify four of your greatest assets (strengths or expertise) and four weaknesses (areas you believe, if they were stronger, would contribute to a better life). The items you identify can relate to career, family, leisure, or any other aspect of your life.

On the second line labeled "M" for each strength you identified (items 1 to 4), suggest one way you believe the item can be a motivator for you.

For each weakness (items 5 to 8), use the second line labeled "S" to identify how you could turn the weakness into a strength. Also, on the third line labeled "M" determine how the "weakness turned strength" could be (or become) a motivator for you.

My strengths are:

1. _____

    M _____

2. _____

    M _____

3. _____

   M _____

4. _____

   M _____

My weaknesses are:

5. _____

   S _____

   M _____

6. _____

   S _____

   M _____

7. _____

   S _____

   M _____

8. _____

   S _____

   M _____

Select one strength and one "weakness turned strength," that you believe are extremely critical for your personal and professional growth. In the space provided under A and B below, outline an action plan (the steps showing what action you will take) for strengthening or improving both of your identified traits, attitudes, knowledge, or skills. Your action plan should include what you believe are appropriate activities, tasks, and timelines to achieve growth. Your plan may also include how you will involve other people, the appropriate environment or surroundings, and other situational elements that are needed for you to take action. Your action plan may have several alternatives to achieve your goal; however, select the best elements possible to take the action you believe will significantly contribute to your improvement. Also in your plan of action, identify how you will contribute to your motivational bank account while strengthening each of your identified areas.

A. My plan of action for further strengthening item ____, is

_____

_____

_____.

This will increase my motivation by

_____

_____.

B.  My plan of action for strengthening item _____, is

_____

_____

_____.

This will increase my motivation by

_____

_____.

Before implementing your plan, you may want to consider adding or building in a support system to help you reach your goals. Let's consider how a good support system can be very useful toward maximizing your successes.

## OPERATING WITH THE STRONG SUPPORT SYSTEM

In addition to contributing to the enjoyment of your successes, a strong support system can help you get through the difficult and really tough times. A support system may involve one or more people and come from several sources. A friend, colleague, or another person in whom you confide and/or with whom you feel comfortable is frequently the best provider of support. One caring, compassionate person can give you a tremendous amount of support. Assuming you will find ways to reciprocate, both of you will benefit from motivational support.

Additionally, or alternatively, you may find a group—baseball team, work group, reading club—that contributes to how you feel about your overall worth and your achievement. Many people also find that a support system is readily accessible by joining a church-related group, participating in a volunteer organization, or becoming an advocate for a worthy cause. There are many ways you can help others, and yourself too, if you just stop and think about it. The following extended exercise will help you further expand your plan to build on your strengths and weaknesses.

| **Value-Added Motivator** | EXTENDING MY ASSETS |
| --- | --- |

Identify a person and/or group you believe provides (or can provide) a good support system for you. Give the reason(s) why you selected that person or group and determine how that person or group will contribute to and foster your support system to make your plan more effective.

_____

_____

_____

_____

Now, based on the two exercises you just completed "My Strengths and Weaknesses" and "Extending My Assets", it is time to put your action plan into motion. Use your support system to good advantage and get started working on the two areas you identified—the two areas you believe have the most immediacy for you to strengthen. Why is it to your advantage to work on both of the items in tandem? Because one can actually augment the other—a great way to get the maximum benefits from both. You may place more emphasis on one versus the other, but both should be enhanced from the effort you give to each.

## THE CHAIN'S WEAKEST LINK

Your action plan, based on the two exercises you just completed, also should be viewed as you would the links of a chain—a chain is only as strong as its weakest link (or links). If you can identify but one single weak link among your strengths and turn that weakness into a strength, you repair the chain. When a weak link becomes a strong one, your other strengths in the chain are enhanced. The new strength becomes part of your other strengths. In turn, the weakness-turned-strength gives meaning to your other strengths. That is, the chain is useful and valuable when all links are strong. You have contributed to your confidence. You know there are no weak links in the chain; thus, the chain can be depended upon to serve its intended purpose.

As you make progress on your action plan, repeat the process with each of the items you identified in "My Strengths and Weaknesses." Replace items (one or both) with new ones as frequently as you make the progress you feel is necessary toward achieving mastery of the traits, attributes, knowledge, and skills that you value. You'll want to frequently renew your commitment to keeping a positive attitude as you work on your plan. Your Card should be a good reminder of the importance of this ongoing activity toward understanding yourself better and learning about the motivators that give you satisfaction.

Keep in mind that your action plan for building your strengths will provide personal and professional growth, but you must focus on and work hard at achieving your desired goal. The results you will get from continuous attention to the activity are directly proportional to your efforts. Additionally, your Card is bound to increase in value if you take your plan seriously.

## DEPOSITS TO YOUR CARD ACCOUNT

The value of your Card, as you already know, lies in how often you use it. Even if you have looked at your Card recently, take it out right now. Notice the five statements on the back:

- ☐ I will keep my attitude positive and guard it as my most prized possession.

- ☐ I will take quick action to replace my negative thoughts with positive ones.

- ☐ I will turn up the air conditioning before my emotions overheat.

- ☐ I will learn more about myself to channel my actions in positive directions.

- ☐ I will continuously work on my weaknesses to mold them into strengths.

These five statements should be viewed as the basis for your motivational philosophy. That is, you need to believe in your Card to make it work for you. You need to value your Card for it to give you value. You need to make deposits to your Card for it to give you dividends—and you need to treat your Card with the same respect you treat your bank cards (or for that matter, your other valued possessions). You know that if you abuse your bank cards, you'll lose them or, at the very least, you will get yourself into difficulty. If you abuse your personal Motivational ATM Card, likewise you'll lose—but your loss will be much greater than you can possibly imagine. If you lose your positive attitude (which is the basis of your Card), you will have lost your most valuable asset for everything you do in life!

So, just how much do you stand to lose? Possibly everything; because without a positive attitude, the losses can be devastating. The losses are compounded if your emotions, thoughts, and actions become negative. Negativity can quickly contribute to losses that can overpower the positive factors that are absolutely vital to your well-being. Negativity can convince you that giving up is the only path you have. And because negativity has such considerable power, you may not recover from it without others' help. Negativity can cripple your motivation so much you could find it extremely difficult to get enough motivation to take one small step toward recovery, let alone the motivation to take the additional steps needed to get you on a positive track toward enjoying your life.

The good news is, no matter where you stand with your own attitudinal and motivational health—now or in the future—*you* are the only one who can make your life better. *You* are the only one who can make your Card work for you. *You*, and *you* alone, have power to be positive and to be motivated. Thus, it makes no sense to procrastinate or postpone action. So take out your Card right now—read it; let it spur you to positive action (or to greater positive action). Take out your Card as often as you need a boost toward a more positive destiny. Reread the statements on your Card; and do something about them—take some positive action to reinforce the value of your Card. Get your Card to help you identify your motivators. Make your Card work for you. Make your Card give you the drive to reach higher levels—to better yourself; to enjoy life. Your Card deposits can grow, but you must nourish them. They will grow only as quickly as you put into practice the motivators you identify to enhance your Card's value.

## A PILLAR OF STRENGTH

By now you probably have found several things that you can say, unequivocally, are your motivators. No matter how many motivators you have, it is to your advantage to identify as many motivators as you can. Why? Because you know that today's motivators may not be as strong tomorrow (and may even become demotivators). By finding several avenues for exploring what motivates you, you will increase your chances for more continual motivation. Your wide range of motivators will act as a pillar of strength—a continuous supply of motivation to minimize the peaks and valleys that life brings.

| Value-Added Motivator | MY 24-HOUR SCHEDULE |
|---|---|

How much of what you do in a 24-hour period is motivational for you? Is it possibly a few minutes, a few hours, nothing, or nearly everything on certain days? If you can identify something interesting about your daily activities, you will find there is motivation everywhere. Note: In looking for motivation, there is a need for a positive attitude. Let's see how this might work for a given 24-hour period.

First, make a list of the activities that might constitute a 24-hour day for you (include everything you do for one or more hours, including sleeping and eating). Once your list is complete, consider how much time you spend on each activity. Then, under the column labeled "Hours Spent," record the approximate amount of time you spend on each activity. Next, in the column labeled "Motivating?", add either yes or no as to whether or not you consider the activity motivating. That is, do you enjoy doing the activity to the point where it helps you get other (possibly less desirable) tasks accomplished? Does the activity spur you to take some positive action? Does the activity reduce some of your stress or give you the rest you need to engage in other things? Does the activity give you more confidence to face life's daily challenges, or similar types of motivating effects?

| My Daily Activities | Hours Spent | Motivating? |
|---|---|---|
| _____ | _____ | _____ |
| _____ | _____ | _____ |
| _____ | _____ | _____ |
| _____ | _____ | _____ |
| _____ | _____ | _____ |
| _____ | _____ | _____ |
| _____ | _____ | _____ |
| _____ | _____ | _____ |
| _____ | _____ | _____ |
| _____ | _____ | _____ |
| _____ | _____ | _____ |

For each activity in "My 24-Hour Schedule" you said was *not* motivating, identify something you can enjoy about it. For example, sleeping may be one activity you stated was not motivating. Think about it, however, and try to find something positive about sleeping. Can sleeping six or seven hours each night give you renewed interest to meet the challenges of the next day? If you have trouble sleeping, can you see the value in giving your body a rest? If you are awake, but resting, are you able to do some creative thinking? Or maybe you can reduce some stress by merely smiling to yourself as you find humor in some of the more stressful parts of the day you just finished.

Finally, study your list more closely and see what it suggests to you. That is, as you evaluate what you do over the course of a day, can you draw some conclusions about how you spend your time? What activities are motivating? Is there a particular time of day that appears to be more or less motivating than other times? The exercise may need to be repeated over a period of a week or so to determine any significant patterns. Once you evaluate your charted items, see if you can draw some conclusions about the type and level of motivation you had on the day you outlined your major activities. Also, consider some of the ways you may improve your motivation. For example, how you can capitalize or draw on your Card's power to improve your 24-hour motivational health? Summarize your conclusions.

---

---

---

Remember, the easiest place to look for motivation is in positive places—and that's great, so do it frequently. On the other hand, the most critical place where motivation needs to be found is in negative places. Finding motivation in adverse situations will require considerable effort on your part. But when you find just one motivator for what appears to be an impossible situation, you will know that it was worth your effort. With practice and time, it will become easier to address each new difficulty as well as to find a motivator that will propel you forward.

Once you have identified one motivator, it's really much easier to identify two or more. You can always make comparisons of what may be the better motivator in a situation (that is, what will contribute to a more positive attitude for you). If you can begin to expand your thinking and find something positive in everything you do, you're on your way to strengthening your motivational well-being, which also points to your giving considerably more value to your Motivational ATM Card.

## Who's Motivated?

 Carrie is a very competent real estate agent. She frequently is the top sales associate in her firm and has received lots of recognition at the local, state, and regional levels. Carrie has an outgoing personality which makes her clients feel at ease. She also seems to be a super mom—always supporting the many activities in which her three children are involved. In addition, she keeps a work schedule that most of her fellow sales associates envy, works out at the gym three times a week, and takes a class over the Internet.

1. Describe what you believe are Carrie's motivators.

2. Which motivators (external or internal) are most important to Carrie? Why?

3. If you were to give Carrie some advice, what would it be?

4. What is one thing you believe you might learn from Carrie? Why?

If you can relate any of Carrie's lifestyle to your own, describe those elements or activities (be as specific as you can rather than merely saying "gym" or "everything").

_____

_____

_____

_____

Based on your review of Carrie's situation, did you give her positive advice (see question 3)? When you compared your own similarities to those of Carrie's, were those elements stated in a positive manner (e.g., stated positively, even if the elements were negative or less than totally positive)? If you can revise some of your statements or "thinking" to be more positive, do it now.

Expressing yourself in a positive manner is important, even when what you have to say is not positive. As you find more positive ways to express yourself, you will become a more positive person who can maximize motivation.

## A TWENTY-FIRST CENTURY CURE-ALL: DAILY MOTIVATION

It should now be quite evident that it is *you*, and only *you*, who determines how positive you want to be and how motivated you are. The external stimulus that helps you move toward this end is important. For example, you may hear an excellent speaker at a seminar or on TV make a sincere, heartfelt appeal. The appeal is so compelling that it fills your emotional bank to its brim. Or you may go to a long-awaited concert and the music is so stimulating that it not only exceeds your expectations, but pulls at your heartstrings. You're happy, relaxed, and probably smiling inside and out.

These external stimuli get you to think strong positive thoughts, and you feel good inside. You may feel so good that, for a period of time, you are more tolerant of a lot of things—other people, your surroundings, and so on—that heretofore may have been problematic for you. Your newly gained tolerance is based on your positive mind-set and good feelings about yourself. You have found an influence that spurs you to action—something that makes you want to activate a motivator. An external stimulus frequently is helpful to change your thinking. You decide you feel better. You decide to be more positive. You like yourself. You've changed your mind-set and positioned yourself to increase your motivation. Because of someone else's help (in a way, an extension of your support system), you have increased your own self-worth.

While external stimuli may be extremely beneficial to you, such stimuli may not be there as often as you need it. That is, you can't go to a stimulating workshop every day or a concert every night. Even if you could, you probably would find that the stimuli begin to lose effectiveness because of the constant saturation you get (similar to the sensationalism we enjoy on TV and in the movies). Thus, too much of a good thing can cause it to become mundane. And that is why most people like to vary their daily activities and continue to seek out and learn new things.

## CONTINUOUSLY REFUELING YOUR POSITIVISM

Finding new and better ways to do things, exploring the unknown, and being creative will contribute to your motivation and avoid a saturation point for too much of a good thing. Your sustained motivation will depend on your ability to internalize it and to find ways to use and apply it to your daily life. Internal motivation comes from your positive attitude or mind-set; it is that "gut feeling" you get that pushes you to take action. Internal or intrinsic motivation is the best motivation you can have because *you* control it. And it can be developed, over time, to such a magnitude that you will find enough motivation to not only carry you through the day, but also to make you excited to get each new day started.

Motivation that virtually propels your life into positive actions and deeds is fueled and refueled by a positive attitude. The more you practice your positive attitude, the more motivators you will find. The more motivators you practice, the more motivation you will internalize. The more you internalize your good feelings, the longer they will last.

Give attention to what motivates you. Do it often—many times during each day. The time you spend on caring and feeding your Motivational ATM Card will never be wasted—for you and for those who come in contact with you!

Fill your motivational data bank until it overflows and spills out all around you.

## CHAPTER 3: MOTIVATIONAL REINFORCEMENT

Reinforce your understanding of the chapter by responding to the following items.

1. Describe some of the characteristics positive people possess.

2. Why is a positive attitude essential for improving your motivation?

3. What is a motivation philosophy and why is one needed?

4. Discuss some of the steps to overcome hurdles in your life.

5. Explain how decision making can be motivating.

6. How does motivation contribute to and "flow" from your confidence and expertise?

7. What can you do to strengthen your weaknesses?

8. Name the five elements of a motivational philosophy that keep your Card healthy.

9. Describe how a 24-hour assessment can contribute to your motivational health.

10. Explain the value of external stimuli in relation to your overall motivation.

11. Why is it to your advantage to protect and care for your Card?

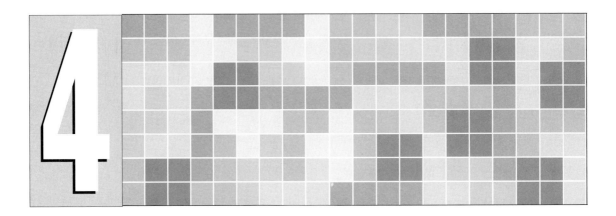

# On and Off Stage . . . and Still Motivated

## APPLAUSE FOR THE CARD

Probably one of the greatest advantages of your personal Motivational ATM Card is that it is available to you whenever you want to use it. It is always accessible, and it is always there when you need it the most. It is as valuable to you as you want it to be; and it can, if you let it, help you maximize nearly everything you do. Your Card gives you a reason to get up in the morning, and it provides the incentive for you to complete your daily activities. It is a powerful asset that contributes to your happiness, and it is a positive energy source to get you moving in the right direction.

How you view your Card can have a tremendous influence on what actions you take, how you meet new challenges, the decisions you make, the confidence you have, the control you exercise, and other elements that give your life meaning and that help you build relationships with others. Your Card is a stimulus for developing meaningful human relationships because as you use it, it is extended to everyone around you. The impact of the Card can be so far-reaching it can help focus you toward success in all your endeavors. In short, the Card, and what it represents, can help you and others enjoy life to its fullest.

## OUT ON A LIMB AND IN CONTROL

To enjoy your Card and the influence it can have on you and others, you need to appreciate what the Card can do for you. That is, to get the most benefit from your Card, you must take control of your life—with a positive attitude. You need to know what strengths and abilities you have, what interests and preferences you enjoy, and when you've reached your limits. You need to know when to forge ahead and when it is time to back off. You need motivation, in varying degrees, at every step of the way. Motivation is important for tackling small as well as big tasks. Motivation is important to your emotional health. Motivation contributes to your confidence, self-control, attitude, and zest for life—whether you are in the limelight or in the background.

Are you in control of your life? Is your attitude positive? These two questions may be very difficult to answer. They are hard questions because the environment has a certain amount of influence on what you do and the way you act. While your actions probably are quite predictable, often you may find yourself in a quandary about when, where, why, how, and even with whom you do certain things.

Being able to predict your actions, of course, depends a lot on how well you know yourself as well as how accepting you are of yourself. That is, understanding yourself is one thing, but accepting and being honest about who you really are is another matter altogether. Do you really accept yourself as you are? Do you like yourself? Do you believe you want to be someone else? Do you think others always get the breaks and you get the short end of the stick? Do you find that the actions of others—even of your friends—are problematic for you? Do you blame others, frequently pointing your finger at them and not at yourself? Do you take responsibility for your actions?

Answering these questions may not be easy, but there are numerous ways to assess each one and take inventory of yourself. Taking inventory is important to your well being because it is your perception about yourself that contributes to the development of a healthy attitude. It is your attitude and basic perceptions that give you the focus for future action. Consider this example:

## Who's Motivated?

Jose is a freelance artist who knows he is creative and skilled, but finds it difficult to get others interested in buying his work. He has never had an exhibit, nor has he displayed any of his work outside his home. While he doesn't market his work at all, he still can't understand why more people don't commission his services and buy his art. Olivia and Kate are so tired of Jose's complaining (and indirect innuendoes that his friends are not very supportive), they set up a web site for Jose to display some of his art. Reluctant at first about a web site, Jose finally gave in to the idea.

1. Why is Jose blaming his friends for not selling his artwork? Yet, why is he so reluctant to let them help him?

2. What are some of the reasons you believe Olivia and Kate set up the web site? In so doing, how could they help Jose and themselves too?

3. How well do you think Jose understands himself and his skills? Explain your answer.

4. If you could help Jose get a better handle on his situation, what are some of the things you would suggest? How could your suggestions help Jose take control of his life and improve his relationships with his friends?

# BEING PERCEPTIVELY SMART IS A TALENT

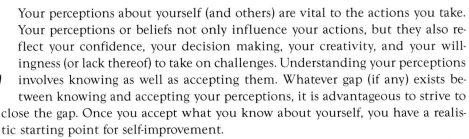

Your perceptions about yourself (and others) are vital to the actions you take. Your perceptions or beliefs not only influence your actions, but they also reflect your confidence, your decision making, your creativity, and your willingness (or lack thereof) to take on challenges. Understanding your perceptions involves knowing as well as accepting them. Whatever gap (if any) exists between knowing and accepting your perceptions, it is advantageous to strive to close the gap. Once you accept what you know about yourself, you have a realistic starting point for self-improvement.

Everyone can benefit from self-improvement. Why? Because you know that no one is perfect and life has enough challenges that most people can improve their strengths as well as their weaknesses. Accepting your weaknesses does not mean you must look at yourself negatively. If, for example, you know your attitude is somewhat negative, accept that reality. But, don't stop there. Accept where you are and immediately take steps to be more positive. Resolve to make the best decisions you can to turn your weaknesses into strengths. Determine the action to take to make your attitude more positive; then practice, practice, practice. You know your chances are pretty good for getting better at the things you practice.

Your motivators truly come into play once you focus and base your improvement (any type of improvement) on keeping a positive attitude and finding ways to be successful (two important elements of your Card). Alternatively, if you do nothing, you'll get nothing—adding zero to zero is still zero. Thus, your motivators are extremely important in making good decisions and taking positive action toward self-improvement.

As you address the unknowns in your life, you draw on whatever previous experience you've had. The more experience you have, the better decision maker you will be. Experience is a good teacher that, by drawing on the lessons you've learned, will help you avoid some of the pitfalls ahead. For example, if you are comfortable with your ability to drive your car in snow and ice, you probably will be quite sure of yourself to take control of a tense situation that is compounded by treacherous weather. Alternatively, if you lack confidence in your driving, your reactions may be very "iffy" on an icy road or in snowy conditions because you are hesitant to take action, react too quickly, or possibly even overreact. The action you take, or the lack of it, is usually a direct result of your ability—or at least a direct result of what you perceive your abilities to be. Your past experience helps you to make decisions.

Your decisions are largely based on your perceptions about yourself, others, and the environment. These same perceptions feed directly into your motivation. Let's say, for example, that you really like chocolate. In fact, your favorite dessert is double chocolate torte and a local restaurant serves the delicious torte. Not too many restaurants you've found even have a torte on the menu, but when you discover a new restaurant that has it, you order it with great anticipation. Because of your past experience, you can nearly taste the wonderful dessert before it is even served.

When the torte is served, you decide it looks great—a bit different than what you've experienced before, but you're still anxious to savor the delicately smooth, rich chocolate. To your dismay, however, you find the torte very disappointing. In fact, if you were to pinpoint what's wrong, you can come up with several things. The torte you thought you really loved is totally unacceptable! How can it be? What has happened to your perception of double chocolate torte? Possibly several things.

As a starter, you had predetermined expectations of the torte because you have always enjoyed it so much. It was your favorite dessert. Your memory of the last time you ate it may have been so strong that it even sharpened your taste buds as you looked at the menu—even before your first bite. But now your perceptions have been changed. You've lost some enthusiasm (and motivation) for the torte, and you may be very critical of the restaurant that spoiled your fantasy.

In the future, you may not be so quick to order a double chocolate torte other than at your favorite restaurant. Or because torte is such a fantastic dessert (and if some time has passed since your unfortunate experience), you may try it again when you see it on the menu—possibly at a chocolate specialty dessert café. Upon ordering it, you find the café's torte really excellent, but it is not the same as you remember your favorite dessert. Alternatively, you may go back to your favorite restaurant and either enjoy the torte just as you've always done (or even enjoy it more than previously) or find that the dessert is no longer as wonderful as you thought it was.

Whatever your experience, your perceptions have changed. That is, even if the torte is still all you originally thought it was, you are now a little more leery to try it in other places than at your favorite restaurant. Or you may decide that the specialty café serves a better torte, and immediately it becomes your favorite. In any event, you have altered your perceptions. You're still in control, but you've found a deviation that may make you more cautious or more adventuresome in the future.

Keep in mind that if you have too many deviations that either change your perceptions or that give you cause to doubt yourself, you may not enjoy the control you need or want in your life. The more you are in control of your actions, the happier you will be, and your actions show in everything you do. Because happiness and a positive attitude go hand in hand, both can contribute to your confidence and to better decision making. For example, if you are a manager or supervisor, your happiness and positive attitude will contribute to how your team perceives you as well as to how you influence them to develop the same characteristics toward enhancing human relationships.

Let's apply this idea of how your control, perceptions, attitude, and decision making can influence your work tasks and interpersonal relationships, especially your daily work tasks and relationships.

| **Value-Added Motivator** | **MAKING THE GRADE** |
|---|---|

Identify a work task that not only needs to be completed on a weekly or monthly basis, but also a task that results in an end product that will go to a friend, colleague, or superior (possibly for review, further action, or acceptance). If you can do this exercise with another person, together you may be able to determine how important the job or task is to each of you and to its intended recipient. Write the task in the space provided:

_____

What is the importance of the task or job to you?

_____

What is the importance of the task to the recipient?

_____

Describe the factors that contribute to the importance of the job (a) to you and (b) to others and why.

a. _____

_____

_____

b. _____

_____

_____

What are the repercussions if you don't get the job done on time or if you don't complete it to the satisfaction of its intended receiver?

_____

_____

What if the job is not well received (with the enthusiasm you believe it should be) by the intended recipient?

_____

_____

How do the answers to these items affect your perceptions about the job or the recipient? How will your perceptions contribute to the way you will do a similar job the next time you have to do it? Summarize your thoughts here:

_____

_____

_____

Now that you have recorded your perceptions about the job you just completed, you may not be as excited about them as you'd like to be. It is natural that your perceptions may not always motivate you to future action. However, you can control your own destiny and motivate yourself by assessing your perceptions and finding ways to change them for the better.

Refer back to your summary. If it was not as positive as it could be, consider how you might change your future action (and thus your perceptions about how you should go about completing the job and what you can expect from it) to make it more positive. Or, even if your summary was positive, consider what action you might take to make it more positive (for you and others). On the lines provided, write a conclusion about this activity. For example, consider how you can successfully accomplish the job task, deal with or take control of the situational factors surrounding it, and how you can work effectively with the involved players for the outcomes to be positive for everyone.

_____

_____

_____

_____

By completing this exercise, you should have found at least one way you can improve the outcome (or the way you approach it) the next time you do a similar task. However, if you did not arrive at such a conclusion, it may be a good idea for you to go back and reassess the job to determine what is standing in the way and what you can do to remove the obstacles to make it a more positive experience.

The value in such an exercise—and in repeating it—is to help you improve your attitude and change your perceptions of how you will approach your next project. Even if you think your attitude and perceptions are the best they can be, there is always room for improvement. Improvement on any front will give you more control of your destiny. The control and confidence you derive from it will contribute to a better environment for you and others.

## ADMIT ONE TO A POSITIVE ENVIRONMENT

Positive people create and enjoy a positive environment. And it's in a positive environment that positivism—positive attitudes and—motivation are nurtured. Positive people are more confident and certainly much happier than negative people because positive people make positive things happen. Your Card entitles you to be positive and, as frequently as you determine is possible, gives you the motivation to turn lemons into lemonade. Your Card helps you to diminish and eliminate negatives toward creating a more positive environment for yourself and others.

You know that you can help yourself and others to become part of a positive environment by the deeds you do, by the words you speak, and by the actions you take. You know it is a positive person who offers an amicable solution or an apology in an unhappy situation, frequently in an effort to try to avoid further conflict. As a result, everyone feels better.

On the other hand, if you are discouraged, there usually are reasons for your less-than-enthusiastic attitude. If you're not as enthusiastic as you think you should be, it will be to your advantage to find the reasons why not. Start your fact finding with yourself rather than with others. You may find it is rather easy to point your finger at others' faults and totally overlook your own. It is also very easy to blame others for why something is not right. If you look for a negative answer, you'll probably find one. It may be that because of your negativity, others may react to you the same way. Consider your answers to the following questions about your happiness or lack of it.

| **Value-Added Motivator** | MY HAPPINESS FACTOR |
|---|---|

**Happiness—some questions to ponder:**

When is the last time I was really enthusiastic or happy about something? Was it something I did or something someone did for me (if it was the latter, did I reciprocate)? Did I share my happiness with a close friend or with someone who is significant to me? How did I capitalize on the situation to make it even more positive? The last time something nice happened to me, did I think of my Card to help me react in as positive a way as possible? And, what did I do to expand the happy moment to others?

**Unhappiness—some questions to ponder:**

When is the last time I was unhappy about something? Was my unhappiness or anger self-inflicted? That is, did I become angry because of what someone said or did? Was it possible I could have looked at the situation differently and either reacted positively, or at least not reacted negatively? If someone lashed out at me (or me at them), did I offer an apology (even if I didn't think it was my fault)? If not, what prevented me from taking the first step to reconciliation? If I expected the other person to approach me or apologize to me, why? (Note: It is not an acceptable answer to say, "because the other person was wrong.")

Write a statement about how you can be happier:

_____

_____

_____

Review your statement. Is it as positive as it could be? Take out your Card and read your commitment on the front of it. Also read the five statements on the back of your Card and apply them to your statement. Can you make the statement more positive? If so, do it. Now, put your statement into practice—as soon as possible and as often as you can.

## AND THE LAST ACT BOMBED

There's another important concept associated with the exercise "My Happiness Factor". That is, if you are a person who *always* takes the blame for a situation, you are at risk too. Being on the other end of the scale by always taking blame can be just as bad as the person who *always* blames others. Taking blame is important; it is a virtue. Taking blame all of the time, however, may be unhealthy. It can actually contribute to your lack of self-confidence. It may even result in others taking advantage of you. How can you possibly believe that you, and you alone, spoiled the whole show? Or, if the last act was rather disappointing, it may be rather presumptuous of you to take full responsibility for it. Above all, it is nearly impossible to be positive when you always feel or act as the scapegoat.

Certainly if your actions weigh in at either extremes of the scale, you need to assess your actions. You should try to find out why you feel the way you do, why you are letting yourself get caught up in playing the role of the underdog, or why you are chastising others for every mistake. Take stock of your motivators—and let your Card help you to focus on the positive. Select those motivators that can help you improve your self-confidence and give you a better balance about your responsibility and that of others. Rely on your Card to give you the motivation to help you improve your own image as well as to help you give others a little slack. You can pick yourself up if you find ways to be more positive, more self-assured, and more motivated toward becoming a person who is in control.

## Who's Motivated?

As Mark returned from a break, he deposited his candy wrapper into the large trash receptacle closest to Peg's and Henry's work stations. In a rather loud voice, Peg remarked to Henry: "The whole office dumps their trash next to us. Maybe we should post signs over our desks that say, 'Dump here: We're the official office trash keepers'." Mark turned around and said, "Gee, I'm sorry." Peg and Henry didn't acknowledge Mark's comment. Mark's inner anger raged; he was determined he would find some way to get even with Peg for her snide remark, a remark she wouldn't even say to his face.

1. Describe what you believe is (are) the problem(s) depicted in this scenario.

2. If Mark considers one of the following avenues, what has he (and Peg and Henry) gained? a) Mark should avoid Peg and never dump trash there again, b) Mark should confront Peg and tell her to either move the trash can or shut up, or c) Mark should go by Peg's and Henry's desks and dump trash as often as he can.

3. Other than those suggested in item 2, what avenues could Mark consider? Which one might be the most successful and why?

4. Even though Mark may not have needed to apologize, why did he say he was sorry? If you say you're sorry for something, do you have to be wrong? What does an apology usually do for a situation?

Rewrite the last sentence of the scenario suggesting the most positive outcome possible. Justify why your rewrite is the best action.

You may have noted in the scenario that Mark could easily have said something like, "What's your problem?", "Get a life", "Stuff it", "What side of the bed did you get up on?", "Is it the trash that I hear speaking?", or similar ugly things. He could have started a dialog that may have turned into an argument. However, he didn't. He just offered a simple apology—not because he was wrong, but possibly because he was sorry Peg felt the way she did about people dumping trash near her work station. He may have even been sorry that Peg wasn't feeling well or was having a bad day.

Remember, a day does not make a lifetime, but one day added to another and another does. And today—right here and now—influences tomorrow and the rest of your life. What you do each day contributes to your destiny. Can you say you're proud of what you did today for yourself (and what may also have had some influence on others)? Did you make good decisions for yourself—decisions that were positive and satisfying? Did your decisions contribute to your motivation and to your taking responsibility for your actions? Your answers should serve as good indicators of how you will approach tomorrow.

## NO STRINGS ATTACHED

For some people, decision making is relatively easy. There are several reasons why this is true. Some people see situations as either black or white. There are no deviations from or caveats associated with their decisions. They may clarify and provide support for their answers, but they do not normally provide any stipulations that may cause anyone to misinterpret or let them deviate from their definitive stance.

Other people may make decisions on the basis that their decisions apply to everyone else but not to themselves. Such decisions can have some disastrous consequences that may be of little or no concern to the decision maker. A decision maker who feels responsible for a decision or who may be concerned about a decision backfiring probably will act in a way to ensure the decision will be the best one for the situation. A consideration for the decision also may be that it will satisfy the majority of people or make them the happiest. Good decision making also will help you keep your life on course. It will contribute to your motivation and your positive attitude.

On the other hand, decision makers who ignore the fact that there are strings attached to decisions or actions are, in fact, shunning responsibility for the outcomes. Because people who avoid decision-making responsibility do not normally get the support of other people, they may not be given the luxury of a lengthy tenure for making important decisions. If they do linger beyond their due time, it is usually because a group or even an individual (via control or support) has permitted them to do so. However, in the end, their decision making has carried with it some consequences.

The consequences of decision making may be short or long term, but there usually are consequences associated with every decision. That is, the decisions that are made by you, your boss, your coworkers, your subordinates, your family, and your friends usually have some strings attached. The decisions are the responsibility of the decision maker. And if the decision maker provides positive direction to those who will be affected by the decision, the outcome has a better chance of being positive too.

Note: If you want a friendship to last, you make the decisions that contribute to that friendship. You choose the path that will strengthen your ties with the individual or group and avoid those that might jeopardize or put a strain on your relationships. There are limits or consequences to your actions; thus, you try to make sure that your actions are positive.

## WHO'S THAT CELEBRITY OVER THERE?

The more positive choices you make—in your home, at work, in social spheres—the better chance you have in fostering positive relationships and reaping motivational benefits from each of them. Motivation is synergistic. That is, motivation exuded from an individual can also be a motivator for another person. Considering the motivation of both individuals together, the combined positive effect can actually be greater than the sum of the positive efforts by each person.

Synergy, when it comes to motivation, is rather phenomenal because of the fact that a little motivation usually leads to motivation that literally seems to mushroom. Mushrooming happens quickly as more and more positive actions contribute to an endeavor or situation, and the motivational magnitude can be quite impressive. For example, it is probably rather easy for you to identify any number of individuals who have influenced and impressively skyrocketed a business or enterprise to successes well beyond anyone's greatest expectations. If you were asked to describe any one of these people, you'd probably say they all have leadership—they display motivation, a positive attitude, and are good decision makers.

Most influential and innovative individuals share many characteristics that get noticed. Their leadership, even if it is subtle, is recognized. However, the way they provide leadership may be done in lots of different ways depending on their personalities, communication, and leadership styles. Some leaders may always appear on stage and really promote their celebrity status. Others stay in the background and remain off stage. Thus, some may be flashy; others low key, outgoing, or quiet. The list may be nearly inexhaustible, but motivation is an underlying factor that plays an important role in their sustained leadership. Their followers have acknowledged their leadership and frequently become motivated too.

Followers trust the leader to take them in a direction that they *want* to be taken. Followers may not know why they want to go in a particular direction, but the leader has exerted the power of influence to take them there. The power of influence may come from the leader's charisma and personality, from the leader's position and authority, or from the leader's expertise and knowledge. Whatever the source of the leader's power, followers have placed trust in that person. If the followers also believe their leader has integrity, especially as it relates to their place in the leader's scheme of things, the leader may enjoy a long positive relationship with followers.

Similar to the leader's attributes and decision-making skills that have attracted followers, there is little doubt that positive relationships are built from positive choices that capitalize on integrity and trust. If you trust someone, you are more apt to value that person's ideas and/or friendship. You are motivated to build a relationship. You trust the person probably because you believe the person's integrity can be trusted—especially as it relates to you. You like what you see and you *want* to be the person's friend. While a friendship requires reciprocity to be built, you have a stake in the reciprocity. You are an important player in the success of the relationship. You, at any time, determine whether or not you want to continue your friendship as well as how strong or weak you may want your association to be. You must decide; the decision is yours.

Test your decision-making ability with the following exercise.

| Value-Added Motivator | MY DECISION-MAKING QUOTIENT |
| --- | --- |

To the left of each item, indicate whether you believe the statement is true or false by marking T or F. If you can't make a decision on an item because the item needs more clarification or is ambiguous, consider the statement as a whole unit. Try not to separate the item into parts. Don't read into it more than what it is. Just determine, for the most part, whether you accept or reject the statement. Force yourself to make a decision for each item.

_____ 1. I am a good decision maker and display confidence as a decision maker; others feel the same way about me and my decision-making ability.

_____ 2. I have many strong friendships that are the result of my ability to make good decisions.

_____ 3. When a group decision needs to be made, frequently I am the one whose idea or solution is accepted.

_____ 4. Making timely decisions that are good for the majority is easy for me because I weigh the facts and seek solutions in my deliberations.

_____ 5. My friends, family, and colleagues consider my decision-making ability as one of my strongest assets.

_____ 6. I take responsibility for my actions; others also would agree that I demonstrate accountability and responsibility in my decisions.

_____ 7. Much of my motivation comes from making good decisions.

_____ 8. Most people would say that my motivation is not only at a high level, but that it influences others to be motivated too.

_____9. I enjoy every opportunity I can find to make decisions because decision making motivates me to further action.

_____10. I know when it is advantageous to involve other people in decision making and I really listen to what they have to say.

Multiply the number of T answers you recorded by 10 to convert your answer to a percent. If you scored 90 to 100 percent, you consider yourself to be an excellent decision maker. A score of 70 to 80 percent suggests you believe you are a fairly good decision maker. If you scored 60 percent or lower, your perceptions of yourself as a decision maker should give you cause to work seriously on improving this skill.

While this exercise may not be scientifically or statistically conclusive, probably you have learned something about yourself. Look at all the statements you accepted for yourself and draw some conclusions about your confidence in making decisions.

_____

_____

Do the same for the items you rejected including those that contained some part of the item you did not accept or did not describe you.

_____

_____

Ask two other persons who know you and whose opinion you value to rate you on the same items. Their ratings may give you further insight about the way others perceive your decision-making ability. Compare your responses with the results of your evaluators and draw some conclusions about yourself. On the basis of the combined ratings, record below what you believe you can do to increase your decision-making ability. Remember, even if you scored 100 percent on the combined ratings, you should still be able to find areas where improvement is possible.

_____

_____

_____

_____

What will it take to become a better decision maker? How can you use your Card to help you improve your decision-making skill? Activating your motivators to improve any skill, including your decision-making ability, provides the stimuli for self-improvement. Thus, "My Decision-Making Quotient" exercise you just completed should help you assess an important perception about yourself—an area where skill development is needed for most people. Of course, you know it's ultimately up to you as to how motivated you are or want to be to further enhance your decision-making ability. If you have several areas to strengthen, take one or two at a time and identify ways you can work on them. Your friends, family, or colleagues may be good resources for helping you determine the factors to consider for improving your decision making. They may be able to give you advice by suggesting ways you can go about addressing the factors that are important toward becoming a better decision maker. Asking for others' assistance also is one of the best ways to build and strengthen positive relationships and friendships. Certainly the motivation you derive from the effort you expend will provide you with yet another advantage of using your Card.

## ONCE UPON A TIME

Creating the atmosphere for making positive decisions and taking positive actions also is up to you. If you can influence the setting or help in its creation, you have made an investment in your own destiny. The atmosphere, to a certain degree, can be what you want it to be. At the very least, you can determine what elements are important to you for your surroundings to be most conducive to your operational style. Your Card acts as a catalyst in assuring your investment is positive toward maximizing your style. But how do you create the setting that will head you in the right direction? It comes from identifying your likes and dislikes. It comes from knowing your interests, and it comes from understanding your strengths and weaknesses—again, the same things that contribute to an understanding of what motivates you.

There are a number of strategies you can employ for creating your own ideal atmosphere—an atmosphere for good decision making and one in which you find high levels of motivation. Strategies include researching your interests and tying your work or leisure activities to your interests, trying out various approaches for attacking your work projects, identifying projects and activities you enjoy (which frequently depend on being completed in a specific setting), taking on an activity that forces you to explore a new area, pursuing the interests of others (including talking with others about why they enjoy such interests), and many other similar things. The strategies you employ do not necessarily need to be tried and tested before you venture into a new challenge. The important thing is that you capitalize on an important premise of your Card—making a conscious effort to expand your horizons.

Moving into new territory can be exhilarating. It may also be a little frightening. However, if you are willing to take a few chances (based on what you already know about yourself and your environment), your risk will be minimal if you consider the alternative of remaining static. The risk itself can be quite motivating. Thus, you really have nothing to lose. But where do you start to broaden your perspective toward expanding your horizons? Your perspective can be broadened with simple activities such as creating a story that starts, "Once upon a time . . . " or by brainstorming and dreaming.

Brainstorming, as you know, is trying to find as many alternatives or solutions as you can to a situation. True brainstorming knows no limits. That is, every idea, solution, suggestion, or alternative that is offered, no matter how bizarre, should be considered when looking at a problem. Brainstorming allows for "thinking outside the box" so all avenues are considered viable—at least in the initial stages. Once you have exhausted all the possible combinations and permutations of ways to look at a situation, you can begin to be more realistic. Then, and only then, do you begin to assess each idea, evaluate its merits, and select the alternatives that may be the most feasible for you to be successful.

Brainstorming works in any setting where decisions are made—and that means nearly everywhere—by any one individual, group, or team. Consider the simple exercise that follows:

| Value-Added Motivator | IF YOU WISH UPON A STAR |
| --- | --- |

List as many different ways you can think of for the use of a paper grocery bag. Number your ideas. (Because the space provided here probably won't be anywhere near sufficient for your ideas, you may want to prepare your entire list on a separate piece of paper.)

_____    _____    _____    _____

_____    _____    _____    _____

_____    _____    _____    _____

　　　If some of your ideas have similar or related uses or results, can you group them in a single category? If you can, do so. Then see if you can add more items as well as more categories. Continue your brainstorming by adding ideas to each of the categories (and hopefully even adding more categories as you get farther away from the reality of what you consider is typically done with a paper bag). Ask yourself questions like, "If I added a waxy coating to a paper bag, what other uses would it have?" or "If I cut and twisted strips of the bag, what could I create?" If possible, get a few grocery bags and experiment what you can do with them. Alter their shape, cut them up, paste them together, and so forth. Continue adding to your list.

　　　To further expand your creativity of brainstorming, do the exercise as a group. Remember, with brainstorming in its purist definition, there is no place for comments such as "that can't be done because of. . . . " You should find your list being further expanded when you discuss the task at hand and actively collaborate with others. Motivation usually is a direct result of brainstorming collaboration.

## DREAM THE IMPOSSIBLE DREAM

In a similar manner to brainstorming, daydreaming also can motivate you. In fact, many creative people rely quite heavily on brainstorming and daydreaming as motivators. Creating dreams and fantasies, as far-fetched as they may be, can be beneficial to motivation. For example, consider a nursery rhyme by speculating, analyzing, or giving it a 3-D introspection as to what it really means. That is, "Jack and Jill went up the hill. . . . Jack fell down and broke his crown. . . . " Did he really "break" his head? Maybe he cracked a tooth, or crushed his hat or . . . ? Speculate about Jack's experience. It was a positive one, right? After all, when "Jill came tumbling after," didn't everything turn out okay? Just like in some movies, they were together and happy in the end! Weren't they?

Certainly you have seen plenty of movies that were unrealistic and yet you came away from them feeling happy, satisfied, and possibly even invigorated. The enthusiasm you derived from seeing and experiencing the movie may have even helped you through the next day or two. The movie influenced you—it gave you the motivation to see a work project through to completion. Wasn't that very project the one that seemed nearly impossible just a few days ago? If it was, and you're now making progress, it may have been the movie that helped you to think a bit differently, reduced some of your stress, and cleared some cobwebs from your mind. The movie possibly even got you out of a rut that you didn't realize had swallowed you.

It probably goes without saying that you can go overboard with nearly everything you do—too many movies, too much work without a break, or overeating. While it's usually inevitable that that too much of a good thing may be bad, you can benefit from varying your routine. Finding the appropriate balance that works well for you should be your goal—a balance that contributes to your being in control. When you do, it truly is quite remarkable where you may find your motivation!

## WOULD YOU LIKE TO BE. . . . ?

A new challenge frequently is a motivator for most people. The challenge may not necessarily need to be one that is grandiose either. The anticipation of starting a new endeavor or even thinking about one may be a strong potential motivator in itself. Why is it frequently more motivating to start a new project than it is to make progress toward its completion? More than likely, it is mainly because of the excitement a new project brings. At the outset, you speculate on where you're going, what you'll be doing, and what path you'll take to get there. Once you get into the project and as you move it forward, you must address all the elements and the consequences associated with the project. Your choices may be difficult, and you find little things or even bigger obstacles along the way that seem to diminish the exuberance and flair that came with the initial challenge.

The project is analogous to the person who seeks fame and fortune. The answer to the question, "Would You Like to Be. . . . ?" comes as a challenge to you. Unless your answer is based on past experience, it is what you believe you'd like to be. The challenge may be attractive for a variety of reasons, but are you willing to pay the price that comes with your answer? That is, if you seek fame and fortune, what are the sacrifices along the way? Will the sacrifices be worth the payoff, assuming you reach your goal? That is, who pays the taxes?

Here's a good example:

### Who's Motivated?

 Trish wants to be a celebrity. She believes that by competing in beauty pageants she can quickly reach her goal. Trish, now 25 years old, has many competitions to her credit; finally, a year ago, she won a major pageant! Last night was her "swan song" after her year's reign. Feeling a big letdown today, she reflected on the past year and questioned her future. The job of beauty queen was extremely rewarding, but she never imagined it would be so demanding. No doubt, though, she has gained an invaluable perspective about herself and life. Her career ambition will become reality in a few weeks when she moves to Los Angeles to start a TV contract. Will it be anticlimactic to her beauty queen title or will it be a stepping stone to something bigger? Is fame and fortune what she really wants? What price will she have to pay to reach it?

1. Why do you think Trish has such mixed feelings about her life?

2. To what degree of satisfaction do you believe she is able to answer the questions she has posed? Why do you think this?

3. Do you believe Trish is being realistic about her life ambition and does she know what lies ahead? Why or why not?

4. What consequences will Trish face if and when she becomes a celebrity?

5. What sacrifices might Trish face along the way to stardom? How does one evaluate whether or not the goal is worth the sacrifices?

## TO BE OR NOT TO BE?

Fame, fortune, and the future are attractive to most people for many different reasons. Regardless of those reasons, you must be willing to pay the price to be successful. And even if you do pay your dues, there are no guarantees. You must face all the consequences—good and bad—that go along with your choice. If the odds seem too great, you are the only one who can make the decision to quit, deviate, or go on. If failure comes, you have to face it.

The price you have to pay for success may appear to be too high or overwhelming. But if you're going to achieve your goal—with a few nuances or even with major redirection along the way—you'll need to stay motivated. In fact, if you continually capitalize on your motivation, and use your Card to its fullest, you cannot go astray. You cannot afford not to make your Card your best friend! Your Card can help you to do the very best you can no matter what path you take.

Relying on your motivation at frequent intervals during tasks and projects throughout life will help keep you focused toward your important goals. You're sure to get some motivating rewards along the way.

## ARE YOU ON TRACK?

Staying focused on your goals is the best way for you to be in control of your life. It follows that focusing on the things you really value is a significant factor to avoid getting sidetracked. Since you are the only one who can be the engineer of your life, it makes no sense for you to sit back and merely be a passive rider on the train of life. In fact, it is dangerous to be anything less than the engineer if your life train is not headed in the direction you believe it should be going.

Reaching your destination will depend on your motivation for making good choices, correcting adverse actions and deviations, and making sure you are in control of how fast or slowly you are moving. Alternatively, if it is the ride that is important to you, then it does not matter which track you are on or where you are going. But if it's the destination that is important to you, it's fairly obvious that you must be sure you're on the right track and headed in the right direction. How much you value your Card (or what your Card means to you), depends on how much and how often you make your Card work to your advantage.

How can you be reassured you are really on the right track? It will take effort on your part. You'll probably need to assess the reality of the situation, the actions you have taken, and the plans you have for the future. And you'll need to keep a keen perspective of not only where you're going, but also how fast you are moving.

Along your life's journey, you may find it necessary to refuel, to refresh your energy levels with some rest breaks, and to negotiate some unintentional stops. If you have identified your motivators to help you through the interruptions—whether scheduled or not—you'll be on your way with renewed interest and determination. The more determined and motivated you are, the better equipped you will be to move toward your goals. If you're in control, you'll know you're on the right track.

## DOING IT MY WAY

Being in control does not necessarily mean having everything your own way, nor is independence a free ticket to do anything you want. If you think you can be independent and avoid the consequences, you'd better think again and consider a realignment of your position. Your motivators may need to be reevaluated for you to avoid disappointment.

Does this mean you can't do it your way? Quite the contrary. You can. But you must stay focused, be in control, and be aware of yourself and your surroundings. If you keep others in mind and how you can contribute to their well-being, you reap many rewards that come with your thoughtful consideration.

Some people believe they cannot be independent if they consider the feelings of others. They believe they lose their free will and actually begin to depend on others. In reality, they can't be further from the truth. In considering other people, you will gain more confidence in yourself, and your increased confidence will contribute to your independence. Additionally, your decision-making ability will increase as a result of finding ways to offer support and assistance to those around you. You will become more aware of your surroundings and more adept at interacting with conflicting elements. You will also contribute to your well-being by becoming more tolerant, more accepting, and more cognizant of your total environment. You're sure to find new motivators that give you and others strength—motivators that, when shared, will expand in significance.

Your personal Motivational ATM Card is a powerful influence for helping you determine what is important to you. Your Card should give you the push to maximize your peaks and sustain you through your valleys. It should help you move off plateaus and stir the stagnant water to find the treasure beneath it. If your Card isn't a comfort and help to you on and off stage, you should ask yourself, "What will it take for me to focus on the important things in life?" And, starting right now, you should pursue (and revisit) that question until you identify or re-identify the motivators that are important to you. Acting like you are in control will not give you the satisfaction of being in control. Thus, you would be wise to stop right now and reassess your old list of motivators. Then, make a new list and a commitment to use your Card to push you toward taking positive action associated with your motivators.

The power of knowing what motivators you have at your disposal cannot be underestimated, but it's up to you to find the power and to unleash it to make your motivators really work for you. No one can force motivation on you, but if you look around, you can see happy people—people who are motivated; people who are enjoying life; people who are embracing life. Thus, no matter at what high or low point you may be in your life at this very moment, you must exert the effort to help yourself. It's your decision to reach out—and everyone can always reach just a little further. A little effort will go a long way. A little effort will make it easier to take each new step toward bigger and better things.

On what do you want to focus? Are you willing to take action? What action can (will) you take *now* toward your target? Can you clearly see the target? If not, move to a better vantage point to get it in focus. When you're positioned and are aiming straight at the bull's-eye, you'll find your goals are easier to reach. Keep focused on your goals with your Card as your guide to keep you steadfast and on track. Take aim—ready, set, go—at being 100 percent in control of your life and actions, making good decisions with confidence and a positive attitude on and off stage.

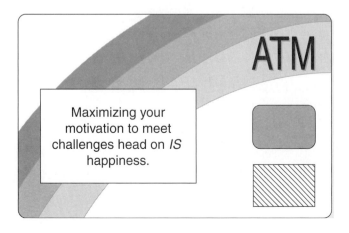

Maximizing your motivation to meet challenges head on *IS* happiness.

# CHAPTER 4: MOTIVATIONAL REINFORCEMENT

Reinforce your understanding of the chapter by responding to the following items.

1. Discuss the importance of being in control of your life and accepting your actions.

2. Explain the difference between knowing and accepting your perceptions.

3. How is happiness, positive attitude, and being in control linked to your confidence?

4. Suggest some of the ways you can create a positive environment for yourself and for others.

5. What can result from under- or over-blaming yourself for mistakes?

6. Explain why it is important to take responsibility for your own decision making.

7. What causes motivation to appear to mushroom around you?

8. Discuss some of the reasons why leaders are acknowledged by their followers.

9. Suggest some ways leaders rely on decision making to enhance their leadership.

10. Name some of the strategies to expand motivation and decision-making ability.

11. How can daydreaming and brainstorming contribute to building motivation?

12. How do you determine if the price of success is too high?

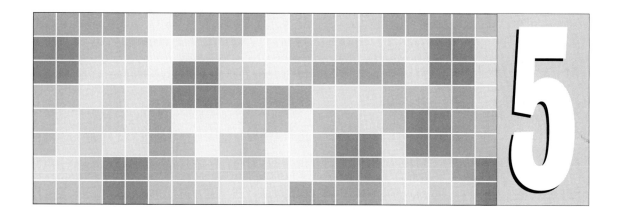

# Always in High Fashion: Motivation with Style

## TRAVERSING THE RUNWAY OF LIFE

When it comes right down to it, most people have many of the same needs and desires: the basics of food, shelter, and clothing as well as other things that contribute to self-worth, satisfaction, and gratification. Because needs, values, and motivation have a close relationship, it is to good advantage to identify your needs and to determine how they contribute to your values (and vice versa). Discovering ways to successfully link needs and values to your motivators and actions to reach your short- and long-term goals are reflected in what may be referred to as your total value system. Your value system reflects your overall philosophy, the goals you strive to reach, and the resources you use to reach them. Your value system also is strongly tied to your likes and needs as well as the importance you place on each of them. Thus, let's start this discussion with what needs are and how they are identified and met.

Most people find that once their basic needs are fulfilled, they move on to find other ways to satisfy their higher level needs and desires. For example, if you have only one pair of jeans and one business suit in your closet, it isn't a difficult choice to determine what you'll wear today if you plan to go to a soccer game. In fact, you'll probably grab the jeans and put them on without even thinking about it.

But if you have several shirts in your closet, you may need to make a conscious decision as to which one you'll wear. By having to make a decision about your shirt, you have already moved on from fulfilling a basic need for clothing to a higher level need. You want to wear a shirt that gives you satisfaction, a shirt that may even contribute to your self-worth. In selecting the shirt you will wear, you may ask: "Should I wear a T-shirt, a golf shirt, or some other type of casual top?" If you are concerned about being comfortable, you may have selected a sleeveless shirt of soft white cotton only to change your mind for one that is more colorful and has sleeves. In changing your mind, you may have given thought to the weather: "Will it be hot, humid, cool, or rainy? Should I be concerned about getting sunburned?"

Even if it is for only a fleeting moment, believe it or not, you may consider a number of other factors that enter into your decision about what shirt to wear. Some additional thoughts that may go through your mind include: "What makes me look my best? Should I wear that really fun, crazy logo shirt? Will it be okay to wear my favorite shirt even if it has a snag or is missing a button? Can I fix it; do I want to or have time to mend it so I can wear it now? Can I wear the same shirt that I had on a couple of days ago?" (You may now be upset that you didn't do your laundry.) Obviously, there are lots of other questions that get answered—probably unconsciously as you continue dressing—long before you even get out the door.

## NEVER IRON YOUR CLOTHES WHILE YOU'RE WEARING THEM

As with the detailed example of selecting a shirt to wear, you probably make hundreds of decisions each day just to address the basic needs in your life. Obviously, many decisions are rather simple, but many become more difficult as your basic needs are satisfied and you move into satisfying your higher level needs. Many of your higher level needs are those that you strive to reach by setting goals—they are the realities in your life or the actualities to which you aspire.

Because, at least partially, your aspirations frequently take time and effort to achieve, they are the things you value greatly. The value you place on them usually gives you the motivation to pursue them because you know the gratification you'll get over the long term is well worth the effort—don't iron your clothes while you are wearing them. You may get the wrinkles out and look good for now, but the burns you could get from your quick action could scar you forever.

The higher level needs become more and more important to you when your basic needs are met or are taken for granted. You no longer have to worry about your lower level needs, so you move up the ladder to achieve the things that contribute to your happiness. Let's consider what some of those needs are:

| **Value-Added Motivator** | BRAND NAMES I VALUE |
|---|---|

For each of the five pairs of items listed, indicate your preference for each pair by placing an "X" on the line before the one that you prefer. Some of the choices may be extremely difficult to make, but try to select your preference to every item.

1. I prefer     ____ making difficult choices     ____ others tackling problems

2. I can't live without     ____ a reliable car     ____ family or friends

3. I value my      ___ honesty and integrity      ___ possessions

4. I live for      ___ my own happiness      ___ making other people happy

5. I hope I can      ___ be really successful      ___ make lots of money

Now, add five additional pairs of items that reflect an item you prefer and an item you do not. The two items that make up a pair do not need to be related in any way.

6. I really enjoy      ___ _____      ___ _____

7. I want to      ___ _____      ___ _____

8. A desire I have is      ___ _____      ___ _____

9. If I could change any one thing in my life, I would      ___ _____      ___ _____

10. If I could wish anything for another person, I would      ___ _____      ___ _____

Now, review your responses to the first five pairs (1 to 5). For each item that you selected for each of the five pairs, consider your rationale for your selection. Write your response for each item here.

1. _____

2. _____

3. _____

4. _____

5. _____

There are no right or wrong answers to your selections; however, consider what decisions you have made on the basis of your needs and wants. If you selected the first item in pair 1, you prefer to take on challenges. You are responsible (or at least feel you want to be accountable) for your actions. If you selected the first item in pair 2 and the second item in pairs 3 and 5, you probably are very materialistic. You believe that material things are more important than certain values and nonmaterialistic goals. Additionally, if you selected the first item in pair 4, you may be selfish and more concerned about your own importance, wishes, and opinions rather than those of the people around you. You may not have considered that if you contribute to others' happiness, you may be rewarded with your own happiness!

Possibly even more important than your responses to the first five pairs of items, are your responses to the second five pairs (6 to 10), the pairs that you developed for likes/dislikes. What conclusions can you draw from each of the second five pairs? Write your responses in the space provided.

6. _____

7. _____

8. _____

9. _____

10. _____

To complete this exercise, add a summary about your responses. Your summary should be related to your value system. That is, what can you say about who you are and what is really important to you? Why?

Summary: _____

_____

_____

_____

Now that you have completed your summary, can you identify any areas of your value system you might want to refocus? If so, take the opportunity to start working on ways to do so right now. Rely on your Card to help you along the way to give you the motivation you need to make changes. If you use your Card to its fullest, you probably will be able to speed your progress toward changing your focus.

## A FAD OR FASHION STATEMENT

The values exercise you just completed should give you some insights into your personality. It should tell you what is important to you and why. Although it may not change your mind about what you want and how you will achieve desired results, it should give you a better understanding of yourself. It should also help you realize that your values may be very different than those of others.

If you like high fashion and your friends may be into fads, who's right? Probably both of you because each of you is expressing yourself through the differences in your value systems. Just because your friends, family, or coworkers do not share your values, you can still coexist and do things together! Further, if you solicit them to complete the exercise above (individually or as a group with you included), everyone should benefit from finding out more about each other. Knowing and understanding the values of those around you should contribute to your being more tolerant of their feelings because they may hold their values just as strongly as you do yours.

Values discussions and comparisons provide an introspection into what you want out of life as well as why you want it. Anyone—students, managers, employees, friends, family members, etc.— can benefit from values discussions to discover how values contribute to better working relationships and, in general, all human relationships. The discussion activity provides the insights, but what you do with those insights is up to you. If you believe your values need adjusting, your Card should spur you to finding the necessary motivation to not only identify the right path for you to take toward reaching higher level goals, but also to help you along the way to work toward and acquire the right things.

### Who's Motivated?

Trevor always wanted a sports car. In fact, not just any sports car; to be specific, he wanted a new, red Corvette. He worked part-time and saved what little money he could throughout high school and college. His goal was to reward himself with the car when he received his marketing degree. There were, however, a few things that happened during his last year in college that changed his ultimate plan. Janie came along; love entered the picture; and marriage vows were exchanged. Janie, with just one more year of college to complete, lost her scholarship—a complete surprise that came only a month after they put a down payment on their first home.

1. Is there anything wrong with having a materialistic goal such as Trevor's graduation present to himself? Is (was) Trevor's goal realistic? Why or why not?

2. Now that things have changed, should Trevor's dream be abandoned? Why or why not?

3. How could Trevor modify his goal (or timing) and still be rewarded? What role could/should Janie play in Trevor's rethinking his goal?

4. What would be the advantages and disadvantages of Trevor's just going out and buying the graduation present he probably deserves?

5. Is there any way possible Trevor might put his marketing degree into the equation? If so, how and what are the possible outcomes?

Using the Card provides excellent motivation to want to do the right things as well as the motivation to want to work, and work hard, toward your goals. That is, your Card should be a constant reminder to you to avoid the shortcuts that give you only short-term gains. While there is nothing wrong with short-term rewards, they should not cloud your vision from seeing the broader picture nor take the place of your long-term goals.

## BUY NOW, PAY LATER

To reach a lofty goal that has value and merit to you may take more time and effort than you believe you have. Keeping your mind focused on the goal may not be easy, but no one said it would. If something is really important and valuable to you, don't be tempted to opt for immediate gratification by jeopardizing what can become significantly greater as a long-term benefit. A quick purchase that means short-term happiness now may mean you'll have an insurmountable bill later—at a time when your long-term happiness may require considerable attention.

If you use your motivators with deliberation to help you get beyond wanting immediate satisfaction, you can avoid at least three pitfalls:

1. Immediate or quick gratification usually doesn't provide sufficient depth or significance to last very long.

2. A Band-Aid approach is just that—a stop gap measure that is temporary. If satisfaction is merely temporary, it may leave you at an even lower level than where you were before you selected the Band-Aid.

3. Once you deviate from your intended goal, you may not have the energy you need to continue on to reach the real reward. The risk you take of not going on may become a setback, or worse yet, it may be the end of your quest for reaching your goal.

## ON SALE FOR A LIMITED TIME

Reaching your goals depends on you, but that doesn't mean you can't get some assistance along the way. You don't need to do everything solo to be independent. Getting some help from others may be a motivator to both you and them. If you tap into a variety of resources available to you, you'll probably expand your perspectives and grow personally and/or professionally.

Being resourceful is a talent that is vitally important in our highly technological society. Information abounds; it is readily available from nearly unlimited sources. Never before has information been so abundant, available, and accessible. It's up to the individual seeking the information to access it by whatever means is most convenient. If there is a challenge beyond finding the best source for the information desired, it is your ability to sort through, in a systematic and timely manner, and select what is really important to you and reject what is not. For example, let's say you truly enjoy shopping. In fact, you take advantage of opportunities to shop whenever you can—going to the mall, using mail order catalogs, ordering via telephone and TV, and purchasing through the Internet on line. What are the advantages of shopping from a variety of sources? If you don't use all the resources available to you, will you be at a disadvantage? While you may have already answered these questions, consider this scenario:

### Who's Motivated?

Tony loves to shop. In fact, Tony would rather shop than do anything else. And whenever he has the opportunity, he's shopping and finding out what's new on the market. His shopping is not limited to any one particular area—he enjoys shopping for clothes as well as for food, office supplies and equipment, hobbies, and vehicles. He's just happiest when he's shopping. Tony says he doesn't really need to buy anything when he's shopping. His friends, however, think differently because Tony always seems to have a little something he has bought for them. In fact, they have made bets with him that he can't go a whole week without buying something.

1. Is Tony's love for shopping unhealthy? Why or why not?

2. What, if anything, do you think Tony's "shopping resourcefulness" brings to his life (including his job) when he isn't shopping?

3. What complications might Tony face if he isn't realistic about how much he buys?

4. What advantages might both Tony and his friends enjoy from Tony's frequent shopping?

5. What motivators are present in this scenario? For Tony? For his friends?

You probably know a Tony (or maybe you're like him) who likes to shop. Why is shopping, especially when there is a sale, so enticing? One of the reasons may be strictly for the enjoyment or gratification it provides. Another reason may be because it's satisfying or motivating to find a bargain or to do comparison shopping. For whatever reason, a sale usually draws people. In fact, lots of people won't buy something unless it has a "sale" tag on it; and, all too often, the item may actually be the regular price (sometimes it is even higher than a regularly priced item from another source). Bargain hunting can be a form of resourcefulness. It can be a strong motivator. Similarly the sale sign is meant to be a motivational influence for you to act now. It's a motivator for the seller to boost revenues. The seller wants to attract buyers, and many potential buyers want to get the best price possible, even if the sale item isn't something they need or really want.

But if something is offered to you and you don't really need or want it, why do you sometimes buy it? One of the most frequent reasons is because the item has been presented to you as something you really do need or should want. If you've shown considerable interest in it (maybe by revisiting the place where the item is sold), you'll be embarrassed not to buy it. Most frequently, you'll probably find the item is marketed in such a way that you need to buy it—right now.

While much of this discussion has focused on shopping (resourcefulness of the seller and buyer, sales and marketing strategies), the same can be applied to many other things. That is, it also relates to the earlier discussion on how resourceful you are at accessing, sorting, and selecting the right information for the right situation and in a timely manner. The motivators are similar, too. Complete the following exercise to see how this discussion applies to you.

---

| **Value-Added Motivator** | **I'M MOTIVATED . . . IN STYLE** |
|---|---|

Identify four activities or actions that you enjoy doing, that you consider to be strong motivators, and that you believe require your resourcefulness to do them. List each of the activities on the lines here:

1. _____

2. _____

3. _____

4. _____

While it may be obvious as to what resources are needed for the activities you've listed, list the necessary resources for each. Record your responses on the respective lines:

1. _____

2. _____

3. _____

4. _____

Similarly, while it may also be obvious why it is necessary to be resourceful to pursue the activities you've listed, give the reason for each. By completing the lead-in sentence, record your responses on the corresponding lines. Make sure your responses are positive (for example, your response should not include a negative such as: "If I don't use the resource, the result. . . . ").

It is necessary to be resourceful because:

1. _____

2. _____

3. _____

4. _____

Now describe what the outcome might be if you don't consider the resources (or if you aren't resourceful). Record your responses:

1. _____

2. _____

3. _____

4. _____

Wanting something and needing it can be two very different things. If you add the element of how resourceful you need to be to get it, the picture can change even more. Being resourceful in assessing the value of something you want or need usually gives you a better reason to try or not to try to get it. If you've made the decision to "go for it" and you have to work to get it, usually it is more valuable to you. This goes for tangible items as well as things that are not tangible.

As you assess how resourceful you need to be to acquire something (and what resources you need to tap into), you may want to ask yourself the question: "Why do I really want or need this?" If you believe you have a valid reason (and that's a judgment call on your part based on your value system) for coming to your decision, you should take some action. Wanting things for the right reasons is important. Just because something is on sale doesn't mean you must buy it. And just because you have taken the afternoon off to go shopping (and have money in your pocket) doesn't mean you have to buy anything.

But how do you know if you have the right reasons for wanting something? If you have weighed the pros and cons for making a decision, you will find the right reason usually will be a motivator. You'll get satisfaction because you value the motivator and what it does for you. You will consider your friends, coworkers, or others and you'll possibly even find ways for them to be valuable resources to you (keeping in mind you'll need to reciprocate). You'll not be stepping on others' toes, and you'll not be tempted to act now and ask for forgiveness later.

Alternatively, even if you believe you've made the right decision and your action still turns out to be a demotivator, you need to regroup quickly and take another path for achieving a more positive outcome. Hopefully you've learned a valuable lesson from the experience. Keep in mind, the more realistic you are about your decisions and the more you find and select appropriate ways and means to help you achieve your goals, the less you will need to worry about demotivators. Your motivators will take over because your Card has you working toward positive outcomes.

## APPEARANCE IS MORE THAN SKIN DEEP

You know that your friends, coworkers, and family can become important resources in building a support system that will move you toward your goals and aspirations. That doesn't mean you may not have to build or mend some  bridges along the way or that everyone's motives are as honorable as yours. Exploitation happens; avoiding it, however, is possible by learning from mistakes, by being realistic, and by assessing the value of your resources.

The resources you value today may not be those you value tomorrow. That is, just as the stock market changes from day to day based on lots of circumstances, you will need to weigh the circumstances that contribute to how valuable your resources are. You'll probably place more value on some resources and less on others at various times during your journey toward your intended objectives. If you are willing to adjust as needed and, as others are involved, are willing to reciprocate, others will be more obliged to do the same. While practicing reciprocity is not a 100 percent guarantee for achieving the results you want, it's a good practice and a good motivator. Doing what you say you'll do will contribute to your integrity. Others will trust you at your word and actions—your value system is showing. Practicing reciprocity based on integrity and trust is a much better posture to take than accepting whatever other alternatives may exist.

You portray your value system in all your actions and words. That is, your persona is more than your clothes and outward appearance. It is all that you do; it is your inward values and how you treat others. It is what you value and how you go about achieving your goals. It includes your motivators as well as how you are motivated. And it includes how you interact with everyone around you. Your appearance is reflected in your beliefs, interests, likes, dislikes, strengths, and weaknesses.

If your appearance is only skin deep, your values will likely be shallow too. You cannot expect others to view and accept you as anything different. Your integrity and honesty, as you know, are two of your greatest personal attributes. They contribute in many ways to your total value system as viewed by others as you practice them in your daily life. They are attributes that also enhance many other things that you value. For example, your dependability and loyalty have a direct relationship to your integrity and honesty. What are the elements that make up your value system? Which ones do you value the most? Complete the following exercise and you'll get a better insight to your value system.

| Value-Added Motivator | MY VALUES WARDROBE |
|---|---|

For each of the items listed here, determine how important each is to you. Use a rating scale of 5-Essential; 4-Very Important; 3-Somewhat Important; 2-Not Very Important; 1-Unimportant. Place the number of your rating in the space provided before each item. Don't leave any items blank; force yourself to rate each one, even if you have to pass it the first time through the list and return to ponder that item. If you wish to add items to the list, use the blank lines for additional items (and rank each of your added items, too).

| | | | |
|---|---|---|---|
| ___ Firm | ___ Patient | ___ Competent | ___ Compassionate |
| ___ Fair | ___ Integrity | ___ Objective | ___ Inspirational |
| ___ Open | ___ Honesty | ___ Dependable | ___ High energy |
| ___ Coach | ___ Resourceful | ___ Self-esteem | ___ Goal oriented |
| ___ Loyal | ___ Decisive | ___ Positive | ___ Good communicator |
| ___ Calm | ___ Political | ___ Charismatic | ___ Knowledgeable |
| ___ Neat | ___ Efficient | ___ Accepting | ___ Self-motivated |
| ___ Proud | ___ Fearless | ___ Consistent | ___ Calm under pressure |
| ___ Happy | ___ Realistic | ___ Innovative | ___ Strong-willed |
| ___ Genuine | ___ Visionary | ___ Ambitious | ___ Even-tempered |
| ___ Tactful | ___ Flexible | ___ Team builder | ___ Enthusiastic |
| ___ Fun | ___ Delegate | ___ Persistent | ___ Productive |
| ___ Lively | ___ Negotiator | ___ Organized | ___ Change agent |
| ___ Kind | ___ Optimistic | ___ Humorous | ___ Inquisitive |
| ___ Loving | ___ Generous | ___ Powerful | ___ Risk-taker |
| ___ Caring | ___ Religious | ___ Creative | ___ Understanding |
| ___ Helpful | ___ Friendly | ___ Intuitive | ___ Well-mannered |

Additional items I value:

___ _____        ___ _____        ___ _____        ___ _____

___ _____        ___ _____        ___ _____        ___ _____

___ _____        ___ _____        ___ _____        ___ _____

___ _____        ___ _____        ___ _____        ___ _____

With all items rated, review your list and add any items that you believe should be on the list but were not included here. Rate each of them the same way (5, 4, 3, 2, 1) as you did the others.

Once you have completed rating the items, note those items you rated the highest (you may want to make a separate list of them). If you have several items rated 5, select the four that you value the most. Again, if possible, place them in the order of their importance to you. Once you have identified your four highest ranked items, record them in the "Essential" category on the lines below (start with the item you rated as the most important in your "Essential" category).

Go through the same process for the items you rated 4; list them below under the heading labeled "Very Important." Do the same for the other items you rated 3, 2, and 1 and record the items on the lines in the respective columns. If you don't have four items in a single category, leave the lines blank for now. Finally, go back to your original scoring and count up the number of items you rated in each category. Write that number on the line under each respective column.

### My Values Wardrobe Summary

| | Essential | Very Important | Somewhat Important | Not Very Important | Unimportant |
|---|---|---|---|---|---|
| 1. | _____ | _____ | _____ | _____ | _____ |
| 2. | _____ | _____ | _____ | _____ | _____ |
| 3. | _____ | _____ | _____ | _____ | _____ |
| 4. | _____ | _____ | _____ | _____ | _____ |
| Totals | _____ | _____ | _____ | _____ | _____ |

From a review of the five categories, what can you say about your value system? Is your value system one that another person might envy? Are your values those that you admire in others? Do you practice the values you believe are essential?

At this point, you may wish to add items to any category above that does not have four items listed. Since it may be difficult to add items, you might want to discuss your values with another individual. Also, once you feel you have completed the exercise and if you have an opportunity to review the above final listing of items with a friend, family member, colleague, or boss, take advantage of it. Another person can offer you important insights about whether or not they see you as you see yourself. Others can also give you their perspective about what some of the items mean to them (which may be very different from the way you view them).

Finally, the main questions you should ask are: Am I happy with my value system? If not, what and how can I change to be more satisfied with my life? What will motivate me to make changes to improve my value system? Write your summary in the space provided.

_____

_____

_____

_____

_____

It should go without saying that to precipitate change in your value system, this listing provides only the preliminary step: awareness. From the awareness stage onward, it probably will take considerable effort on your part to make changes. Values are deep seated; they are what you are and what make up your everyday actions. Thus, to make even small changes, you'll, no doubt, need the help of your Card to stay motivated as you work on making values changes.

The effort you expend to alter some of your values may be the most important thing you can do to get you headed on a more positive runway of life. If you select your values "wardrobe" which capitalizes on your inward appearance, your outward appearance also will be enhanced. That is, your values should be able to meet the test of time—the values that feed your positive momentum and motivate you to do your very best in life.

## WHAT YOUR ATTIRE SAYS ABOUT YOU

As you dress for a formal occasion, you probably wouldn't consider wearing a casual outfit that may not be appropriate. Why? More than likely, part of your decision is based on your values system and part of it on what makes you feel good. To feel good, you want to look good. That may mean you will wear something that you know looks good on you. Some other considerations in wanting to look good may include wearing something that will stand out, that will be impressive, or that is unique in some way so as to be noticed. Alternatively, you may want to wear something to blend in and be comfortable with others at the event.

Comfort may be another consideration; however, lots of people may not list comfort as their first motivator in dressing for a formal occasion. You may have even considered what others will be wearing and what the occasion demands. For example, if you are going to a formal wedding or a formal party at a friend's home, you may consider what to wear on the basis of wanting to please your host and hostess. You may want your attire to say, "Thank you for inviting me. I am pleased to be here and want to show my respect to you for the occasion you have planned."

Whatever your attire, you have made a statement about your personality and about your values. You have considered your own values in either what pleases you or what pleases someone else or both. If you have considered other people, you know the importance of fostering relationships with other people. Your values are showing.

While this example of dressing for a formal occasion does not offer any real insights as to how you should dress for success, it does stress the way your values may appear to others from your outward appearance. Other people may want to get to know you because, at least initially, they like the way you dress. You, too, may find you want to work with someone who dresses in a certain way. You may even subconsciously select someone to work on a project because you believe that person is organized, knowledgeable, and can deliver a quality product. Why? It is likely because of the person's professional, neat, and clean appearance. The person has given you a specific impression from the clothing the person is wearing. You believe or perceive that the person really is "wearing" a value system.

## Who's Motivated?

Rosa and Darla are best friends. They like many of the same things—Thai food, casual clothing, and many leisure activities. Even their career choices are uncannily close; both are computer programmers. Their modes of operation, however, are another matter. Rosa is systematic, deliberate, and sequential in the way she works and lives. She likes to complete a project to her exacting satisfaction before moving on to another. Darla, on the other hand, can be described as more or less a free agent. She enjoys many different kinds of things, is always coming up with new ideas, and finds pleasure in jumping from one thing to another. She truly enjoys having lots of things in progress all of the time (at work and home) and frequently loses track of time because she is engrossed in a project. Rosa has learned she must be patient with Darla. In fact, whenever they make plans to do something, Rosa knows she'll probably have to wait for Darla.

1. From the similarities and differences in Rosa and Darla, what values are of importance to both of them? To each of them individually?

2. Why is it difficult, if not impossible, to determine who has the better value system and who will be more apt to succeed in life?

3. If you could select just one person, would you want Rosa or Darla as a friend? coworker? boss? subordinate? Why?

4. Form a mental picture of Rosa and Darla, then describe the images you have of them and of their offices and homes.

## EVALUATE YOUR IMAGE

The runway of life, no doubt, provides plenty of challenges for people to express themselves on a daily basis. Of course, the image you convey each and every day does not depend on other people—it depends on *you*. If you are concerned about your image and how others perceive you, you may be rather careful in the choices that contribute to the image you reflect. Keep in mind that the choices you make include your actions, deeds, and words as well as your clothing and physical outward appearance. Evaluating your image on a regular basis will help you to build

and reflect the image you believe is important. Your evaluation should help you to prioritize your values, emulate characteristics you admire in others, and find the right balance of the elements that work to your advantage.

Working toward developing the image you believe is important for your own well-being should be your goal. However, we know that most people also want to ensure that others have the right assessment of them. Conveying the right image carries certain challenges with it—challenges that can be met most successfully with a strong value system and good motivators to achieve the goals associated with your needs and values. With the challenge for achievement and personal success in life, motivators and incentives become value-added elements to everyone. Thus, you probably will find your Card a handy resource to tap into the motivators that contribute to the assessment and development of your personal and professional image—a whole image that is packaged to reflect your attitude, personality, and style.

Don't let anyone tell you that a positive attitude and being motivated are not in style. They are! And they are so critical to your other values as well as to the challenges you meet every single day that you will do well to take considerable pride in keeping them polished and protected. With a positive attitude and the motivation you need to meet the challenges that lie ahead of you, you will always be in style—and, definitely, always in high fashion.

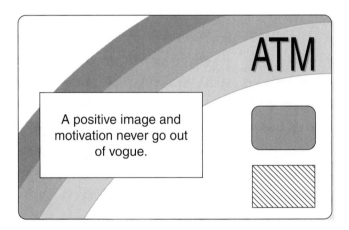

A positive image and motivation never go out of vogue.

## CHAPTER 5: MOTIVATIONAL REINFORCEMENT

Reinforce your understanding of the chapter by responding to the following items.

1. Discuss the significance of the various levels of a person's needs.

2. How do your preferences determine your value system?

3. If your values differ from others, why can you still enjoy diverse friendships?

4. Identify some of the risks that are associated with opting for instant gratification.

5. What are some of the important elements of selecting good resources?

6. How do you know if you have the right goals and reasons to achieve them?

7. Suggest some ways your friends can be significant resources to reach your goals.

8. Name at least five elements that make up your value system.

9. How can you change or alter your value system to make it more satisfying?

10. Suggest some ways you can determine how your values are portrayed to others.

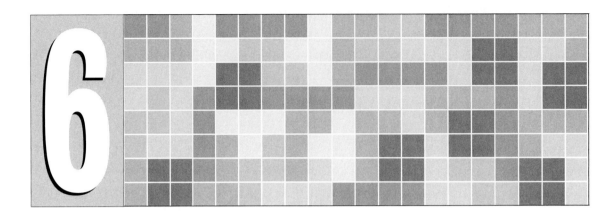

# Your Motivational Road Map: The Signs Along the Way

## RACING WITH THE COMPETITION

If you've ever had the opportunity to watch a Grand Prix, NASCAR, Pike's Peak, or some other major road race, you probably can appreciate the tremendous skill needed by the drivers as they work the course. They not only need to be skillful in their driving, they also need to keep tabs on how their car feels, maximize their speed, negotiate traffic, avoid lots of potential negatives, and stay alert to a variety of other things. Their goal is to win (or, if they are newcomers to the sport, to move up in their position) while being aware of considerable challenges that could quickly turn into devastating consequences. Because there is competitiveness in all aspects of the race, the drivers and their crews focus on many different components that can give them a competitive edge. They are motivated toward a goal; they minimize and avoid negatives at all costs.

Obviously, you don't have to be a race car driver to be motivated by competition. Competition can be very motivating for nearly everyone. And competition can work to your advantage, especially in difficult situations. Competition can make you more aware; it can make you concerned about the surface of the road. It can also help you through rough times—through those hairpin curves and the unknown debris on the road created from the traffic ahead of you. That is, to keep your interest and competitive edge in life, you must negotiate a lot of challenges along the way. If you are motivated to meet these daily challenges, you have a better chance of not only meeting life's competition head on, but also enjoying your life considerably more than if you just let things happen.

Many of the challenges you face each day come in the form of small bumps in the road. Others are similar to dangerous potholes, construction areas, and major roadblocks. You must be ready for these unexpected deviations if you're going to ride or drive the road of life. Can you do it? How well can and do you meet everyday challenges, especially when they are negative? Are you overly concerned about the unknowns that lie ahead? On the other hand, are you just taking one day at a time with little or no concern whatsoever for the future? Keep in mind that, even if you're somewhere in the middle, your personal Motivational ATM Card is there for support.

## WHAT DO TRAFFIC SIGNS TELL US?

No matter what course you take, frequently you'll find lots of warning signs along the way to alert you of the dangers ahead. For example, your boss's behavior may tell you emphatically to *stop!* While her actions may be positive or negative, she definitely has your attention. Her words, posture, or even silence sends a strong message to you to be on the alert. If you have been astute in reading your boss's signals, you view the stop sign as a warning that you must be cautious or tread softly. Stop is a negative indicator that gets your attention so you'll probably be much more alert in your future actions—at least for a while. As you proceed, you may even be looking for hidden potholes that present further challenges that you may encounter.

Whether you realize it or not, you learned very early in life to react to negative indicators—no, stop, don't, can't, etc. As a child you were warned of many dangers and were taught repeatedly you couldn't or shouldn't do certain things. You probably heard such things as "don't touch the stove," "no, you can't go and play next door," "you've ruined your best shirt," "you can't have cake now because you won't eat your supper," and similar types of warnings. All of these warnings are negatives. The fact of the matter is, that by the time you became a teenager, you were subjected to hearing negative warnings repeatedly. It has been estimated that negative reinforcement happens literally thousands of times—even in the most positive, nurturing environments—to every child by the time a child reaches his teen years. It is further reported that negative reinforcers outweigh positive reinforcers by at least five to ten or more times! Here's a sample exercise that will give you a fairly clear indicator of how negative your environment may be:

| **Value-Added Motivator** | TRAFFIC LIGHTS I'VE ENCOUNTERED |
| --- | --- |

Using the green, red, and yellow color scheme of a traffic light as categories, think of some of the experiences you've had in the last week that are positive (go), negative (stop), or warn of an upcoming negative (caution). As you think of an event or activity, determine into which category it should be entered. For example, one of your coworkers or subordinates may have given you a compliment in a meeting for a job well done. That event should be entered in the go category. Be sure to identify the event or activity first; then determine the category that it represents. Write down the event or experience in the appropriate category in the spaces provided. If you have difficulty completing one or more of the three categories, try to complete at least one category (3 events) and provide at least one event in the other two categories before you continue reading.

Go events:

1. _____
2. _____
3. _____

Stop events:

1. _____
2. _____
3. _____

Caution events:

1. _____
2. _____
3. _____

Did you have difficulty completing any one category? If so, which one and why? Which category did you complete first? Did you find more than enough events to fill one of the categories? If so, which one and again why? Is there any significance as to why one of the three categories was the easiest to complete? Draw some conclusions about your responses to these questions.

_____
_____
_____
_____

Probably there are numerous activities and events in your life that you take for granted. You may never have considered associating activities into groups representing green, red, and yellow traffic lights—situations that are positive, negative, or warning of an upcoming negative. However, every day of your life you are forced, consciously or not, to encounter traffic-light activities and events. Some of those situations you expect to be positive; others you expect to be negative. When a positive event, or what you perceive should be a positive event, turns out negative, it frequently sticks in your mind a lot longer than if the event had truly turned out positive. That is, many people tend to remember negative situations much longer and more frequently than they do positive ones.

If this is true, then what happens when a negative event turns out positive? Surprisingly enough, a negative situation that turns out positive may still cause you to be skeptical (negatively cautious) and a little surprised. Furthermore, because of your past experience, you may even be a little cynical and consider the positive event with caution. You may wonder why the situation turned out positive and you may continue to look for a less positive alternative or more realistic outcome. You may even look for reasons to turn the positive situation into a negative one just to confirm your assumptions that it can't possibly be positive. Consider Ulga's experience:

## Who's Motivated?

Ulga, a senior vice president of a major bank, has attended many social events on behalf of her organization over the past five years. In fact, possibly too many events! Since she is the most recent employee promoted into a senior executive position, she feels she usually draws all the second-rate events. Gradually, over the years, however, she has totally changed her attitude about her role—and it shows. What has caused such a dramatic change of heart? At a charity ball about four years ago she met Geraldo, a prominent attorney. She and Geraldo, now happily married for nearly three years and with two beautiful children, attend most of the bank's social events together.

1. Do you believe Ulga's persona or behavior at social events may be different today than four years ago? If so, how? Why?

2. How do you believe Ulga represents her bank (or is perceived) at the social events she attends now versus those she attended early in her promotion? Why?

3. Why is one's perception about a situation so important?

4. Whose decision was it for Ulga to project a more positive role and why?

While it is possible that Ulga may have grown into her role, consider what may be a very different ending for Ulga. Let's say that 10 years from now, Geraldo believes he has made a terrible mistake in marrying Ulga and their marriage ends up in a messy divorce involving a custody battle over their children. Is it possible that Ulga would blame the bank for the whole mess? Possibly, yes. In this scenario, it would be a positive turned negative at least twice over. That is, her promotion was positive, but attending the social events was negative, then meeting and marrying Geraldo was positive until the divorce turned her feelings negative. In fact, if a divorce were pending, meeting and marrying Geraldo would be a big negative too. Ulga's children would factor into her attitude, too. If Ulga's feelings really turn, she might even view her promotion (as well as her job, colleagues, and life) as negative.

We know that the scenario of Ulga and Geraldo, and many others with similarities, is a part of life that people must face every day. People—students, employees, leaders, nonworking persons—have to make choices. Most people have the choice of whether or not their lives are going to be positive or negative. That choice is made on a daily basis and probably many times during a single day. Certainly it isn't always easy to display positive behavior when there are so many negative things around you. And no matter what the reason, every person with whom you have contact is influenced by your behavior. All too frequently it takes only one negative event to overshadow many positive ones. What behavior do you portray? Are you perceived as someone who is positive or negative? When things get rough and you become negative, how can you overcome your negativeness?

| **Value-Added Motivator** | **PERCEPTIONS ANONYMOUS** |
|---|---|

Identify three people with whom you work or have daily contact. List a positive and a negative behavior you see in each of them. Record your responses on the lines labeled PB (positive behavior) and NB (negative behavior). Then, if you have a suggestion for improving the negative behaviors you identified, write that suggestion on the line labeled S.

Person A: _____

PB _____

NB _____

S _____

Person B: _____

PB _____

NB _____

S _____

Person C: _____

PB _____

NB _____

S _____

Now look at the responses you provided regarding the negative behaviors and suggestions for each of the three people; then answer the following questions:

1. If someone described me, would I have any of the negative behaviors that I identified for any one of the three people? ___Yes ___No

   If no, how would others describe any negative behavior I have?

   _____

2. If someone offered me the suggestions I noted to correspond to the negative behavior I identified for any of the three people, would I be offended? ___Yes ___No

   If yes, could I modify the suggestions to be less threatening? ___Yes ___No

   If yes, how? (Add your responses to the S lines above.)

3. If I demonstrate any of the negative behaviors I identified, would I want to change my behavior? ___Yes ___No. Explain:

_____

_____

Also, would I want someone to help me change my behavior? ___Yes ___No. Why or why not?

_____

_____

4. What would it take for me to accept assistance from another person to improve any of my negative behaviors?

_____

_____

5. How can I personally help Person A, B, and C become more positive?
   Person A: _____
   Person B: _____
   Person C: _____

Your responses to question 5 may be similar to or exactly the same as your suggestions for each of the three persons. If so, you may have a keen sense of how to help others. If not, you may be disinterested in or totally insensitive to others' needs. Alternatively, at this point, you may not know what suggestions to offer to negative people. Possibly it may be helpful for you and others to do the same exercise together. On the other hand, if your responses to question 5 are somewhat different than your original suggestions, you may have (a) learned something about yourself and (b) expanded your sensitivity to others' needs.

Note: Ideally, the "Perceptions Anonymous" exercise can be an excellent group activity for three or more persons. Before undertaking the activity, however, each person needs to make a commitment to the activity. Even then, there could be potential negative fallout. The success of the activity will depend on each participant's commitment: each must *want* to participate and learn what others perceive as weaknesses (negative behaviors), be willing to accept others' perceptions and consider the outcomes (keeping a positive attitude while considering one's own negative behavior as perceived by others), and have a sincere desire to make changes (taking action without pointing fingers at the person who described a negative behavior). This is not an easy exercise because most people may not even be aware of their negative behavior—as perceived by others—and may become defensive. "I'm not that way" or "How could someone think that of me?" are typical responses (verbalized or not). However, each person needs to keep in mind that the activity is focused on a perceived *behavior* and not on the *person*. The success of such an activity depends considerably on sincerity and trust among group members.

As a starting point for conducting the group exercise, the group may benefit from role playing. Role playing (suggesting various ideas as plausible solutions for a situation, even those ideas that may not mirror your beliefs) is a more cautious approach to self-analysis than using your own personal situation. That is, role playing can be less personalized, and less threatening, because members of the group can decide on how to make more positive an identified negative behavior that is not associated with any specific person in the group—a way to avoid conflict with each other yet consider difficult issues. As the group becomes more comfortable with role playing, subsequent activities can be more personalized. That is, each person may suggest a negative behavior he believes someone else perceives he has. In either case, the group discussion centers on possible suggestions and solutions for changing the described behavior. As each person offers a contribution to the discussion and buys into the problem, solution, and course of action (with sensitivity and compassion), the benefits of the discussion have value to everyone.

The real value of the group exercise comes as several people contribute to a situation. Collectively, the group usually can provide more alternatives for action than might be possible when viewed only from one's own narrow perspective. Also, when each person makes a commitment to participate in the issue at hand, each person is apt to become more self-analyzing to internalize, consider, or apply the situation.

Self-analysis, especially as you look at ways to improve and foster your personal and professional growth, is a healthy and rewarding activity. As you become aware of your behavior and gain a better understanding of yourself, it is easier to identify appropriate actions to take toward more positive behavior.

## WHEN THE ROAD GETS ROUGH

Everyone experiences negativeness at some time or another. The point at which you recognize it, however, is critical—and, the sooner the better. That is, if you find the road getting rough yet you speed on without heeding it, you could face additional consequences. Alternatively, once you recognize or become aware of the change in the road, you can determine what caution is necessary as you proceed ahead.

If there are steps in the process of improving negative behaviors, the first step toward altering your behavior is awareness. If you are aware that you are acting in a certain way, you have the choice to continue or to change your behavior. To make a change toward more positive actions, you need to understand why you are acting in a negative manner.

A next step toward changing or correcting your behavior is getting a better understanding of yourself. Be honest with yourself as you answer such questions as: Am I aware that I am acting in a negative manner? What clues do I have to why I'm acting (or reacting) like I am? Can I explain (explain, not justify) my actions? The answers to these questions will give you better insight into understanding (yes, understanding, not justifying) your actions. As you understand why you do as you do, you place yourself in a much better position to identify how you can change your actions to be more positive.

A final step in adjusting negative behavior is taking positive action. Your action may need to be evaluated carefully to avoid your selecting a not-so-positive action by merely justifying the action as positive. You also may seek others for their advice and suggestions to help you make the right decision toward positive action. If you are a manager or supervisor, you may feel you cannot win in a negative situation involving subordinates in your work group. Yet dealing with negative behavior via a team approach can be a good way to get people with varying personalities and views to better understand themselves and each other. It also can lead to fostering good human relationships. Thus, if a team can successfully work through the problem, the result could be helpful to building a stronger work group. And because relationship building is a long-term process that takes patience and time to achieve good results, everyone benefits from buying into the effort to achieve more positive outcomes.

# NEGOTIATING THE STEEP GRADE AHEAD

Working and dealing with people who display negative behavior will take awareness, understanding, and action on your part if you expect to foster any type of meaningful interaction or relationship. If you try to determine why others are behaving as they do, you know you will gain a better understanding of them, the situation, and even yourself. Understanding the reasons behind why a person is acting (or reacting) in a certain way gives you more room to interact with the other person. It gives the other person space too. It may take a little time to gain understanding, but the time is well spent versus speeding ahead as you go over the hill (and possibly becoming involved in an accident on the downhill side of a steep grade).

## Who's Motivated?

Gary, an 18-year-old and the youngest employee in your department, has been clinging to your coattails for nearly six of the seven months he has been in your company. He can't let you pass his desk without coming up with some type of comment to detain you. Questions, questions, and more questions—many of which are just totally irrelevant and some even bizarre. It seems that he'll do anything just to talk with you. Frankly, he has become a real pain in the neck. You're now avoiding going by his work station and are at the point of closing your door just so he won't stop and bother you. Gary seems to be a very happy, positive person and a nice guy, but you're counting on the day he'll grow up and get a life!

1. Why do you think Gary drops everything to have a conversation with you?

2. What could you do to try to change your perceptions about Gary?

3. If you knew that Gary was a neglected child and starved for attention all his life, do you believe you could be more tolerant of his wanting your friendship?

4. How could you support Gary in promoting his self-confidence and in creating a more positive working environment for both of you?

As you gain a better understanding of others, you can be more positive about why they act as they do. Your understanding and concern usually will result in becoming more tolerant and accepting of their viewpoints. In turn, you may even alter your behavior (for the benefit for everyone) and accept others more willingly because you are aware of their situation. You understand them. Similarly to you, they are probably just trying to get through their day. More than likely, they are focused on their own challenges rather than yours. Your interest in them may be just the help they need to see their world from a different perspective. As a result, they get a better view of their behavior. They may not be aware of their negative posture and may be appreciative of your efforts to help them make some changes (and you can assist them in getting their own personal Motivational ATM Card too). Both of you benefit from the experience. You gain a better understanding of yourself and you are now in a position to offer others support while helping yourself.

## PASSING IN A SAFE ZONE

PASSING LANE AHEAD

Helping yourself and others improve negative behaviors can be a real challenge. However, it is a challenge that is worth taking since there is nothing to lose and everything to gain. It is important to remember that you want to try to deal with a person's negative *behavior* rather than seeing the *person* as someone who is negative. That is, you want to understand the reasons why negative behavior exists and help work out solutions for that person to have more positive behavior in the future. You want to avoid making personal attacks against the other person. Your plan of attack, so to speak, should be aimed at helping the person change negative behavior rather than aimed at the person. Because anyone displaying negative behavior is probably caught up in negative thoughts and emotions, that person will be vulnerable to and even threatened by personal attacks. There are numerous reasons why people do as they do, and, no doubt, the challenge and opportunity to help another person become more positive will always exist.

| **Value-Added Motivator** | EXPANDING WHAT MOTIVATES ME |
| --- | --- |

Identify someone you believe displays negative behavior. What makes that person's behavior so negative? Is it that he is petty and nitpicks at things you or others do? Does he keep you from doing your work or try to get you to help him with his? Is the person critical of others (and probably of you behind your back)? Does he live in the past rather than the future? Is the person selfish, making sure he comes out ahead on everything? Answer some of these questions by describing a person you know who displays some type of negative behavior. You don't need to name the person, but have a specific person in mind as you respond to the above questions.

Behaviors of Person X: _____
_____
_____
_____

Do you know why the person displays negative behavior? Can it be that you perceive his behavior as negative when it really may be *you* who needs a behavioral change? If you are sure of whose behavior needs changing as well as the real reason(s) behind the negative behavior, do you have any suggestions that could help the person you identified (and help you, too) to be more positive? How can you be sure the person will be receptive to your assistance? While these are just a few of the difficult questions that confront people in trying to resolve negative situations, write some of your ideas and responses to the questions.

Suggestions for Person X: _____

_____

_____

_____

It bears repeating that the more you are aware and understand yourself and others, the greater your ability will be to identify negative behaviors and their causes. Once you become astutely aware of your behaviors and actions, you can capitalize on finding ways to make them more positive. The commitment you make, with the help of your Card, to take positive action for yourself will be valuable in assisting others to be more positive too. To gain yet a better understanding of why you and others act in certain ways, consider some of the following signs, questions, and suggestions.

## LIGHTS REQUIRED IN TUNNEL

The sign "Lights Required in Tunnel" reminds you as a driver entering a tunnel to turn on your vehicle lights. Its purpose goes well beyond just turning on your lights; it is a caution to you to be a little more careful while driving through the tunnel. A sign at the tunnel exit frequently says, "Lights on?" or "Turn off your lights" to remind you to turn off your lights because you no longer need to exert the caution associated with the tunnel. Of course, if you drive a late model car, you may not have a choice to turn on or turn off your car lights—the car manufacturer has made the choice for you. However, the tunnel signs still serve their purpose. The signs are prominent to alert you to be cautious.

In a manner of speaking, your personal ATM Card is analogous to the tunnel entrance and exit reminders to turn on or off your car lights. Your Card is a reminder to improve your negative behavior. It is a reminder before you enter the tunnel or a potential challenge, and it is a reminder after a hazard (or negative situation) that you need to stay alert—to be positive as you proceed. If you have negative behavior or are confronted with a negative situation, do you know when to be cautious? Do you know when to forge ahead or to back off? Further, do you know when to stop and just let go? That is (to use a cliché), don't beat a dead horse. If there's nothing more you can do to make a situation better, just move on to other things that you *can* influence and change. Consider the following scenario:

### Who's Motivated?

Paul gets his share of unsolicited mail, phone calls, and e-mail. He is particularly sensitive about the calls for wireless service since he switched carriers about eight months ago when he was offered a very attractive package of "free this" and "free that" with a low monthly fee. At first he was quite pleased with his service. But after the first month, the service went downhill to the point it has become unacceptable. He has been frustrated on many occasions when he's tried in vain to contact the wireless provider. In fact, as he has told his friends so many times, he can't believe how unresponsive the company is when he sends an e-mail. When he calls to leave a message, he frequently gets a busy signal. If he does get through, a recording says to go to the company's web site and send an e-mail!

1.  If Paul is so unhappy with his wireless service, why doesn't he respond to some of the unsolicited offers he receives asking him to change providers?

2.  What prompts Paul to continue to tell his story over and over to his friends?

3.  How is Paul's behavior affecting him? His friends?

4.  If you were a friend or colleague of Paul's, what advice would you give to him?

Negative behavior frequently comes in the form of repeating the same old story over and over. The story usually doesn't help anyone—especially if what happened is in the past and you don't plan to (or can't) do anything about it. Instant replay is useful to learn from mistakes, but to replay an event (especially if it is negative) over and over again for whatever reason can be harmful to you and others. By replaying an old, worn-out, negative event, you lose because you are living in the past and are feeding on negative thoughts. Others lose because they are tired of hearing the same old negative story. You and they probably have better things to do than to get a repeat performance from a person who seems to thrive on the past negative thoughts. Even replaying a positive event over and over can become a negative if it has served the test of time and needs to be retired.

If you find yourself playing reruns of negative events, ask yourself: Why am I reliving a negative event? What benefit does it have for me (and others) to repeat it? How is my behavior affecting my (and others') work and relationships? What can I do to be more positive? As you seriously consider the answers to these questions, ponder the possible responses and their consequences. You may find it has been a burden to continue to live in the past and you're just as tired of it as those who have heard your story again and again. You may not only find it easy to alter your behavior, but also find it is a relief to get the event behind you so you can move on with your life. You have a lighter load and you can forge ahead.

Thus, if the negative event of the past can be changed, the best thing to do is to take action to change it! Benefit from the past, but get your emotions into positive territory. That is, if you can drive your action into a positive zone that has been based on a tough experience, you can benefit from the negative experience. You must, however, let go of the experience. If you don't, there probably will be some negative fallout that mires you down even further. Get the negative event out of your mind as quickly as you can. If you're having difficulty letting it go, find something positive either about the experience or about an outgrowth of it. If necessary, continue finding positive associations only until the positive elements associated with the event remain. Try it (and use your Card to back up your desire to do so) because it does work.

## SPEEDING TO THE LIMIT . . . AND BEYOND

Let's say you have a credit card that is "maxed" out to its limit. You are barely making the minimal payment (including the high finance charges) each month. Apply the following three levels to this situation: 1. Awareness level: Is your credit card a problem? 2. Understanding level: Why is it creating a challenge for you? What are the real causes of your dilemma? 3. Action level: How can you get out of your predicament?

As you answer these questions, assess your motivation for changing your spending patterns. If you are motivated by buying something to boost your spirits, consider the consequences of how the instant gratification can work against you. Remember that instant gratification can hinder your long-range goals and can actually become a devastating demotivator. For example, your credit card problem could become an even more debilitating problem if it impacts your overall credit rating. So, before matters get worse (and they usually will if you don't take some positive action), make a pact with yourself that *now* is the time to do something about your uncomfortable situation. Renew your commitment to your Card and devise a plan of action that will move you into positive terrain.

In developing your action plan, you should carefully, but quickly, consider all possible options. In the case of a credit card problem, several options may be plausible. If you can't stop spending, have a close friend or relative hold onto your credit card for a specified amount of time when you'll have your debt paid down to a certain level (or better yet, fully paid off). Give that person enough particulars about your plan to avoid your coercing him into giving the card back prematurely. Alternatively, cut up your credit card (yes, it may seem to be a drastic measure). You can always apply for a new card when you're back on your feet. Or consult a consumer credit counseling service to help you devise a plan for better management of your finances. Whatever you decide, take positive action to correct the situation and take it quickly. Left unattended it could become disastrous to you by affecting your work, your personal and professional relationships, and your self-esteem.

## LEFT LANE CLOSED AHEAD

A simple warning about some action that needs to be taken can be worth everything to you. Heeding the sign, "Left Lane Closed Ahead" gives you a warning you need to merge to the right lane. If you start planning immediately upon seeing the sign, you can identify the best way to merge right and possibly avoid a wreck in heavy traffic. The same is true about seeing a warning that is or could result in a negative situation. If you are alert to a potential problem, you can take precautions to avoid or diffuse it. If you don't take action, are you willing to accept the consequences? One alternative may be that you could hold your ground, rely on (or force) another person to take action, and not worry how the situation turns out. Consider Rita:

## Who's Motivated?

Rita is one of six supervisors working in an inner-city company that distributes perishable goods. She and the other five warehouse supervisors meet at least once a week to assess the movement of their products. Rita doesn't like to have a scheduled time to meet; it is too restrictive for her even though the others have suggested a set time each week for their meetings. When they did follow a meeting schedule, Rita would usually have them reschedule because she couldn't make the meetings due to any number of her many crises. The other supervisors (all men) have given up fighting Rita—after all she has been at the plant longer than any of the rest of them. Rita is so negative about so many things, she definitely retaliates when someone doesn't see things her way.

1. What may be some of the reasons or factors why Rita's counterparts let her determine the supervisor meeting times?

2. Speculate as to what you believe causes Rita to be so strong headed. Are her colleagues helping her or feeding into her negative behavior? Why?

3. Do you believe Rita is happy with always getting her own way for meetings with the other supervisors? Why or why not?

4. What might be some of the possible courses of action the five supervisors could take to be on more equal ground with Rita? Suggest an alternative that may contribute to Rita's chances for better working relationships as well as to like herself more.

If you are a strong-willed person who may have some rather inflexible behavior (whether or not you know it), you may think your opinion is the best one. You're always right. You have the best solution. You're sure your coworkers count on you—depend on you—to come up with the best plan; and, sometimes, it's a real burden to see yourself as having to carry the whole load. We all value our own opinions, but holding your ground "no matter what" can create, as well as fuel, a negative situation. That is, in your quest to be right, other elements can get in the way. You focus on winning because you are right. After all, don't others "know" you are right? They depend on you to take control, to find all the answers. It follows that you must be forceful or people would run over you . . . or does it?

There is right and there is *right*. With forcefulness, even if you are right, there still are consequences. The consequences take into consideration many different elements. Some are vitally important such as friendships and relationships. But, when interaction with other people becomes secondary, overconcern about winning may sacrifice your future. In essence, you've won a battle, but lost the war. The end result usually makes everyone suffer, gives people unnecessary stress, and causes lower productivity—all because people do not remain motivated very long in a negative or unhappy environment.

## DEFENSIVE OR OFFENSIVE DRIVING?

Usually there is no way of knowing how "out of proportion" a negative situation may get, especially at the outset. By quickly seeing the potential volatility of the situation or behavior (awareness), it's your choice—based on what you know or try to find out (understanding)—to get involved or stay out of it (action). Along the way there are many warning signs of upcoming negative situations that people encounter every day.

The warning signs should tell you, "Prepare to stop" or "Watch for something ahead that, if I don't slow down, could cause a problem for me." Warning signs from your boss (or subordinates), coworkers, friends, and family come in all forms, shapes, and sizes. Being ready for the unexpected, while keeping a positive attitude, can give you the edge you need to cope and handle a situation in an acceptable manner. Your behavior not only will be appropriate, but you will help others see you are in control. Others will benefit from your positive actions because you both find ways to encounter the roadblocks and look for alternatives that will contribute to minimizing future obstacles.

This is not to say that you should be so cautious that you avoid action, but that you should "keep your eyes open" while staying positive and optimistic. For example, an offer comes in the mail, and you think it seems nearly too good to be true. Probably it is; probably there are strings attached which you need to consider. Or a colleague tells you about a stock that he knows is going to pay big dividends in a short period of time. You invest (or overinvest) in it. Then some unforeseen news sends the stock plummeting and you're either forced to sell or hold on while your losses continue to grow.

These two examples of handling caution should help you see the difference between being positive and having blind optimism. Optimism is good to have because it is fostered by a positive attitude. It can help you approach every situation. However, blind optimism will not help you be prepared for life nor will it yield any insights into meeting future challenges.

## ALERT AND MOVING ALONG THE "M" HIGHWAY

With a positive attitude and your eyes wide open, you can be alert and move with deliberate speed and confidence along the M (motivational) highway. As you do, you will be able to consider the ways you can prepare for a positive future: What warning signs do I frequently encounter? How can I recognize them quickly and ward them off before they become negative (or get out of hand)? If I recognize a warning sign early enough, of what benefit will it be to me (or to others)? What can I do to turn potential negatives into positive situations? These and similar questions will help you channel your thoughts and emotions to more positive things. And your action-based responses, spurred on by relying on your Card, will help you avoid unnecessary stress and time dwelling on something that is not productive.

In this chapter, you've encountered several considerations for and ramifications of identifying and changing negative behaviors to positive ones. You know that negative behaviors are based on negative thoughts, emotions, actions, and perceptions caused by a variety of factors—discouragement, stress, depression, whining, disgust, obstacles, disappointment, embarrassment, setbacks, disenfranchisement. You also are keenly aware and, it is hoped, are encouraged by the fact that negative behaviors can be changed. If you want to, you can travel the M highway. If you want to, you can help yourself and others meet the challenges that confront you each day.

Ultimately, *you* are the only one who can help yourself turn negatives into positives. Study the ideas, examples, and exercises presented herein and revisit them as often as needed. With your Card in hand as your motivational road map, remember the importance of heeding the signs along the way. As you do, you will be able to continuously work at improving your surroundings and, in turn, your quality of life.

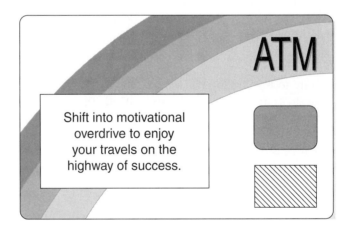

## CHAPTER 6: MOTIVATIONAL REINFORCEMENT

Reinforce your understanding of the chapter by responding to the following items.

1. How does motivation contribute to competition and vice versa?

2. Discuss why negatives are so much more prevalent than positives.

3. When a negative event turns out positive, what do people usually remember and why?

4. Why is it easier to identify others' negative behaviors than your own?

5. Describe what is meant by "perceived" behavior.

6. Why is it important to understand why people act as they do?

7. How can your negative perception of someone's behavior actually be your problem?

8. Suggest some of the negatives of repeating the same old story.

9. Why is it important to take quick action to improve or avoid negative situations?

10. Why should you prepare for "expecting the unexpected"?

11. Explain why you are the only person who can turn negatives into positives.

# SECTION III

# Mobilizing Your Motivational Portfolio

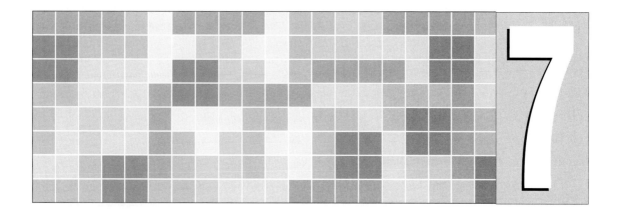

# A Patent for Motivation: Your Positive Attitude

## YOUR MOST VALUED TROPHY

You know that you value the things that are important to you—the greater their importance, the higher their place in your personal value system. Why certain things are important to you may also be linked to the "color" of your mood or behavioral characteristics. That is, are you aware of the elements that suggest or reflect the color of your attitude? Before answering that question, let's look at the significance of how your accomplishments, rewards, and satisfaction contribute to your self-esteem—to your positive attitude.

Can you think of a time you won a prize, received a trophy, or were given an honor for something you did? Can you recall what a good feeling you had about both the prize and your accomplishment? You probably felt really good about the reward; you enjoyed the inner satisfaction associated with the positive reinforcement. If the award was the result of someone recognizing you or selecting you as a winner, you were pleased the display of honor was in front of your peers. The award and the recognition you received represent external (extrinsic) recognition. The good feeling about what you did as well as the good feeling about receiving the award gave you internal (inner or intrinsic) satisfaction.

Probably there are several reasons you may still remember the event. You may recall that it was satisfying because your colleagues recognized you. Maybe you were honored for your "beyond the call of duty" efforts or for a job well done. If you received your prize or honor as a result of considerable effort on your part, you value your recognition more than if you had put little or no effort into the activity that resulted in your recognition. Furthermore, because you know you gave your best effort rather than only a partial or half effort, you have increased the value of the award. It represents something very important to you. Consider Michelle's honor:

## Who's Motivated?

Michelle, an Italian restaurant owner of seven years, recently received the city's "Outstanding Service Award" and was honored at a gala dinner where the sixteenth annual award was presented. The host of the event gave a wonderful presentation about the service as well as the food at Michelle's restaurant. Michelle prides herself on high-quality food that is always served with a creative flair at its prime and presented by courteous and attentive wait staff. Undoubtedly she will always cherish the award. She should be reminded of it for a long time because she's sure the recognition will bring considerably more customers into her place of business. She still muses to herself, "finally, my hard work is paying off!"

1. Identify the rewards associated with Michelle's honor. Which ones are internal and which ones are external?

2. Is the timing good for Michelle to begin to cut a few corners in the quality of her ingredients, to raise prices, or to consider similar things? Qualify your answers.

3. How do you believe Michelle's wait staff have and will benefit from the award?

4. Suggest some reasons and ways Michelle may (not) be motivated to continue her restaurant's reputation.

Rewards, such as Michelle's, are frequently given on the basis of an outstanding accomplishment. Michelle has devoted her life to her restaurant. She works long hours and is constantly striving to improve every aspect of her business. She loves what she does and is motivated to give her all. The award is definitely the "icing" on her Italian cream cake. And, even though she has worked hard to achieve the prestigious award, she has kept other things in proper perspective along the way.

Can you relate to Michelle? Do you have the desire and drive to achieve at high levels? Of all the things you have done in your life, what is your most prized accomplishment? Why does it stand out over other things? What reward(s) (including both tangible or nontangible rewards) did you receive for that accomplishment? What satisfaction (your internal, intrinsic, or nontangible reward) did you enjoy from your accomplishment and reward(s)? Complete the following exercise to answer some of these questions.

| **Value-Added Motivator** | MY MOST IMPORTANT ACCOMPLISHMENT |
|---|---|

Reflecting back on the questions in the previous paragraph, write down what you consider to be your greatest accomplishment. Describe the satisfaction you experienced. Also, describe the type of rewards you received and tell why they were external and/or internal.

Accomplishment/Reward   _____

_____

_____

_____

_____

If you received recognition in the form of a tangible award or a verbal citation (an external or extrinsic reward), you probably can recall the event and the satisfaction you derived from it. You may even remember shedding some tears of joy, hugging colleagues and friends, or showing your appreciation to others who may have given you support along the way. Why? Because, without a doubt, you really felt good inside (an internal or intrinsic reward of satisfaction). Your emotions, thoughts, and actions were happy ones—positive ones. Your positiveness probably made others feel good too.

On the other hand, let's say you may not have received an extrinsic reward for one of your most important accomplishments. Was the intrinsic satisfaction of your accomplishment motivating enough to contribute to your positive attitude? Consider Martin's situation:

## Who's Motivated?

Martin, a talented and successful historical writer, cannot help but think back to his high school days when, as a senior honors student, he submitted an essay in a national competition. He knows it was an excellent piece on the Civil War—in  fact, it has been cited as such in recent years. But, he didn't win the national prize; he didn't even get an honorable mention. Why not? The judges said his topic was not aligned as closely as it needed to be to the purpose of the award. Martin finds it interesting to note that Candice, the award winner two years ago, wrote on a similar topic! Candice recently gave a lecture on her essay that Martin attended and she even referred to his earlier (nonwinning) work as a major influence for her essay. Candice expressed surprise, appreciation, and that it was "an honor" that Martin came up and introduced himself to her after the lecture.

1. Does Martin have legitimate feelings about the judges decision or is he just a poor loser? Why or why not? Why can't Martin let go of the fact he didn't win the national competition over 15 years ago?

2. How could Martin have been rewarded in other ways, maybe even some that are more important than when he was a senior in high school?

3. Play back the conversation (or variations of the exchange) you believe may have taken place when Martin introduced himself to Candice.

4. For Martin to foster a positive attitude, on what aspect of this scenario should he focus?

The outward, tangible, external or extrinsic rewards are always nice, but it is the inner, nontangible or intrinsic rewards that give more staying power to motivation and a positive attitude. You don't have to win a prize to be a winner; you don't have to receive a tangible award to be rewarded. The most important aspect of any reward is the *feeling*—the internal satisfaction that you have achieved a goal, accomplished an objective, completed a project, or extended kindness to another person.

## RECIPIENT OF THE ULTIMATE PRIZE

Your self-esteem is closely linked to your aspirations and expectations. Your self-esteem and self-worth also are dependent upon the value you give to your accomplishments and the emphasis you place on rewards. That is, your attitude is your most prized possession. Your positive attitude is your trophy—the ultimate prize. It is something that you should value greatly because it contributes to everything you do; and it is yours, and yours alone. If you keep your trophy (your positive attitude) in plain sight and polish it frequently, it can be the most powerful motivator you own. And, yes, *you* do own your positive attitude so you should protect and guard it so others don't take it from you, step on it, or damage it.

Your personal Motivational ATM Card can contribute to the value of your positive attitude by helping you keep your emotions, thoughts, and efforts positive. For example, let's say you are expected to give a short acceptance speech on the value of your attitude. Can you make your speech upbeat and focused on an "I can" approach? Think of your acceptance speech; think of the importance of your positive attitude; think of how your Card can keep you focused on positive things; and think of how your attitude is your most prized possession. Plan your speech to reflect your innermost, heartfelt feelings—feelings so compelling that your positive attitude will constantly be at work helping you to keep your actions positive.

| Value-Added Motivator | MY ACCEPTANCE SPEECH |
| --- | --- |

In two or three sentences, write out a summary of a speech you believe represents your ultimate prize: a positive attitude. Refer to the previous paragraph for suggestions to make your speech reflect your positive attitude, what you want your attitude to become, and realistic ways to motivate you to keep your attitude positive. That is, consider how you will use your Card to your best advantage.

_____

_____

_____

This is not an easy exercise unless you've taken the "I can" approach to complete it and are convinced you really can be successful. If you've been realistic about what you can do and will do whatever it takes and as often as necessary, you'll enjoy your decision. Transfer your summary speech to a sticky note and attach it to a prominent place you'll see often (for example, next to your bedroom clock so you'll see it first thing in the morning and the last thing at night). Whether you realize it or not, just by thinking about and writing your speech, you've already made progress in the right direction toward a more positive attitude. Every time you read your summary speech (and reading it morning and night is a good suggestion) you will be reinforcing your commitment to a positive attitude. In fact, when you read your summary, you should smile to yourself because you know your speech is there to help you improve.

Whenever your summary speech needs to be refocused to get you going at maximum speed in the right direction, rewrite it; and rewrite your sticky note, too. Work, and work hard, toward the goal represented by your speech. It goes without saying that the result will provide you, and others, with immeasurable benefits. Just think of the high returns you'll yield from the use of your Card toward being more positive about your life!

## A TALE OF TWO PERSONALITIES

Practicing your speech often via your thoughts, emotions, and actions will reinforce your commitment to improving your attitude. That is, your actions should reflect the direction you have mapped out to take. Because you want to be more positive, you will need to act in a more positive manner on a consistent basis. You cannot expect to think one thing, do another, and hope everyone around you will respond in the way you believe they should. Similarly, you cannot expect others to react to you in a positive way if you practice your positive attitude on merely one or two occasions. Neither can you expect to help or inspire others to activate their motivation if you are not motivated or are not showing your motivation.

Focusing on your own motivation first may seem selfish, but it is not. In fact, it is just the opposite. You cannot expect others to want to include you if you don't want to be included, especially if your attitude indicates otherwise. Put another way, displaying your motivation makes perfect sense from a "what you see is what you get" approach. If your actions say you really want to establish a working relationship and your thoughts are in sync with your actions, there is little left for speculation.

Keep in mind that your positive attitude will rub off on others, but it may not happen as quickly as you hope it will. Also, your motivators may act as demotivators to others and vice versa. You may be able to see the paradox of a motivator also being a demotivator. You may also be able to quickly identify other incongruities of motivators and demotivators. However, other individuals may need a little more time to see the paradox or possibly they may not see the incongruities at all. Similarly, you may have already mastered the art of juggling lots of activities associated with eliminating or diminishing demotivators. That is, you may have put aside activities that are not important, that are not worth your effort, that you don't want to do, that you can't do to your satisfaction, etc.—assuming these activities do not affect your job or that of others around you. While others may not be able to successfully follow your lead, your consistent behavior will encourage them to see how important your positive attitude is to you and they will respond accordingly.

## FIRST IMPRESSIONS ARE LASTING ONES

You know that consistent positive behavior is not only desirable, but vitally important to the interactions you have with other people. You, like everyone else, want to be known as a person with a positive attitude. To do so, you know you must nurture your positive attitude by thinking positive thoughts and doing positive deeds. You also know you need to be on guard to avoid negative emotions and thoughts that quickly project a negative attitude. A negative thought, even for a minute, can prompt an adverse situation. You know that a first impression can be one that lasts for a long time.

If you strive to be and do your very best every day, you won't need to be worried about the impression you make. Just be yourself and your positive attitude and motivation for positive action will be far-reaching. To repeat: It's up to you whether or not you have a positive attitude—it's only *you* who can truly motivate yourself. Although there are lots of ways to be motivated and get motivational assistance, ultimately it's still your decision whether or not you are motivated and whether or not you have a positive attitude. Your Card provides you with this wonderful challenge! There's probably no other challenge, or a more important one, that you, and you alone, can control to your own satisfaction.

## WHAT COLOR IS YOUR ATTITUDE?

Your Card tells you that your positive attitude is priceless. Because you have sole control of your own attitude 100 percent of the time, you also know it is possible to continuously build on it to improve it. Making your attitude "shine" so to speak, is similar to wearing certain clothing and colors to maximize your best features. While you probably don't wear the same color every day, you enjoy how the various colors can change how you look and how you feel. If you think about it, you've probably even said on occasion, "I feel like wearing (color) today" and possibly have even given a reason why you plan to do so. What colors do you enjoy? Which ones enhance your attitude?

Let's look at some of the colors and what they say about your attitude. Applying the colors to your attitude is another "I can" example. Colors can alert you when to be cautious or when to take a bolder stance. As you consider each of the colors, think of how you can foster a more positive attitude with the motivational influence they provide.

**RED:** Red is a color of strength and passion. It is prominent and eye-catching. Red says "I love you" and that you care about the other person's well-being. It is a color of confidence and makes a bold statement. On the other hand, red also says "stop; don't come any further." It warns that if you do, you could get into trouble.

If your attitude is red, you are secure and probably will provide security for others. You want to do what is right and want others to do the same. You know the importance of being disciplined and organized. Red also says you're willing to take action and there is no time like the present to get started before something gets in the way to halt it.

When your attitude is red, you should exercise caution because you may flare up and quickly let your anger show. When you "see red," others need to be on the alert. You may act on impulse because you are confident (possibly even a bit over-confident). Slow down and think things through. It may be easy to act now and apologize later, but your positive attitude will probably suffer as a result.

**YELLOW:** Yellow is a color of light, liveliness, and exuberance. It is a creative color and, similar to red, suggests confidence and self-assuredness. Yellow is a color to be seen—its significance shows up well when surrounded by other colors, especially dark colors. Yellow is a happy, bright color and represents your concern for happiness and your well-being, as well as others', too.

If your attitude is yellow, your self-esteem is at a high level. You portray the assurance that you are not only in control, but that you also like it. Because of your self-confidence, you may take some risks that others would consider questionable, but you're willing to back them up with strong support for your decision.

When your attitude is yellow, you need to be aware that you can go beyond your limits before you realize it. Your successes in exploratory and creative endeavors of the past may give you overconfidence to forge into new territory. If your ideas outnumber the plausible solutions for implementing them, you may be in danger of never really getting anything of substance accomplished. Others can quickly sense your lack of follow-through. They also may become skeptical of your ability to change; thus, your recovery from others' perceptions of your abilities may be very slow.

**BLUE:** Blue is a color of serenity and calm. It is soothing and sends a very positive, nonthreatening message. Blue says "I want to interact with you and establish a meaningful relationship." It expresses the strong value of sincerity and trustworthiness. Blue is a very stable color that also expresses strength and power.

If your attitude is blue, you are a peacemaker, and you're in a position to help others improve their attitudes. Your sense of commitment and honesty will let you "tell it like it is." You have the stability to be leaned on, and your willpower gives you the strength to avoid being abused. You're firm, but also sensitive to other people and their needs.

When your attitude is blue, you may have the tendency to communicate with a little too much calmness, finesse, and good intent. You may also be straightforward and sincere, which can get you into trouble if you are a little too blunt with your comments. Should communications break down or a crisis occur (not usually because of you, however), you probably will remain strong and calm, but others won't count on you to acquiesce because you're not about to just "roll over and play dead."

**ORANGE:** Orange is a boisterous and busy color. It says "Come take a chance with me" because it is adventuresome and lively. Orange combines the boldness of both yellow and red as well as merges the confidence of the two colors. Orange is the life of the party, and will and get others involved; and, of course, orange will be the last to leave.

If your attitude is orange, you want to do everything for everyone. You have lots of energy and enthusiasm, and you want to get on with things. You find fun things to do and get people involved. You are not afraid of jumping into the middle of any kind of activity. Because you find pleasure in nearly everything, you like variety and excitement.

When your attitude is orange, you need to be aware that your commitment may not mean the same to you as it does to others. That is, you enjoy a party so much that you get bored with the mundane chores of life and want to move on to where the excitement is. You may have trouble completing projects because your interests can be pulled in many directions. You are someone everyone likes to be around, but not necessarily on a team where deadlines are important or where a complete, quality product needs to be produced.

**GREEN:** Green, a mixture of yellow and blue, benefits from the positive, self-assuredness of both colors. It has the lure of yellow's happy environment and the stability of blue's steadfast mission. Green is peaceful, soothing, and compassionate. It depicts a generous spirit and giving nature—and that is why it is easy to "go" with green. Green provides a safe way to move ahead.

If your attitude is green, you are the stabilizing force for your friends, family, coworkers, boss, and subordinates. You provide them with a comfort zone for moving steadily down the path. You are helpful and reassuring. People are very comfortable to be around you. You get things done because you have the drive to get going and provide solid direction. You concentrate and stay on task, and you follow a project to completion via a systematic and orderly process.

When your attitude is green, your overly safe direction for the task at hand may be a hindrance. That is, your leadership may be so even-keeled, it is dull and boring. Even though you are a self-starter, some people may be somewhat concerned and reluctant to join in your activities because they may not be able to sustain the same type of "stick-to-itiveness" motivation that you have. You probably will apologize to them (for their disinterest) and end up finishing the project (or putting the final touches on it) yourself.

**PURPLE:** Purple is a color of stature and royalty. The product of red and blue, purple represents authority, strength, and outward confidence. Purple provides inquisitiveness, mystery, and creativity. It represents undisputed leadership, and you will always be counted on for strong and forceful decisions.

If your attitude is purple, you can tackle the impossible. You have charisma, leadership, and power—all of which attract followers. You give empowerment to your followers because they are loyal to you. You're a winner, and both you and they know it. Your deliberateness lends itself to tackling tough projects. You find inventive ways to solve complex problems and are dedicated to accomplishment. You thrive on results—results that are even more important to you if they are flashy.

When your attitude is purple, you may be dangerous because of your considerable power to change the world. While people like that quality, you must be cautious that your strength doesn't overwhelm them. You may squelch others' creativity and devalue, discredit, or even stop their input. In empowering others, you may find you totally withdraw from an activity after giving others all the authority, responsibility, and accountability they need for a task. Once your followers realize you've moved on, they can become disenfranchised with your self-centered leadership and view you as pompous, arrogant, and selfish.

| **Value-Added Motivator** | WHAT COLOR IS MY ATTITUDE (STRENGTHS)? |
|---|---|

On the lines provided, describe a behavior you believe you display that is reflected by your positive attitude. List one behavior (strength or positive element) for each of the six colors discussed previously. Be specific in your descriptions. That is, if you show confidence, indicate how and when your confidence is displayed (for example, you put a major building project back on the right track because you were decisive about replacing some beams that most likely would have caused problems at a later date).

For each of your positive attitude elements, a line labeled M is provided for you to add a motivator that you believe will enhance the positive element. The motivator should be something you can do, will do, or have done to help you continue developing a more positive attitude.

RED: _____

_____

M _____

_____

YELLOW: _____

_____

M _____

_____

BLUE: _____

_____

M _____

_____

ORANGE: _____

_____

M _____

_____

GREEN: _____

_____

M _____

_____

PURPLE: _____

_____

M _____

_____

By completing the "What Color Is My Attitude (Strengths)?" exercise, you have achieved at least two important objectives:

1. You have described something that you believe contributes to your positive attitude. In so doing, you must think about your strengths (and weaknesses). By describing a positive element, you reinforce your belief in that behavior.

2. Adding a motivator to augment or further expand your positive attitude suggests a motivating action you believe can (does) work for you. It gives you a strong message that you can further enhance your behavior and be motivated toward developing a more positive attitude.

As you completed the exercise, you probably thought of several of your weaknesses before coming up with a strength for each color. The exercise forced you to find positive behaviors and you were forced to think about and describe positive actions. You can further benefit from this exercise if you try to practice the elements, via your motivators, as often as you can. Further, when you feel you have maximized an element, exchange it with another, and so on. Rely on your Card to provide the incentive for continuing to expand your positive attitude horizons.

| **Value-Added Motivator** | **WHAT COLOR IS MY ATTITUDE (WEAKNESSES)?** |
|---|---|

Just as you did in the preceding activity by describing your strengths, do the same thing for your weaknesses. That is, describe six elements (one for each color) you believe are weaknesses or negative elements of your behavior. You may include negative behaviors you believe should be eliminated or changed to give you a more positive attitude. As you identify your negative elements or weaknesses, also consider how you can turn them into strengths and positive behavior. Add a motivator to each one to spur you to take some action. Then follow the same procedure to continue your personal and professional attitude development.

This activity may take some serious thinking on your part. Don't rush it. You may move on to further reading before you finish it; however, mark the activity in some way so you will remember to come back to complete it. The time you spend doing it will provide you with many satisfying rewards.

RED: _____

_____

M _____

_____

YELLOW: _____

_____

M _____

_____

BLUE: _____

_____

M _____

_____

ORANGE: _____

_____

M _____

_____

GREEN: _____

_____

M _____

_____

PURPLE: _____

_____

M _____

_____

Obviously, this is a long-term assignment, but you should not wait for another day to get started on improving your most prized possession. Don't let procrastination contribute to precious time slipping away when you could be working on enjoying your life more with a positive attitude. Your Card should help you stay on track if you associate the elements you identified with the bands on your Card.

If you haven't noticed the "color" bands on your Card, stop right now; take out your Card and look at it. The "rainbow" bands of your Card should be a constant reminder of why you need to work on this exercise. Your Card should be saying to you, "Don't postpone action; there is no time like the present to take action." Your initial motivation to get started will help you get on a positive roll and find the self-development experience enjoyable and the results rewarding. If you work diligently at describing and really dissecting your behaviors while finding ways to make them more positive, there is no doubt whatsoever you will enjoy the pleasure of displaying your positive attitude.

## PAINTING WITH A RAINBOW PALETTE

You probably display, to some degree, at least one of the characteristics represented in each of the six color categories relating to attitude. Why? Because, as your likes and dislikes are expressed, they reflect the color of your attitude or attitudinal mood. The strength of your attitudinal moods is directly related to the type and amount of motivation you have and need to take to achieve some desired action or result.

If your mood is a little down, your motivation may not be as strong as it should be to produce a positive outcome. The result may be an undesirable action, but this should not discourage you from quickly getting back on track. Painting with all the colors of the palette can give you many alternatives, in all shades and hues, that will help you achieve positive results. If you use the boldness of the primary colors—red, yellow, and blue—you may find the inspiration you need to take more deliberate, positive action than if you avoid the elements represented by these colors. Capitalizing on the characteristics and behaviors associated with the secondary colors—orange, green, and purple—you may discover your actions can be just as rich and compelling as taking on the attitudinal actions associated with the primary colors. The elements related to the secondary colors, however, offer a buffer to the boldness when you need a change. You can create a bold environment for yourself or one that is more subtle by blending the colors of your identified behaviors, actions, and motivators. The combinations and permutations of the ways and means to be more positive, and more effective in life, incorporate each of the colors of the rainbow. In turn, your motivation to achieve the goals engrained in your value system is as powerful and meaningful as you want to make it—and your Card suggests that your actions spurred by your motivation can be as colorful as the rainbow.

## THE POT OF GOLD AT THE END OF THE RAINBOW

The rainbow should be a good reminder that the power of your positive attitude should never be underestimated. If you follow your motivational rainbow, you will find it has the lasting power to lead you to the pot of gold at the end.

You, however, have everything to lose if you ever consider your attitude as anything less than a pot of gold or, even more importantly, your ultimate reward. Its value is up to you—it is what you determine it to be. You choose its value. You decide when, where, why, and how your attitude can work for you. You determine what effort you want to devote to it, as well as the circumstances under which and how fast its value is increased.

Using your Card to enjoy your journey of life will definitely contribute to the increased value of your ultimate prize. Along the way toward developing a more positive attitude, the rainbow represented by your Card should give you an awesome view and an inspiring perspective. And, it truly is your assurance that the pot of gold at the end of the rainbow is of real value to you.

## A FINAL NOTE: PATENTS CAN RUN OUT

So, why can't you take a Pollyanna approach all the time? Because it's difficult, if not impossible, to be positive all the time when there are so many negative elements that touch your life. There is no magic solution for staying positive. However, because you know that your Card appreciates in value as it is used, your positive attitude cannot help but get more positive each time you display it, but your positive attitude will need rejuvenation.

Undoubtedly, you'll need to be prepared to renew your Card from time to time—usually when you least expect it. Under both positive and negative circumstances, plan to renew your commitment to a positive attitude as often as necessary; keep your positive attitude active. Truthfully respond to the question that you ask yourself frequently, "Would I want my attitude patented?"

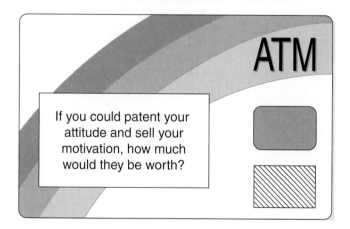

## CHAPTER 7: MOTIVATIONAL REINFORCEMENT

Reinforce your understanding of the chapter by responding to the following items.

1. Discuss why people feel good when they are recognized.

2. What makes you feel so strongly about your valued accomplishments?

3. Define internal versus external satisfaction, accomplishment, and reward; discuss their similarities, differences, and/or interrelatedness.

4. What is the significance of taking an "I can" approach to things?

5. How can a positive attitude contribute to a good impression?

6. Who really controls your attitude and why?

7. Suggest several attitudinal behaviors associated with each of the primary and secondary colors (red, yellow, blue, orange, green, and purple).

8. How can you benefit from associating your attitude with a color?

9. How can your mood affect your motivation and vice versa?

10. How can your Card help you rejuvenate your attitude?

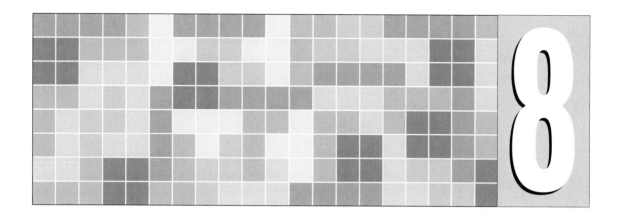

# Motivation for All Seasons

## CAN SUNSETS LAST FOREVER?

If you've ever yearned for the sunset to last just a little longer, you know the peace and solace associated with the wonderful feeling you get from the beautiful blending of sunset reds and oranges that fill the sky. You look well beyond the present. Your thoughts are lost in a panorama of breathtaking bursts of purple and gold playing with the other colors and patterns of light on the horizon. You get caught up in daydreaming and thinking of the pleasantries of life. In your mind, you paint a mental picture of things you enjoy and you recall wonderful, warm memories.

As you watch the sailboats effortlessly weave graceful paths along the glistening blue water, you wonder what adventures the occupants have had. You dreamily wish you were sailing away somewhere—nowhere in particular—just somewhere. You may even drift into a fantasy where you picture some far-off exotic destination. Bringing your thoughts a little closer to reality, the beautiful scene makes you smile as you recall some of the events of the day. Somehow the sunset has helped you view your day with a much more positive attitude.

In essence, the sunset has offered an incentive to your attitudinal perspective—you've taken it and adjusted your attitude. You've actually let yourself get lost in the warm glow of the dying colors on the horizon. The sunset's beautiful deep red, brilliant burnt orange, dancing yellow, and muted gold interspersed with the majestic purplish hues have helped you to dwell, even for a few minutes, on comforting, friendly thoughts. You've taken advantage of a natural resource provided by the environment to give you enjoyment. You chose to find something good in your surroundings. As you took time to enjoy the beauty and serenity of the ending day, it was your decision to think positive thoughts and express your emotions.

## CHOOSING YOUR IDEAL CLIMATE

Like so many things in life, a beautiful sunset contributes to your senses and emotions. It acts as a motivator for you to experience an attitude adjustment. You can choose to accept the challenge or ignore it. You must, however, make a timely decision to take advantage of the motivator because a sunset usually fades quickly into darkness (yet, if you're fortunate, you'll get another motivational boost from the full moon just appearing). By choosing to let the sunset contribute to your attitude, you may have a more enjoyable evening and even start tomorrow on a relaxed and pleasant note. Your attitude has benefited from the experience. In turn, if you experience enough events that give you a motivational boost similar to the effect of the sunset, the collective experiences could contribute to a personality adjustment. Consider Alicia:

### Who's Motivated?

Alicia hasn't always been successful. In fact, up until about nine years ago you could say she was destined to failure. As a child, Alicia grew up fast. Her family was on the edge of being disfunctional and she acquired street savvy at a very early age. She was capable of doing well in school, but it had no value to her. Alicia always had a mind of her own. As an independent thinker she managed to get into more than her share of trouble. In fact she attracted trouble and lots of negative friends who nurtured it.

Alicia learned early she had natural talent for leadership—her gang was quite powerful and it was easy to influence her friends—probably too easy since that's what contributed to her boredom. When Alicia decided she no longer was challenged, she decided to look for other friends who were independent like herself. Fortunately, the friends she found were quite positive—a trait she was already beginning to see as valuable. It didn't take Alicia long to figure out she could be liked a lot more as a positive influence than as a bully. One little positive attitude change at a time led her to a total personality change. She completed her high school equivalency exam, started taking business classes at the local community college, and now is the proud owner of a growing business. She knows her waste recycling company is going to be highly successful because she has the right attitude and motivation for continuing to work hard and to persevere through the challenges. Nothing can stop her now!

1. Is it just coincidence that Alicia's energies turned positive? Why or why not?

2. How did Alicia's independence lead her to a change of attitude? Compare the many challenges facing her now with those of her early years.

3. Describe Alicia's attitude and what motivates her.

4. Could Alicia's personality adjustment have occurred if she hadn't practiced being positive for a period of time? Why or why not?

5. What can be learned from Alicia's life development?

There's probably not much that can stop Alicia now. Her positive attitude is firmly in place—her personality reflects it; she sees the value of it. A personality adjustment generally results from a number of repetitive attitude adjustments, frequently in close succession, rather than from a single event. It is a difficult and long process to change one's attitude, as Alicia found out. But with dedication, a positive attitude can be achieved. It takes just one step at a time—turning negative energy into positive actions. As you take action, *you* will motivate yourself to value and think positive thoughts.

Staying motivated is harder when you can't view sunsets (or similar things that give you motivation) throughout the day. And, even if you could, too many beautiful sunsets may reduce their effectiveness if you lose interest in their beauty. You know that it takes a concerted effort to stay motivated. That's why it is so important to highly value your positive attitude. If you carry your positive thoughts with you throughout the day, your horizon will become wider and your peripheral vision broader. Your tolerance and acceptance of others will expand. Your creative thinking is energized. You will be more observant. You'll find ways to express and balance your expression and freedom from the increased perspective you've developed and from keen observation. That is, your attitude will be displayed according to how you access the motivation that prompts you to action. The motivation you derive from the resources available to you is in your hands; its effect depends on how you decide to use it.

## THE FOUR SEASONS OF MOTIVATION: WINTER, SPRING, SUMMER, OR FALL

As you know, your behavioral attitude and motivation are influenced by both positive and negative factors. You also know that your attitude and motivation are directly tied to your personality, values, and the characteristics that make up your personal style. Your style suggests you enjoy certain things and reject others. Your style also gives substance to the way you communicate and interact with people.

Whether or not you like it, your personality, values, and style are reflected in your interpersonal relationships. In fact, your own personal style may sometimes come through much more strongly than you'd prefer. The better you understand yourself, as well as understand your motivators and the factors that contribute to your overall behavior, the greater success you'll derive from your interactions with others. That is, if you know what motivates you, you'll understand why it is easier for you to interact with some people and not others. If you know what motivates other people, you'll also better understand why some interactions are successful and others are less so.

Understanding yourself leads you to learn, and want to learn, more about others. As you do, you become aware of how sensitivity to others' styles will contribute to more effectively interacting with all types of people. You begin to enhance and maximize your interactions. Also, learning as much as you can about yourself (and others) will give you insights into how you can modify your personality and style in an effort to become a more positive you. If you find your personality, values, and style aren't what you believe they should be, you can work at changing them—and with practice and perseverance (boosted by the influence that your Card gives you to continue on when you're tempted to slack off or quit) you should be successful. Furthermore, understanding your preferences and those of others gives you the edge for motivation to work for both of you. To make the point, let's look at some additional elements that contribute to your personality, values, attitudinal behavior, and style—specifically, elements that contribute to your motivation or motivational style.

Your predominant motivational style may be viewed as winter, spring, summer, or fall. Why? Because each of the four seasons may represent many of your personal preferences—likes, dislikes, and interests for activities, accomplishments, and even productivity. For example, you may find your motivational style can best be described as winter because of the way winter makes you feel and act. If you consider what really motivates you during the winter season, you may find it rather surprising how many things you enjoy. If the winter season really motivates you more than other times during the year, it can be said that your motivational style comes predominantly from one season. On the other hand, you may find your style relies on a little spring and a lot of fall. Or your motivational style may definitely be summer, but you need the other seasons to maximize it.

If one season does not come close to describing your style, your motivation may still be linked to the seasons. For example, your motivation may come from change—a seasonal change, a weather change, or a combination of influences associated with a season. Through a comparison of what the seasons mean to you, you may find that pleasant experiences and events in the past suggest a pattern for your particular style. The pattern or lack of it could give you additional insights into your personality and style of communication.

But you say you don't live and work in an environment that clearly has four distinct seasons. Believe it or not, you may have unconsciously or specifically selected where you live and work and/or especially where you vacation on the basis of what the weather or season offers you for personal satisfaction.

What are some of the elements that suggest your motivational style can be associated with one or more of the four seasons? What is your motivational style—winter, spring, summer, or fall? You may find it interesting to discover why you are motivated by some of the things that relate to specific times of the year and possibly not to others. As you look further at what motivates you, you may gain insight as to what season describes you best.

**Winter:** You wake up one morning and find the ground covered with snow and the white stuff still coming down. You know the day is yours—it's a holiday! It's a day you can use for catch-up on some work you need to do at home or even in the office (where you'd have few or no interruptions). Before you decide on these options, you quickly consider further: You can sleep in, go for a walk in the fresh, crisp air—or, what a perfect day to go to your cabin by the lake. You're sure your elderly neighbor would also appreciate your shoveling the snow from her walk. Your options are nearly endless.

On the other hand, it's so nice and warm under your down comforter that you ponder: Just to turn up the heat, you need to get out of your cocoon. There's the issue of traversing that cold floor to make coffee; yet a nice hot, steaming cup of coffee would be a great way to get the day started right. Should you quickly take a hot shower and get your day started, or would you rather watch the snowflakes fall gracefully to your windowsill as you snuggle further down in your warm bed? It would be a wonderful day to read the novel you just bought. Better yet, why not have breakfast at the deli–bookstore. You could hang out there and read for awhile, and they're sure to have a crackling fire in the fireplace. You probably would also run into some of your friends at the bookstore—some good conversation on a wintry day always adds warmth.

---

| **Value-Added Motivator** | **MY WINTER MOTIVATORS** |
| --- | --- |

What do you enjoy about the winter season? Why is it one of your favorite or least favorite times of the year? Are there specific things you like to do during the winter months—possibly some things you can't do during other seasons of the year? Why do you find winter exciting, invigorating, depressing, confining, or transitional? Further, what do you dislike about the winter season?

Describe your emotions that are associated with the winter season. If you have specific likes and dislikes, events and activities, or past positive and negative experiences that can be associated with winter, include them too. Use the space provided below as a starting point for your list. That is, don't be limited by the amount of space provided here for your list. Get a pad of paper and label two sheets as follows: Sheet 1: My Winter Motivators (Things I Enjoy About Winter), Sheet 2: My Winter Demotivators (Things I Dislike About Winter). With two lists, you can continue to add items as you think of things along the way. You may wish to number each item for ease of reference later.

### My Winter Motivators and Demotivators

(Things I Enjoy About Winter)                    (Things I Dislike About Winter)

_____         _____

_____         _____

_____         _____

You will be asked to refer back to this activity later in the chapter. Thus, complete as much of it as you can now to maximize the benefits of the entire exercise.

**Spring:** It seems that you've waited forever for spring to arrive. In fact, the anticipation may have been just a little too long, so spring's arrival is just a bit anticlimactic. You can finally get out of the cold, depressing doldrums of winter. Already you see the grass beginning to perk up its color (and you wonder how long you can hold off before it has to be mowed). The crocuses are blooming, and the tender green shoots of the tulips and daffodils are just beginning to peek through the ground. It's time for mulching and planting—how good those vegetables from your garden will taste later (but is it worth the energy now?). Freshening up your yard is always nice, but doing it seems like a never-ending, tedious chore. Maybe spring is not really your favorite season after all. The spring winds are playful with the sweet scents of dogwood, but your allergies also are in full bloom. The rain is hampering your tennis game and outdoor activities. Yet, the rain is so refreshing, it seems to tell you it is cleaning up the air for you to breathe just a little deeper.

Springtime is invigorating and gives you a burst of energy. You've decided you're going to start exercising in earnest to get rid of the few extra pounds you know you added during the winter months. You have lots of new spring projects that you want to get started; however, cleaning out your closet is not your idea of a spring project, nor is it a part of your new exercise program. The spring season is the time to plan your summer vacation (after completing your income tax) and it's a great time to shop with the abundance of new merchandise in the stores. Your enthusiasm is high even though the fresh, new season has always been a bit problematic for you. That is, you have the tendency to overspend a little—probably the result of being cooped up so long over the winter months—and end up having to downgrade your summer vacation plans. Spring is really a paradox for you—a catch-22.

| **Value-Added Motivator** | **MY SPRING MOTIVATORS** |
| --- | --- |

What do you enjoy about the spring season? Why is it one of your favorite or least favorite times of the year? Are there specific things you like to do during the spring months—possibly some things you can't do during other seasons of the year? Why do you find spring exciting, invigorating, depressing, confining, or transitional? Further, what do you dislike about the spring season?

Describe your emotions that are associated with the spring season. If you have specific likes and dislikes, events and activities, or past positive and negative experiences that can be associated with spring, include them too. Use the space provided as a starting point for your list. That is, don't be limited by the amount of space provided here for your list. Get a pad of paper and label two sheets as follows: Sheet 1: My Spring Motivators (Things I Enjoy About Spring); Sheet 2: My Spring Demotivators (Things I Dislike About Spring). With two lists, you can continue to add items as you think of things along the way. You may wish to number each item for ease of reference later.

**My Spring Motivators and Demotivators**

(Things I Enjoy About Spring)                    (Things I Dislike About Spring)

_____              _____

_____              _____

_____              _____

_____              _____

As noted for each season activity, you will be asked to refer back to this activity later in the chapter. Thus, complete as much of it as you can now to maximize the benefits of the entire exercise.

**Summer:** You enjoy summer more than another time of the year because of what it represents. For example, there's the warm weather (although it is sometimes much too hot for your comfort) for outside activities such as after-work socializing, baseball games, working in the yard, or cleaning out the garage for a yard sale. Summer seems to bring on a more relaxed atmosphere at work, too. People dress a bit more casually and seem to treat projects somewhat less critical (but the deadlines are still there). Everyone discusses a planned or just completed summer vacation—the competition is stifling with everyone trying to outdo each other with the biggest and best. There are always numerous weddings and related events—they're usually fun, but there is a limit to how many gifts you can buy.

Summer just plain goes by too fast. It's hard to put your finger on why you feel you never really get into summer before it's gone. Maybe you have difficulty jumping into summer because there are just too many choices to make. Maybe you spend too much time planning and organizing your time so that you don't have time to execute your plans. Maybe you need to be more spontaneous. But you remember the trouble you got into last summer when you really practiced that laid-back feeling at work. You recall enjoying summer to the fullest, but you truly paid for it later by not meeting some of the more-than-generous deadlines that appeared to be so far away when summer started. Your boss definitely sent the wrong message when the casualness became all business. It wasn't really fair to you when you truly did contribute in so many ways to making the work environment more pleasant for your coworkers. Some reward!

| **Value-Added Motivator** | **MY SUMMER MOTIVATORS** |
|---|---|

What do you enjoy about the summer season? Why is it one of your favorite or least favorite times of the year? Are there specific things you like to do during the summer months—possibly some things you can't do during other seasons of the year? Why do you find summer exciting, invigorating, depressing, confining, or transitional? Further, what do you dislike about the summer season?

Describe your emotions that are associated with the summer season. If you have specific likes and dislikes, events and activities, or past positive and negative experiences that can be associated with summer, include them too. Use the space provided below as a starting point for your list. That is, don't be limited by the amount of space provided here for your list. Get a pad of paper and label two sheets as follows: Sheet 1: My Summer Motivators (Things I Enjoy About Summer); Sheet 2: My Summer Demotivators (Things I Dislike About Summer). With two lists, you can continue to add items as you think of things along the way. You may wish to number each item for ease of reference later.

### My Summer Motivators and Demotivators

(Things I Enjoy About Summer)                    (Things I Dislike About Summer)

_____          _____

_____          _____

_____          _____

_____          _____

_____          _____

As noted for each season activity, you will be asked to refer back to this activity later in the chapter. Thus, complete as much of it as you can now to maximize the benefits of the entire exercise.

**Fall:** Fall is definitely the season made for you. The weather finally turns cool and there's mystique in the air. Football season starts and you plan to go to a lot of games or at least watch them on TV if you are a little short on cash from too much summer fun. You like the fact school is back in session. Of course, this means a constant shuffle of kids back and forth to what seems an endless array of activities. The fall clothing line is out and you're already enjoying the new styles; you've opted for a different haircut and the change makes you feel good. Fall is always when you have to decide what volunteer projects you want to do and how involved you want to be. That is, should you help with the mailing to raise funds for Thanksgiving baskets or should you run yourself ragged by distributing food to people less fortunate than you? There are so many other special fall events where you can assist—you wonder if you'll get overcommitted like you did last year and end up with a miserable cold during the few days you will have to enjoy the social events around the New Year.

The beautiful fall colors give you such a good feeling and you enjoy long solitary walks to solve work problems that frequently mushroom at this time of the year. Everyone seems to have "before-the-end-of-the-year" deadlines. Yes, fall creates a panic; no, it's really more like crisis upon crisis. You wonder why it's so imperative to rush when enjoying the fall and winter holidays can be so much greater if you have a little time to plan and get ready for them. Fall is a time of mixed emotions for you: happy because of family and friends getting together, but sad because some of them are no longer living.

| Value-Added Motivator | MY FALL MOTIVATORS |
| --- | --- |

What do you enjoy about the fall season? Why is it one of your favorite or least favorite times of the year? Are there specific things you like to do during the fall months—possibly some things you can't do during other seasons of the year? Why do you find fall exciting, invigorating, depressing, confining, or transitional? Further, what do you dislike about the fall season?

Describe your emotions that are associated with the fall season. If you have specific likes and dislikes, events and activities, or past positive and negative experiences that can be associated with fall, include them too. Use the space provided below as a starting point for your list. That is, don't be limited by the amount of space provided here for your list. Get a pad of paper and label two sheets as follows: Sheet 1: My Fall Motivators (Things I Enjoy About Fall); Sheet 2: My Fall Demotivators (Things I Dislike About Fall). With two lists, you can continue to add items as you think of things along the way. You may wish to number each item for ease of reference later.

### My Fall Motivators and Demotivators

(Things I Enjoy About Fall)　　　　　(Things I Dislike About Fall)

As noted for each season activity, you will be asked to refer back to this activity later in the chapter. Thus, complete as much of it as you can now to maximize the benefits of the entire exercise.

Now that you have completed the four seasons of motivation, it is time to reflect back on what the seasons mean to you. Look at your winter statements first. Have you listed more motivators than demotivators or vice versa? Is there a theme or pattern to your responses? Can your motivators (and/or demotivators) apply to any other season? Add a summary about what your winter motivators and demotivators say about you. For example, do your actions reflect that your personality and communication are cold to certain people? Is there a pattern of negative versus positive in a single category? Are there other patterns such as shunning group activities for those you like to do alone either in a specific category or across other categories? Look for the clues and patterns that tell something about your personality, values, and style. Ask a friend or colleague to help you dissect your responses.

| Value-Added Motivator | MOTIVATED FOR ALL SEASONS |
|---|---|

Complete a summary for each of the four seasons by responding to some of the questions posed in the preceding paragraph. Then, in the section labeled Season Reflections, draw some conclusions about your personality and communication as they are reflected in your motivational style. For example, are you concerned for other people or just for yourself? What behaviors can you identify that truly reflect your style? What did you learn about yourself that might help you avoid or eliminate your de-motivators or add to or strengthen your motivators?

Winter Summary: _____
_____
_____
_____

Spring Summary: _____
_____
_____
_____

Summer Summary: _____
_____
_____
_____

Fall Summary: _____
_____
_____
_____

Season Reflections: _____
_____
_____
_____

As a result of the winter, spring, summer, and fall exercises, you have learned a little (maybe a lot) more about your personality and your motivational style. If you've also identified additional motivators (and demotivators to avoid) to add to your list, that's even better. Further, if your Season Reflections conclusion suggests you need to make some changes toward maximizing your positive attitude and your motivators, you know there's no time like the present to get started. You probably don't need to be reminded that you're in the driver's seat to get your weather satellite in full operation. But if you do need a little boost, take out your Card and read it. Force your Card to give you some sunny skies for making your day brighter—make today "happen" as it definitely is the first day of the rest of your life.

# FORECASTING POSITIVELY SUNNY WEATHER

The future will depend on your commitment that you make today. Why not take positive action right now? Ask yourself, "What weather forecast would I like to see and hear if the weather person on my local TV station were to broadcast my attitude?" The answer to that question may be somewhat scary—if it is, change your attitude for the world to see. You should find comfort in knowing that the answer is not nearly as important or critical as it is for you to take immediate action to use your motivators to make your attitude more positive.

## Who's Motivated?

Lijun, a recent graduate of pharmacy school, waited in the busy airport for her international flight to return to New York after a wonderful visit with her family. Her emotions were so confused—she was happy that she had such a great time with her family, but she was sad that she was leaving them for another extended period of time. She also was excited about her new position starting next week at a large pharmacy in Chicago, but she was a bit apprehensive about whether or not she was fully prepared for moving to a new city and starting a new job. She wondered if she would like her coworkers, and even more importantly, if they would like her. She questioned whether or not she could keep a positive attitude especially if the atmosphere at the pharmacy was cold and indifferent. She took out her Card and asked herself why she was so stressed over everything. She quickly came to the conclusion that it was okay to question these things, but that she needed to move on with positive determination. After all, her greatest asset is her positive attitude—and it's a perfect motivator. "That's settled," she thinks. She will give her new environment and her coworkers her best "season's greetings."

1. What do you think Lijun meant by her best "season's greetings"?

2. If Lijun's attitude truly is positive and she knows how to motivate herself, what challenges face her? How can she meet them? Be as specific as possible.

3. Why do you believe Lijun was having mixed emotions as she left her family? How can her positive attitude and motivation help her if she revisits such thoughts along the way?

4. If asked, how would you describe your best "season's greetings"? What elements would be in your greetings?

5. Which holiday gives you the most motivation? Why (e.g., describe your motivators)? How can you use your favorite holiday's motivational factors to your advantage during the rest of the year? Be specific.

# AIR-CONDITIONING MAY LOWER ATTITUDINAL HEAT AND HUMIDITY

People with the most positive attitudes, like Lijun, can have lows once in a while. If you are an extremely positive person, you know that to be true. You also know that if you let your Card help you change, you can pick yourself up quickly and get back into your positive frame of mind. Let's say, however, you're not the most positive person (or you know of someone who you wish would be more positive). What causes the down time? Why does it last (or seem to last) longer than it should? How can the negative or less-than-positive behavior be turned around?

Obviously, the answers to these questions vary so widely that it would be impossible to list all the possibilities. But what is common to all probable causes and reasons for negative behavior as well as the duration of each is: your emotions affect everything you do. Your emotions can be swayed or turned by events and behavior of others. Your emotions can change with your surroundings. Your emotions permit you to think thoughts that make you reject trying things, such as air-conditioning to lower your attitudinal heat and humidity. Your emotions are affected by what you see, smell, hear, taste, touch, and experience. Your senses and emotions are influenced every moment of the day—just think of how many times each day you have the opportunity to be positive!

Choosing to let negativity take over may be an easy way out, but it carries with it tremendous consequences. Once you start on a downhill grade, your progress toward discouragement and negativity can be very rapid. You feel sorry for yourself; you console yourself; you think, "Poor me." You're probably right because there may be many good reasons why you're down, including reasons that are no fault of your own. You do, however, have a choice. Remember this: There is always someone out there who is less fortunate than you. Do you want to trade places with that person? If you give up, would you want to end up the same way? If you think you are at rock bottom, it is possible things could still get worse— and they will if you don't do something about your situation.

If you want to trade places with someone who has it better than you, you can't (that happens only in the movies). Furthermore, is there really anyone with whom you'd want to trade everything—lock, stock, and barrel? You may want *most* of the assets of some other person, but there are always a few things that may make you unhappier than you are right now. "I wish I could be . . . " is an ideal that can work only in fantasy land. To move toward bettering yourself—and maybe closer to the premise of that ideal—you must adjust your attitude. An attitude adjustment is the only way you can keep from falling even further into a deep, dark hole. And adjusting your attitude to be more positive may be extremely difficult to do because your emotions take such strong control of you. However, the sooner you start thinking positive thoughts, and begin letting your Card really work for you, the quicker your downward skid slows down. The stronger your motivation is to focus your thoughts into a positive realm, the easier it is to stop your negative slide and turn your out-of-control free fall into upward, positive momentum.

## WHEN IT RAINS ON YOUR PARADE

You know that you must depend on your motivators to turn negative thoughts into positive ones. It follows that if your cache of motivators is rather large and the strength of your motivators is extremely robust, you have everything on your side. Building your motivators into a wealth of resources is your goal. You stockpile your motivational resources by seizing every opportunity you can to turn negatives into positives and by turning positives into even greater positives and so on. That is, when it rains on your parade, find a positive element in the event.

Don't let a passing inconvenience hamper your style. If you let anything eat away a little of your positive attitude, it can result in permanent damage. Find a bright side. After all, the rain may be a positive motivator to someone else and lead to a very powerful motivator for you. Consider how others view the rain and adopt a positive perspective of some aspect of it. Don't underestimate how many positives you may be able to find if you look for them. Smile; the rain may bring long overdue cooler weather; the rain may provide a very nurturing result once it's over. The rain could turn a muddy puddle into a picturesque pond you can enjoy. If the birds enjoy it too, you have a value-added or extended motivator.

## MOTIVATED FOR ALL SEASONS

Never underestimate how value-added motivators can help you to be motivated throughout the year. And they can actually extend your favorite season long after it's over. How? If you have a favorite season, consider how and why you may be motivated more during that season than another one. By capitalizing on your dominant season, you can identify the elements that interest you and then find ways to extend those elements into the other seasons throughout the year. You may need to be creative in extending your seasons, but creativity is one of the best motivators you can have. If at first you don't come up with anything tangible to extend your dominant season beyond its current parameters, try hard to discover what it is that you enjoy about your favorite season. Do some brainstorming about the things that are associated with your favorite season's activities. You'll probably be surprised at how easy it is to get value-added benefits from merely thinking and daydreaming about what really gives you joy and satisfaction.

So what is your favorite season? How can you capitalize on your dominant season? How can you carry over your motivation from one season to another? And how can you truly be motivated for all seasons? The answer to these and similar questions become your ultimate challenges to extend your motivation throughout the year. As you accept the challenge, you'll discover there is a rainbow and a pot of gold at the end of it. You'll be keenly aware that your Card is important to you because you are the only one who can determine what goals you want to pursue and what value you place on your rewards. What is paramount to you is the fact that the value of your attitude and your motivational weather is totally up to *you*. Your Card is definitely an all-weather card. It can and should be used throughout the year. So go ahead—use your Card to its fullest—and be motivated for all seasons!

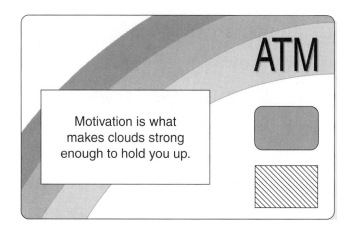

## CHAPTER 8: MOTIVATIONAL REINFORCEMENT

Reinforce your understanding of the chapter by responding to the following items.

1. How can something you enjoy, such as a sunset, relate motivation?

2. When you really value something, how does it show in your personality and style?

3. What is meant by a "motivational style that comes predominantly from one season"?

4. List several positive and negative factors associated with a winter motivational style.

5. List several positive and negative factors associated with a spring motivational style.

6. List several positive and negative factors associated with a summer motivational style.

7. List several positive and negative factors associated with a fall motivational style.

8. What is meant by "your emotions affect everything you do"?

9. Can you stockpile your motivation? Why or why not?

10. How can your motivators extend your favorite season?

11. Why is the Card an all-weather asset?

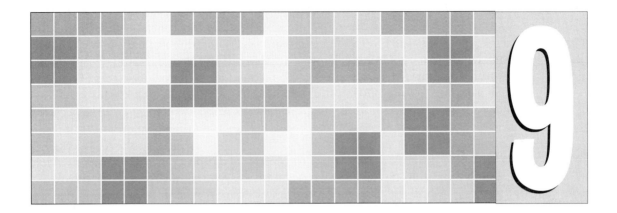

# Hitting Motivational Home Runs

## WHAT'S YOUR BATTING AVERAGE?

Have you ever thought about what it takes to be a good baseball player—to be a strong hitter who scores for the team consistently time after time? Whether in baseball or the game of life, scoring for yourself and the team, hitting home runs, and winning don't just happen by accident. Success comes with practice—practice that is based on a good understanding of yourself—your strengths, weaknesses, and style. That is, you need to know a lot about yourself so you can work on the right things to help you reach your goal.

Similarly, a good baseball player must develop and sharpen his skills and abilities to be successful. Long before a batter steps up to the plate, he must think about hitting the ball, capitalizing on the pitch he gets to avoid striking out. The batter also must practice hitting all types of pitches and demonstrate confidence that he is capable of hitting all types of pitches. Finally, the batter must maximize the skill he has developed to act on a pitch that will send the ball into the field or maybe even over the outfield wall. The successful hitter will establish a record as his consistency is shown, and others will expect the batter to perform based on that established record.

Motivation works in much the same way as you would go about earning an enviable batting average. It starts with knowing what you can and cannot do, knowing what inspires you to achieve, knowing the strengths and weaknesses about your behavioral attitude and style, and taking steps to achieve your desired goal. Using your personal Motivational ATM Card for self-motivation can be most rewarding if you are aware of and follow some basic steps to achieve motivational success. The steps are: Thinking positive thoughts and thinking about success; practicing positive behavior and practicing the best posture to take in a variety of situations; demonstrating confidence and demonstrating an "I can" attitude; maximizing motivation and maximizing positive strategies; acting on those strategies and putting 100 percent into the respective actions; establishing a pattern of continuing motivation; establishing consistency in all aspects of positive behavior; expecting success; and knowing others expect you to be successful too.

Three things bear repeating: The course of action that leads to success (a) is defined by you; (b) depends on how well you understand your strengths, weaknesses, personal style, and motivators; and (c) depends on taking action and assessing your actions. If you are already headed toward and making progress in a positive direction, your effort may be minimal to reach your goal. That is, you may need to do only a little polishing of your skill if your goal is clearly in sight. On the other hand, if your goal is unclear or further away, you may need to put considerable effort into your practice. You may even need to stand back and reassess your assets so you can capitalize on them. If you want confidence that you are taking the right course of action, you shouldn't miss evaluating any of the steps along the way to reaching your goal.

## Who's Motivated?

Kylie, a civil engineer, knows that she is good at what she does. She has a solid education (holds a BS and MS in civil engineering) and she is confident in her abilities. She likes what she does, and she is energetic and positive. Kylie has worked on a number of projects as well as with several managers at her firm. She works well with coworkers and managers. She is one of the company's best field engineers. Management has already noticed Kylie's abilities and sees her moving up into the ranks of senior management. Kylie has a very bright future with her multinational engineering firm and is excited at the new opportunity she has been offered: to head up a new unit of 25 engineers in South America. She is one of six managers the firm is sending to the company's new, expanding South American operation. What an opportunity! Kylie realizes the new challenge will be significant to her lifelong career goal. It is an opportunity that cannot be passed up; she's excited. Kylie is bound to gain a wealth of experience that would help her continue moving up the corporate ladder.

1. From what you can ascertain, what are Kylie's strengths?

2. What are Kylie's weaknesses?

3. Assess each of these challenges Kylie believes she faces: a) she does not have any management experience, but she has good technical knowledge; b) she no longer would work side-by-side with a team in the field, but would still provide expertise in directing field operations; c) she has never had an opportunity to travel and this would give her a great perspective of another culture; d) she would need to leave her church and friends behind for three years,

but would be back for a visit twice each year; and e) she can more readily re-
locate now (she is single) than possibly later when she settles down.

4. Is Kylie being realistic about the five major challenges (or are there others that
may be more challenging for her)? Justify your answers.

# TAKING ANY OLD PATH MAY GET YOU "THERE" FASTER

An introspection into your strengths and weaknesses can be extremely beneficial
when you need direction to make progress toward an intended goal. If your goal
is clearly defined, you can assess your progress to make sure you are moving toward it. Without a clear and realistic perspective of your goal, it will be impossible to know whether or not you are headed in the right direction. Thus, you will
need to develop the best skills you can in formulating goals that are realistic for
you. You will also need to be realistic and honest with yourself in evaluating your
goals.

Most people need to evaluate their goals on a frequent basis. The assessment
process is healthy. It is a confidence measure. It says that you are willing to look
closely at yourself. It says you want to better yourself and make changes. Assessment,
however, is only as good as knowing what you are evaluating and how accurate you
are in your assessment. How can you do a good evaluation? How can you be sure it
is accurate? You should be able to easily identify with the answers to those questions. That is, the more you understand yourself—your likes, dislikes, personality
traits, communication styles, motivators, strengths, and weaknesses—the more confidence you should have in making an accurate assessment of yourself.

You know that your self-analysis depends on you and that it can be only as
good as you make it. You must approach it with an open mind and view it with
honesty, even if the result may not be what you would like it to be. Also, if you
are truthful about what you need to do to better yourself, you will probably try
hard to make an accurate evaluation of yourself and will take action to change
whatever behaviors need to be changed. The changes you decide to make will depend, to a large degree, on your desire or motivation to make them. That is, you
can rely on your motivators and can mobilize them with vigor at critical junctions to help you on your way without serious interruption.

Along the way, to assure you are heading toward your intended goal or even
the right goal, you must still continue your assessment. Taking any old path will
probably get you someplace quite fast, but not necessarily in the direction you
need or even want to go. Using your personal Motivational ATM Card can help

you stay on track, especially if you use it often. It can keep you focused on your defined course of action. And the more you use your Card, the more practice you get for improving your batting average—and maybe even hitting home runs.

## EASY FOR YOU TO SAY

Motivation

A baseball player's success depends on her contributions to the team. It is not realistic to believe that only one team member's batting average is important, but it does play a major factor in how the team scores. Consider how motivation works in a somewhat similar manner. That is, the greater your motivation, the more significant it is for you and others—or if you expect to score by hitting a home run, you have to work at it. And you know there are home runs and then there are grand slams. You can't expect to hit the ball out of the park in a major game if you have done it only a few times in practice. Even if you have demonstrated consistency in practice, there are lots of elements that contribute to a very different environment when a scrimmage is exchanged for a game with an opposing team. Additionally, some teams are considerably more threatening than others. Some teams may be truly major league and you will not only need to get used to them, but you'll also find they have a unique style. The factors that enter into how you will perform in a real situation (in front of a rousing crowd, so to speak) are what contribute to your overall performance.

It is a good analogy to compare a baseball player's performance to your own motivation. You need motivators every day, day after day, throughout your entire life. In a way, there is no beginning or ending to your need for motivation. The need to "turn it up" at times, just as in a baseball game, can help take you out of a slump—slumps that are caused by getting down on yourself, negative interactions with other people, and a variety of other external factors. The picture in which you find yourself, in fact, can be quite variable. Yet, few external stimulators rarely change that much. That is, you'll still meet negative people. Not everything goes according to your plan. You find yourself in a quandary because even the best decision may be poor, mainly because of changing circumstances. Thus, while each situation that you encounter can be quite dissimilar, the major elements pretty much remain the same.

Most people know that meeting the situations of daily life may not be particularly easy, but they can be less monumental and even more enjoyable and satisfying if a person has confidence, pride, and self-worth. Confidence is based on the feeling you really *can* do something. It is a feeling that is strengthened by your positive posture and being successful. If you experience a snag, setback, or what even seems to be an impossible situation, confidence is what tells you to go on and try again. Similarly, it is motivation that moves you to take action. Your motivators help you reach success.

You, of course, also know that each success you experience, no matter how small, adds to another and another until several small increments of success make a real difference for you. Each success motivates you to further action because you like what you see; you are proud of your accomplishments or actions. Your pride builds and adds to your motivation that contributes to your success. You value what you've done.

The more you value your actions, the more confident you become. Your pride has increased; you've increased the value of your total image. It all sounds so easy and straightforward. You know it is, but when you put everything into practice, you are still challenged—sometimes challenged much more than you feel you can handle. That's when it is vitally important to think about your successes. That's also the time it is essential to call on your Card to give you the boost you need to motivate you to positive action. It's the time you are glad you know what motivates you because you have a good understanding of yourself.

The following exercise will add to your understanding of yourself. Have fun completing the exercise even though you'll need to make some difficult choices for some of the items.

| Value-Added Motivator | MY PERSONAL STYLE IS . . . |
| --- | --- |

In the following exercise, you have four choices to place in a rank order for each of 25 items. With 1 as your top choice, 2 as your second-highest choice, 3 as your next choice, and 4 as your least-acceptable choice, number each of the choices for each of the 25 items. Force yourself to make a 1, 2, 3, 4 rank-order decision for every item. Your choice should be based on what you believe, not what you *think* you should believe. There are no wrong answers for this exercise, so be sure you rank each item according to how you really feel about each one. Above all, enjoy expressing yourself as you work through the items.

1. I am happiest when I
   A. apply a procedure to a work task
   B. add flair to an assigned product
   C. make a new friend from a work project
   D. get a report or task done in record time

2. I read the newspaper
   A. starting with a specific page and methodically moving through it
   B. totally at random, but definitely include the comics
   C. focusing on sports pages or other personal interest stories
   D. as quickly as possible, mainly for the news

3. My actions are best represented by a
   A. calculator
   B. hot-air balloon
   C. teddy bear
   D. steamroller

4. I'm proud of my work area (desk, drawers, files, etc.) because it is
   A. well organized and I can find things easily
   B. a hub of lots of projects going on at once
   C. available to my coworkers—they can call on me for anything
   D. completely clean—all projects are done or moving along

5. My favorite movie is one that has
   A. a well-developed plot
   B. a pleasant, happy ending
   C. lots of good relationships
   D. lots of fast-paced action

6. Food I am most likely to enjoy would be
   A. a well-balanced combination
   B. anything, just lots of variety
   C. a medley of complementary flavors
   D. whatever is handy

7. I particularly feel good about myself when I wear
   A. a coordinated ensemble or suit
   B. lots of accessories and jewelry
   C. comfortable, easy-to-wear clothes
   D. basic casual or rugged clothes

8. If I could be described as a power tool, I would be
   A. a multifunction power screwdriver
   B. a jigsaw or paint sprayer
   C. a sander or car buffer
   D. an automatic stapling gun

9. Everything in my kitchen
   A. has a purpose and function
   B. reflects a cheery atmosphere
   C. is easily accessed
   D. is something I use frequently

10. A value I most cherish is
    A. dependability
    B. happiness
    C. friendship
    D. success

11. Computer jobs I might enjoy would be
    A. programmer or developer
    B. salesperson or marketing representative
    C. ergonomic designer or evaluator
    D. expediter or distributor

12. I'd be lost without
    A. a clock and a daily planner
    B. a cell phone and unlimited long distance
    C. voice mail and a missed-call feature
    D. e-mail and the Internet

13. My most productive working style is
    A. knowing that everything is where I know I can find it
    B. knowing who I can depend on if I can't find what I need
    C. talking with others to assure I have what I need
    D. moving on if I can't find something quickly

14. My idea of a perfect vehicle is a
    A. reliable, economical luxury car
    B. fun, fast sports car
    C. versatile sports utility vehicle or van
    D. fast, reliable car or truck

15. An ideal vacation would
    A. be well planned and even may be combined with a business trip
    B. have few restrictions to enjoy excitement and adventure
    C. include my friends or family and go to a mutually agreed-upon destination
    D. maximize the time spent at the destination rather than on getting there

16. My behavior can be best described as
    A. even-keeled, thinking before I act, and finding solutions to problems
    B. fun, being the life of the party, and enjoying life to its fullest
    C. considerate, valuing others' opinions, and making sure others are happy
    D. solid, taking direct action, and getting the job done

17. My preference for a fragrance is
    A. a muted, somewhat ordinary scent
    B. a fruity or friendly scent that is noticed
    C. a light, friendly scent
    D. wearing none at all; it's too much bother

18. I view myself as a person who is
    A. organized
    B. free-wheeling
    C. people oriented
    D. assertive

19. Life would be more fun if my colleagues
    A. would be interested in getting the facts and prioritizing tasks
    B. could lighten up a little, socialize, and make work enjoyable
    C. would just try to get along and be a team
    D. could just get going on a project

20. My sock drawer is best described as
    A. neatly arranged by color or style
    B. in disarray, messy or helter-skelter
    C. arranged around other more important stuff
    D. in no particular order, but handy

21. When I have a conversation with people, I like to
    A. plan what I'll say next
    B. be as spontaneous as possible
    C. assure them I am listening
    D. be as succinct as possible

22. I approach mundane household tasks
    A. in an orderly fashion doing what makes sense to do first, second, etc.
    B. by doing whatever seems pressing at the time
    C. while taking others' needs into consideration
    D. by attacking them head on and just getting them done

23. My biggest concern for the world is to assure
    A. there is a solid future for generations to come
    B. everyone finds enjoyment and happiness
    C. peace and goodwill are fostered
    D. major problems are resolved now

24. If my personality were an animal, it would be a
    A. fox
    B. monkey
    C. rabbit
    D. lion

25. I really like working with people who
    A. are concerned with details of the task
    B. have lots of ideas for a project
    C. get everyone to contribute to the effort
    D. just want to get the job done

You will now need to total your responses by counting the total number of responses you ranked for each choice. That is, for each of the 25 items, how many first choices did you give to A responses? Record that number in the chart that follows.

Now, count up the total number of second choices you recorded for each A response. Record that number in the chart.

Next, count up the total number of third choices you gave to A responses. Record that number in the chart.

Finally for the A responses, count up the total number of fourth choices you recorded for each A response. Record that number in the chart.

Now that you have counted all your choices for A and entered them on the appropriate lines, follow the same procedure for totaling all the B, C, and D responses. (Note: If you wish to check your tally, total each row and each column. Each of the rows and each of the columns should total 25 indicating that you completed and recorded responses to all 25 items. This step is offered only to give you a way to check to see if you've recorded all your responses in the table. It has no other significance to the scoring of the exercise.)

| 1st Choices | 2nd Choices | 3rd Choices | 4th Choices |
|---|---|---|---|
| A = 1 ____ | A = 2 ____ | A = 3 ____ | A = 4 ____ |
| B = 1 ____ | B = 2 ____ | B = 3 ____ | B = 4 ____ |
| C = 1 ____ | C = 2 ____ | C = 3 ____ | C = 4 ____ |
| D = 1 ____ | D = 2 ____ | D = 3 ____ | D = 4 ____ |

Now look at each column. For the first column, which category (A, B, C, or D) received the most 1 choices? Record the letter of the category in the blank below under 1st choices. Now do the same for your 2nd choices, your 3rd choices, and finally your 4th choices.

| 1st Choices | 2nd Choices | 3rd Choices | 4th Choices |
|---|---|---|---|
| Category ____ | Category ____ | Category ____ | Category ____ |

On the following graph, chart the results of your four choices. Make a wide vertical line starting at the base (0) and continue upward, stopping at the number that represents how many responses you had in that category. Note that the choices you recorded may *not* be in the same order as the categories in the grid below. Chart your responses for categories A, B, C, and D, in that order, so it is easier to refer back to the categories as you read further.

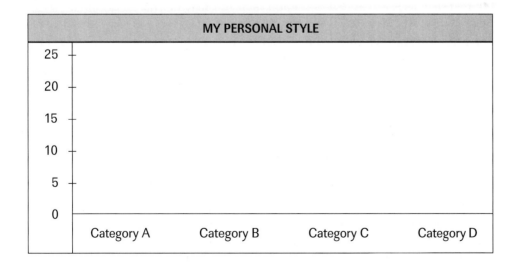

To determine what each category means to you and your own style, here's a brief summary of each category:

Category A Style: a person who is process or procedure oriented. He likes to plan out a project and get all the facts (who, what, when, where, why, how, etc.) associated with it. He may need considerable details to get the job completed.

Category B Style: a person who is change oriented. She tries to make a job fun and likes to be involved in lots of activities. She is happiest with changing elements as well as moving between and among projects.

Category C Style: a person who is people oriented. He has great concern for people and their welfare. He is a relationship builder who wants people to get along with each other and work together as a team to achieve a result.

Category D Style: a person who is results oriented. She just wants to get the job done. She may provide considerable structure to control the way a project is done, but the important thing is to get it completed.

Before going into more detail about the categories and what insights they may offer for understanding your own behavior, you may wish to look back at your summary responses for each of the categories. That is, look at the first column and the category that you recorded as having the greatest number of first-choice responses. How many of the 25 possible first-choice responses did that category receive?

For example, let's say you have 13 first-choice responses for category D. Let's say further that you have 5, 4, and 3 first-choice responses for each of categories A, B, and C, respectively. Because category D represents considerably more first-choice responses than the other three categories, your style probably reflects that your motivation is aimed at a goal to get a job done (category D) rather than to plan a project (category A), to have fun doing it (category B), or to assure everyone is happy doing the project (category C). In this example, category D (with a focus on results) has considerably more responses than the other three categories; thus, you probably can easily identify with the style represented by category D.

On the other hand, let's say your first-choice responses were more evenly distributed such as A = 7, B = 6, C = 7, and D = 5. You may not have a dominant style for everything you do, but rely on several styles to live your everyday life. Further, you may now want to look at the second column for a secondary style and on to the fourth column that represents the style you most often reject.

To give you more insight about your style and the styles of others, consider the following expanded discussion about each of the styles:

**Category A Style:** If you identify with category A, your style is focused on procedures or processes. You are more concerned about the way a job is done than what is done, when it gets done, or who does it. Your planning and organizational skills are emphasized; you like things in an orderly array. You may be quite detail-oriented because you want things to flow in a logical, step-by-step manner. You enjoy challenges that rely on your collecting facts and information. If you don't have a way to analyze a situation, you are somewhat at a loss and feel things may be proceeding without direction. You may be frustrated with people who operate in other styles, mainly because they may not be as orderly as you are.

Because the category A person is process oriented, the process is more important than the decision itself. It is so important to collect information and get the facts that you may be known as someone who is extremely thorough (and that may drive others crazy if they don't operate in your style). You also may be relied on to always have the best information as well as to know where to get it. Your attention to analyzing a situation, however, may not permit you to feel there is enough information or resources for making a final decision; thus, you may be very slow to make a definite commitment. Also, you probably communicate in a very low-key, unobtrusive way. Your ultimate desire to get the facts of a situation may have you searching and planning a process for the best way to get them.

The category A person is further characterized by someone who thinks and acts in a very logical, systematic manner. That is, you like to evaluate each element of a situation and don't feel comfortable if you can't. You would never react on rumor and would feel very uncomfortable being a part of a group that did. In essence, your style is reflected in an orderly, middle-of-the-road behavior where the best way to reach a solution is to get solid, substantiated information. You need a well thought-out road map to guide your decision-making process. As a result, you don't reach closure quickly, but continue to plan out a course of action that you evaluate (or want to evaluate) at each step of the way. Planning is definitely the key to your management style. In fact, you may continue planning so long, that making a commitment based on your desire to get all the facts is difficult if not impossible.

**Category B Style:** If you identify with category B, your style is characterized by finding enjoyment in most everything you do. You are a free spirit and thrive on lots of change. You are not concerned for any type of process or even a plan. You are mainly interested in having a good time with whatever you do; you probably see something interesting in nearly everything. If you don't find an activity interesting, you probably won't finish it. You'll find all sorts of reasons to have many things going at once. Your creativity works overtime and you have lots of ideas for projects and ways to do things. You may be somewhat impatient if others want to slow down on a project to get more facts or evaluate what step to take next. You probably find positive elements in most situations—and can cope with a boss who seems to always be on your back to get a job done. But you may drive him crazy as he tries to get you to complete a task; or he may be disappointed in you if you don't complete a job to his satisfaction.

You want to get started—to take some action—but not necessarily to get the job done. As a result, your conversational style may by fragmented or reflect a little impatience because you frequently jump from one subject to another. Also, you probably go along with people from the other styles, especially with people who can get things done. Since your outgoing style attracts people, you have lots of friends. You don't miss anything because you want to get the most out of life. As a result, you don't hang around any one person for too long a period. People with other styles may sometimes misinterpret your style to be one of less substance because of your many interests. You enjoy going in a lot of directions, whichever seems important at the time. You may not be very well received by the person who wants to get things done or a person who likes to plan ahead.

**Category C Style:** If you identify with category C, your style is focused on people. Fostering good, strong interpersonal relationships is your goal. You want to get the opinions of everyone and try to make everyone happy. You're the peacemaker and will find something—anything—to try to get people to work together to become a cohesive team. You don't like to work independently, and you do not like it when others work independently—your perspective (and theirs) may become too narrow for all people involved to be rewarded for and to enjoy the outcomes. Thus, you would rather spend time discussing a project at its outset as well as discussing it at many junctions along the way so the project becomes a group effort. The time spent in discussions, in your mind, is vitally important to ensure the group is working together.

Because establishing good working relationships is more important than getting the job done, you may find it difficult to meet deadlines. That is, your last resort—especially if the timelines have slipped significantly—would be to assign the project to someone who could just complete it quickly. You are so concerned that people contribute to the process or product, you may be very popular as a supervisor. Your subordinates like you, and even if their styles are different than yours, they like working for you and will get the job done. On the other hand, those who just want to get on with things may find your style just a little too laid back. If your concern for involving people is extremely strong, you may not make timely decisions because you desire group involvement. You probably are extremely uncomfortable if you are forced to select the best people to do a job and make sure they do it.

Your leadership skills may be excellent if you combine some of the elements of the other styles to assure there will be a quality product in the end. The empowerment you give to subordinates may be viewed by some as giving out a task that has responsibility and authority, but somewhat lacking in accountability. That is, because you don't want to tell anyone the job was not completed to your (or your boss's) satisfaction, you may have a tendency to buffer bad news to assure everyone works together.

**Category D Style:** If you identify with category D, your personal style is product or end-results oriented. That is, your objective is to get the job done and move on to your next project. You probably are rather productive; you can complete nearly anything you undertake. You may, however, be a little blunt in finessing the people around you. Your people skills may actually lack polish because you don't see the real value in taking the time to establish good interpersonal relationships. Relationships may, in fact, stand in the way of taking the action that is needed to get something done. Frequently, your communication may be, or appear to be, rather abrupt and to the point. You know where you're going and you want to get there as soon as possible. Some people will like this direct approach; others will find it objectionable.

People with styles similar to your own really like having the freedom to get started on a project and to get it done as quickly as possible. Other people who need more detailed directions about a project may have difficulty working with or for you. You know where you're going, but you sometimes don't share the direction with those working on the project. You may feel there isn't time to get into discussions about other solutions because you already have the best solution to get the job done. For your coworkers or subordinates, following blindly may have its merits. Some coworkers and followers, however, will need more interaction with you to get a project done in the most satisfactory, efficient manner.

On the other hand, if your intensity to get things done is coupled with over-supervision, people may either totally depend on you (for everything, including motivation) or totally reject your direct style to drive them. That is, your style can be rather intense—you have your own standards and you expect others to join in or get out of the way. Some may like that quality; others will balk at your lack of interest in meeting their needs, your impatience for their wanting to get all the facts, or your taking all the fun out of work.

# BEATING THE COMPETITION

So, what does this really mean to you? Your predominant personal style is based on your likes and dislikes, many of which you can define and have indicated in the exercise you just completed. Your style reflects a pattern that encompasses many different kinds of activities and behaviors. Knowing you have a pattern that depicts a particular style (or possibly two styles), you may now better understand why some motivators work for you and others don't. Your personal style is significant to you because you can accomplish a task and get satisfaction out of doing it if you operate within your own style. You can grow into other styles by being aware of what each style represents. Also, you can now look more closely at your preferences to relate them to your strengths and weaknesses as well as to your motivation.

Thus, your motivation is closely linked and aligned to your personal style. In fact, you may not be able to distinguish between your motivational style and your personal style because they are so intertwined or integrated into your life. In any event, your style gives you insights into why you like and do certain things and not others. You understand your style. You know why you are motivated to do certain tasks and to be around certain people. That is, if you are not comfortable in your environment (possibly because you must adapt to someone else's style), you cannot expect to be as highly motivated as you might be if you were in an environment that is conducive to your style. An understanding of behavior styles helps you compete in many environments. It gives you an edge for healthy competition. Your efforts are rewarded because you can employ strategies that will enhance your own style (and others' styles too). You get a degree of satisfaction from the results; you are motivated.

Once you know your predominant style(s), including the personality traits and motivational elements that describe your actions, two distinct things give you an advantage for all your future actions: 1. You identify and understand your dominant behavior patterns that give you clues to which areas you want to strengthen and which ones you want to change. You see how your style may closely mesh with or be in conflict with others' styles. 2. You are now in a better position to understand other people's styles, which helps you improve your interactions with them. You can better appreciate the similarities and differences between your style and those of others. You can see things from other people's perspectives, capitalize on their needs and strengths, and downplay or avoid the things that cause them concern. Everyone benefits from your new insights.

The benefits from understanding your own style and, in turn, others' styles, help you stay motivated when a situation gets tense. You know there will be those situations that will try your patience and goodwill; you know it's very difficult to try to be positive and happy all of the time. But by understanding your style, you can be more cognizant of how you *should* and *want* to react to a situation. You can look at both the forest and the trees to make the best decision for controlling how you *expect* to and *will* react. If you base your actions on what you know about the styles, you can speculate on some of the consequences, based on your own and others' reactions associated with the styles. You can see the styles at work; you can contribute to a situation versus making it worse.

It's your choice to control your emotions and thoughts. It's your choice to jump into the thick of things or to back off. That is, you don't have to win the prize to beat the competition. You win when you're in control. You win when you keep your attitude and actions positive. You make the best of a situation because you understand how the competition works.

## WINNING THE PENNANT

In addition to knowing the competition to channel your efforts in the right direction, you know you must work hard to get the best result from everything you do. Your winning equation for maximizing your positive attitude requires effort, practice, persistence, and patience. It doesn't come automatically—at least not all of the time. It requires improving your skills and strengthening your weaknesses to the point you act and react in a consistently positive manner. As you get better at reading a situation (or reading the styles of the people involved), you can help to create the right atmosphere for maximizing results.

That is, your motivation can contribute to the environment through your actions, which are based on your understanding of your own actions as well as your understanding of others' actions. You help others gain a better understanding of themselves (even though they may not realize it or appreciate it right now) and help them to see the viewpoints of their colleagues. Your contribution of motivation and a positive attitude is significant—and will rub off on others. Your experience and understanding will also contribute to finding and fostering the right mix of things for creating a balance that can diffuse a tense situation. You may not single-handedly resolve a problem, but if you can contribute your knowledge to improve a situation, your contribution is important.

### Who's Motivated?

 Glen, a women's varsity basketball coach, is one of the most positive, upbeat persons you could ever know. He finds something good about everything and everyone. If you need a lift, it's Glen you call on to give you a pep talk. He seems to know what you need and truly reads people extremely well. Glen can be counted on to step into difficult situations to help ease the tension. He is supportive of everyone and doesn't seem to take sides. He's a true professional and never misses a game. He is a strong disciplinarian—an attribute he applies both to himself and to his team. On Glen's basketball court, no one gets any slack cut in practice; no one seems to really want it. Glen's team members work hard for him, and he is always there for them.

1. What style(s) characterize Glen? Why?

2. Why do some people who first meet Glen think he is not for real?

3. What makes Glen an ideal coach?

4. Apply Glen's style to (a) yourself and (b) a colleague. What changes might you (your colleague) consider making to be more like him?

5. Speculate as to what may be motivators for Glen. Why?

## THE IDEAL COACH

You know there are several elements that contribute to Glen's style. There are also elements of all the styles that characterize Glen. You, too, have found your style to reflect a crossover of elements among the styles. It is the combination of characteristics that provides uniqueness to your own (and others') style(s). Some characteristics also are more desirable than others. For example, a coach who has a positive attitude, is supportive and encouraging, and provides team incentives is someone who will motivate her team more quickly than one who is not.

Being a motivational coach is an awesome responsibility. To motivate yourself is one thing, but to motivate a whole team is quite another matter. But does Glen really motivate the team or does he provide the motivational influence for his individual team members to motivate themselves? Consider the following two questions about motivation and how you can help others with their motivation: What does it take to stay motivated over time? Can your motivation be transferred to others?

To stay motivated day after day, you know that it's essential to maintain as positive an attitude as possible—and you know your positive attitude needs to be nurtured with positive thoughts, emotions, and actions. That is, your positive attitude doesn't just happen, but you control it. The more you practice being positive, the more positive you will be and the more likely you will enjoy longer-lasting positive benefits. Positivism breeds positivism, yet you're the only one who decides on the extent of your positive outlook. This means that you and only you hold the ultimate power in what happens to your attitude.

Motivation is the go-between that makes your attitude what it is. If you choose to be motivated, you can be; you've taken advantage of believing in your Card. But it still takes effort on your part. Others may influence your motivation. Events and activities may influence your motivation. Influence is wonderful, and even though others and things can influence or spur you to action, your motivation is still yours. Your Card is yours. You motivate yourself. You control your own motivation. How much or how little motivation you have is determined only by what you want it to be. Motivation cannot be transferred to you from someone else. They can influence you, but they cannot directly motivate you. You must make the choice in the direction you take. You must take the action.

Since you know that literally everything around you influences you in some way, your environment can be a positive, a negative, or even a mixed influence. It is how you act within that environment that is important. Let's say you and a number of other people are caught in a severe lightning and thunderstorm that has cut off electricity in the area. The storm has broken out the windows of a large department store. Some of the people around you rush into the store to take whatever they can. In fact, people are rushing in and out of the store in a wild frenzy. You have a choice in this negative situation to either join in the looting or take some other action. No one is forcing you to take action, but you are being influenced by your surroundings. What action will you take? What motivators do you have to avoid joining in a negative, illegal activity? How will your thoughts, emotions, values, style, and positive attitude contribute to your actions?

If you decide against joining in a negative activity but continue being subjected to other negative surroundings (possibly more than positive ones), it may not take long for the continual negative influence to rub off on you. You know it is extremely difficult to totally ignore your environment whether it is positive or negative. If your actions are negative, you unmistakably devalue your Card. Your Card loses some of its value whenever you decide against taking positive action. Its usefulness to you is diminished and can only be reinstated by reversing your actions. But because it's still your decision, the sooner you decide you want to be on the winning team, and take action toward that decision, the quicker you will get back on track.

## BE A TEAM PLAYER ON A WINNING TEAM

Picture yourself as the batter who plays for a baseball team—a team with a winning attitude. You are influenced by your positive team members. In this metaphor, you see some of your teammates hitting home runs. To you the home runs really represent motivational home runs and you are determined to follow the lead of the strongest batters. You find success because you look for it; you plan your actions—positive actions. You avoid negative situations as much as possible because you know that to consistently hit motivational home runs, you must surround yourself with positive people and operate within a positive environment. You count up your assets: You have a strong, upbeat, supportive coach (and, possibly you are the coach—the manager, leader, etc., who must lead your team to victory). Your team works hard and is motivated to excellence. You and your team members are positive on and off the field. And, of course, you and your teammates practice, practice, practice . . . to bias success on your side. The positive environment created by everyone's winning attitude is a motivating influence. You can't lose!

You are a winner—because you are determined to be a winner. Yet, there are so many negative influences that abound that you may feel, at times, it is sometimes impossible to avoid or get out of a negative environment. It may be very, very difficult to rise above it, but it is not impossible. It may take all the effort you can muster to maintain your positive attitude and you may even want to give up at times. If and when you're confronted with these times, you must pick yourself up. You must believe in your Card and the rewards your Card can provide to you. You must value your Card because the value you place on your Card will determine your choice.

Every moment of every day you have the power to accept or reject various elements in your environment toward what action to take. If you surround yourself with positive people and become a part of a positive team, some of the positiveness of the other players will probably influence you. Similarly, your attitude and motivation also project vibrations to those around you to influence their actions. All of these influences and influencers are important, even critical at times. If you can project a positive, motivating influence, your team members will value the influence generated by your positive energy. They, however, still must act on your influence—they must motivate themselves (and, you hope, they will be able to do so because your influence is so strong).

Similarly, others can provide a very powerful influence for you, but it is you who takes action. It may be easy to exert a little less effort or even drop off the team, but you'll probably always regret the consequences if your decision isn't reversed. You are the owner of your own motivation just as you are the owner of your positive attitude. Choose to be on the winning team and continue striving to hit motivational home runs.

And, as a reminder for reaching your goal: practice, practice, practice.

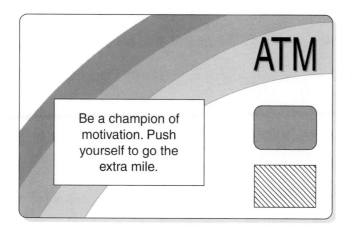

Be a champion of motivation. Push yourself to go the extra mile.

# CHAPTER 9: MOTIVATIONAL REINFORCEMENT

Reinforce your understanding of the chapter by responding to the following items.

1. Make the comparison of how motivation may be somewhat similar to achieving success at improving one's batting average.

2. Why is expecting success a good course of action?

3. Explain the importance of doing a personal goals assessment or a self-analysis.

4. What is the basis of a person's confidence and how can it be strengthened?

5. What is the importance of learning about your (others') style(s)?

6. Describe some of the elements associated with each of the four categories of styles.

7. Discuss the pros and cons of ways you might work best with each of the four styles.

8. How does knowing your style contribute to creating the right atmosphere?

9. How can you be a coach of motivation?

10. How can a team contribute to the motivation of each of its members?

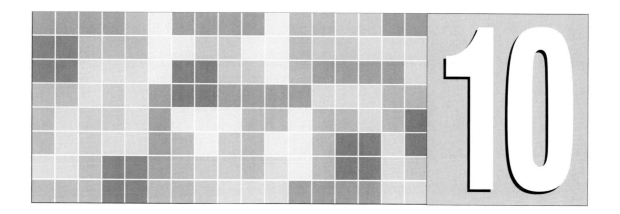

# Motivation Via Personal Project Management

## A SYSTEMATIC APPROACH TO LIFE

You know that to be successful in reaching your goals in life, it takes planning and effort on your part. If you select the right goals and find the right motivators to get you going down the right path to your destination, you can find satisfaction in both the journey and the end result. You know, too, that you can circumvent a variety of obstacles along the way and meet other challenges that require selecting among alternatives yet still find your goals rewarding. But how do you know if you have the right goals even though you have the motivation to take action? The answer is not always clear, but you will be more confident that you do have the right goals if you take a systematic approach to selecting them. Consider Lydia and Bradley.

### Who's Motivated?

Lydia approaches everything she does with a goal in mind. She has goals for her education, for her health, for her savings, and even for shopping. Lydia is extremely well organized and it seems to her friends that she may reach her life's mission more quickly than anyone around her. Lydia's friend, Bradley, also is a very disciplined individual whose life ambition is to help young people achieve their life dreams. Bradley believes he can realize his ambition from a variety of avenues: he can become a major league coach (his athletic abilities have already earned him several prestigious scholarships), a franchise owner (maybe a restaurant, sports team, child care facility, etc.), work for or establish an organization which promotes kids' achievement (*Fortune* 500 company, health/fitness center, nonprofit or volunteer organization, etc.), or become a teacher/trainer (public or private school teacher, sports program trainer, etc.). One evening Lydia and Bradley got into a rather heated conversation about their lives. How would you respond to some of the following conclusions each of them made? Give some rationale to support your responses.

1. Lydia doesn't believe Bradley has any goals at all.

2. Lydia thinks Bradley may never accomplish anything because he doesn't have a clue where he is going.

3. Bradley believes Lydia may have a lot of short-term goals, but no real life mission.

4. Bradley thinks that Lydia overorganizes her life; that she has so much structure she must have a goal before she can proceed with anything.

5. Both feel they could never change places with each other in terms of the way they approach their lives.

Many people approach life similarly to the way Lydia and Bradley do. Lydia has taken a short-term perspective to accomplish things that are important to her. She makes plans, focuses on them, and then drives herself to reach them. Her plans, however, could be much broader if she hopes to realize her full potential. Bradley, on the other hand, has a very global perspective about his life. He seems to know what he really wants to do with his life—in general—but has not zeroed in on ways to get there. It is good he evaluates lots of alternatives and options. But unless he begins making some critical decisions related to his ambition, he may be not be able to count on reaching his expectations.

Both Lydia and Bradley could benefit from developing a personal plan through an understanding of project management. That is, if they were to develop individual plans to help them reach their goals, they could benefit from evaluating the components of their plans. In developing their plans, they probably would find many of their plan components similar to those elements found in project management. A basic premise of project management (or how to manage a project or activity) is to identify and assess the factors (including the mission, goals, steps, resources, timelines, etc.) that contribute to the accomplishment of the project. The goal is to develop a well thought-out plan for the project to be completed in the most successful manner. A plan usually helps the planners and facilitators to approach a project with much more confidence and determination than would be possible with a haphazard approach. Thus, project management is aimed at and follows a game plan to reach a goal.

Developing a plan (or several plans) for the important things you do in life will help you to prioritize what's really critical and vital to you. A personal plan offers you the structure you may find essential to proceed at a good pace in a positive direction. A plan provides a guideline for you to follow, which reinforces your confidence for wanting to reach your goals. A plan also provides you with incremental steps that you can evaluate periodically to make sure you are actually making progress each step of the way toward your goal. And as you develop a plan (or two or three) that really works for you, you get better at the planning process and selecting courses of action to yield the results you want and need. You become good at planning and at integrating your plans to take advantage of the variety of elements and situations you encounter along the way toward your goals.

## THE VALUE OF A MOTIVATIONAL BUSINESS PLAN

Having a plan of action for reaching your goals (or for completing a project, an activity, task, etc.) is similar to a business plan developed by a company. That is, a business plan, simply stated, is a plan that describes the company—past, present, and future. The plan acts as a guide to direct where the business wants to go and be over a period of time. For example, the company's leaders need to ask where they want their business to be in a few months, a year, 5 years, 20 years, or some other specified period of time. A business plan outlines what is important to the company. It includes such things as the company's vision (what the business wants to become), mission (what its purpose is and the end results to be achieved), goals (strategic components, steps, tasks, or achievements to move the business toward its mission), and objectives (smaller components which make up and help to achieve the company's goals). A business plan describes what the business does and how it does it, what resources it has and needs (especially human and financial resources usually based on a budget), who its customers and competitors are, and what uniqueness it brings to the market (including its marketing strategies). A business plan takes into consideration the challenges and issues it faces and determines a course of action that helps to focus it on being successful.

Can you see how important following a business plan can be to a company in a technological, information-saturated, competitive society? Equally as important, you probably also can see how you can benefit from developing a business plan which focuses on your own success. That is, if you develop your own personal plan, you can determine where you want to go and what you hope to achieve based on your identified vision, mission, and goals. You can develop a plan that will guide your career and your life. If you follow your plan and assess your progress along the way, you know when you are on target and when you may be getting off track.

Thus, what your strategic personal plan does for you is similar to what a strategic business plan does for a company. Yes, there still are risks and no absolute guarantees even with the best plan; and there will, no doubt, be plenty of challenges (and maybe even failures) along the way. But, a well thought-out plan is a much better way to approach the unknown—to anticipate some of the roadblocks and alternatives—than to just let life happen without any preparation. Your planning can help you develop good strategies to make progress toward your goals, to capitalize on your strengths, and to maximize your motivation. What a wonderful tool you have to become the successful person you desire to be!

Once you develop your strategic personal plan to help you guide your career and stay on track, it becomes easier for you to develop other types of plans. For example, your personal plan usually focuses on a broad perspective. To achieve your broad perspective or vision, you'll probably want to have smaller plans for your goals, projects, and activities that contribute to your personal plan. Each of your plans—broad or narrow, general or specific—becomes a strategic plan that provides the framework for an endeavor or project. And the basic components of any type of strategic plan are similar and quite logical: determine a starting point, identify the steps you will take to move you in the right direction, and define your expectations to assure you really have reached your goal.

In developing a strategic plan (personal, project, etc.), you will find there are certain components of each of your plans that must be done immediately. Others may be critical in importance. Some of the elements may be interesting and others may not. If you assign weights to the elements you've identified as necessary to reach your goal, you will further determine what emphasis you need to place on each one. You can then decide how to assess and evaluate the elements as well as identify what alternatives are open to you or how they can be created. Finally, once you've determined you have the best plan to proceed, you will need to take your plan seriously and follow it with dedicated determination.

## NOT FOR ME!

What if you feel you don't really need a plan because you know where you're headed and how you will get there? That's great! However, it has been found that for even the most disciplined person as well as for an individual who feels he doesn't need a plan, a plan is vital. Why? Because a plan can be systematically evaluated at critical junctions—junctions which may not be seen if a plan is not developed. Thus, the person who says he doesn't need a plan may be just the person for which this discussion is intended!

Many people believe they know where they are going without actually developing any type of strategic plan. They feel confident they are headed in the right direction. They believe if they are moving forward, they are progressing toward a goal. Possibly they are; however, many people are surprised at how different an approach they could actually take once they sit down and analyze what it is they really want to do and what goals are truly important to them. Others find they know what they want to do, but have difficulty in identifying and taking appropriate actions to reach their goals. Many people find the real value of a strategic plan is in seeing the upcoming challenges and potential roadblocks that may be obscure without a plan. A plan can help avoid being blindsided and will give you focus for moving ahead at the right pace.

While there are no easy answers to assure you are headed in exactly the right direction and at the right speed, you can benefit greatly from knowing and considering how you can better reach your goals through the concepts used in project management via a business plan. Keep in mind that project management can be applied to everything—from a project or a vacation to your motivation or career. Let's look at project management from the perspective of developing a personal plan—that is, a motivational business strategic plan for your life. Once you see the big picture of where you are going or want to go, you can apply the steps to everything you do.

# MY LIFE'S EXPECTATIONS

What are your expectations about your life? An excellent place to start in identifying your expectations is to ponder where you want to be 5, 10, or 20 years from now. And even if you have an immediate need staring you in the face—such as a project or other rather tangible desire such as a vacation, house, car, etc.— you would do well to start with your life goals. Why? Because your immediate needs and wants may turn out to be less important than you think they are right now. Alternatively, they may be even more critical than you believed once you have looked at the bigger picture of where you're going in life.

| Value-Added Motivator | MY EXPECTATIONS |
|---|---|
| In the space provided write down your life's expectations (where you want to be in 10 to 15 years). | |

_____
_____
_____
_____

At this point you may want to refer back to the general components of a business plan. Using the business plan elements as a general guide, develop a vision and mission you have for your life. Your vision and mission should be rather global and overarching. A good example may center around your wanting "to become a leader whose impact makes a significant difference to society." Obviously this statement is very broad and less tangible than wanting something that is materialistic or tangible (such as wanting money or something money will buy).

Your vision should be one that could have many different goals. The statements you develop for a vision and mission should be broad because you want to leave some room for alternatives as to how you will reach them. Your vision, and subsequent statements, should give you excitement and drive—something that will energize you every time you think about it. You should be reminded of your vision, and its value to you, each time you look at your Card. Thus, your vision should be motivating—you want to pursue it and you want to start now.

If you find you have several directions you want to take, see if you can fold them all into an encompassing vision statement. But, do not be disappointed if you don't come up with a good statement immediately. You may need to give your statement considerable thought—most people do—and write out several drafts (over a period of several days or weeks for refinement) to reach a statement that truly is your vision. You may also need to do the same with your mission statement (and if, for now, you cannot see the real difference between mission and vision, the important thing is that you get into a frame of mind that starts you thinking along the lines of your global aspirations).

| Value-Added Motivator | MY VISION AND MISSION |
|---|---|

Even though you may not have ideal vision and mission statements right now, you can start by putting into words what you believe each is:

My vision is:

_____

My mission is:

_____

As suggested above, read and reread your vision and mission statements. Over a period of days and weeks you will probably rewrite and modify them to where you find satisfaction, excitement, and motivation in them. Your vision is what will guide you to reach your goals. It should not need to be changed even though you take different paths and change goals along the way. That is, your vision should, in a way, be like a big, sturdy umbrella that is useful in all types of weather—rain, sleet, sun, or wind. If your statement isn't large enough or strong enough, it (similar to the umbrella) will not stand the test of time. So make your vision and mission statements something you really believe in and trust— statements that give you excitement to want to reach them. Then translate your vision to your Card; that is, your Card should represent your vision. Every time you look at or think about your Card, your vision is right there to motivate you to action.

Even though you may not, at this time, have statements that are refined and finalized, it would be beneficial to you to developed tentative vision and mission statements so you can proceed to develop goals which will contribute to an overall plan for your life. Based on these broad statements, determine a goal or two that will contribute to your vision and mission. Your goals should still be somewhat broad (such as "to become a community leader" to tie this statement to the earlier example) and may have a timeline attached to them (such as "within 8 years"). To assure you have a goal that will work for you, you should ask yourself several questions: How long term is my goal (does it contribute to my life's vision and mission)? Is it realistic (both in scope and timing)? Can I be expected to achieve it (develop incremental steps, etc.) if I work at it?

Write down one goal you believe will work for you to achieve the vision and mission you identified earlier:

_____

_____

The next step in the process of developing a plan for yourself is to identify the elements and steps that will make your plan work. To help you see the whole picture of what you want your personal plan to accomplish, here are some important steps to follow as you look at your expectations:

---

### MY MOTIVATIONAL BUSINESS PLAN

1. Identify a (several) goal(s) you want to reach. Important questions to ask are: What are my vision and mission? Is my goal exciting and aimed at achieving my vision and mission? Are my expectations realistic, yet challenging, and reachable with effort?

2. Do a SWOT* analysis. That is, write down your strengths, weaknesses, opportunities, and threats to your vision (mission and goals). Questions to ask are: How can I maximize my strengths? How can I minimize my weaknesses or change them into strengths? How can I can take advantage of or capitalize on my opportunities? What threats or potential threats stand in my way or can be circumvented to reach my goal?

3. Identify the strategic elements and the basic steps of your goal. Questions to ask are: What are the critical elements needed to achieve my goal? What steps can I take (or motivators can I employ) to assure I will stay headed (and will make progress) in the right direction?

4. Evaluate each of the strategic elements needed to reach your goal. Questions to ask are: What is the value, need, and timing of each of the critical elements of my goal? What alternatives are available to me when challenges enter the picture? (Challenges may be factors within your control—internal; or factors outside your control—external.) What measurements can I make and what quality measures can I put in place to assess each element to assure I will be taking the right course of action toward my goal? What resources will I need for each element to accomplish my goal?

5. Determine the time, place, and emphasis for reaching your goal. You should strive to become a "satisfied customer" of your goal. Questions to ask are: What is the most conducive environment (or my options) for implementing my goal to my greatest satisfaction? How much effort am I willing to give to make my goal a reality? How will I "market" (implement) my goal?

6. Revisit and revise any of the steps as needed. Questions to ask are: Do I need to reevaluate my choices? What alternatives may be open to me if I recycle, revamp, or take another approach to the elements and steps in my plan? Is this the best plan I can develop? If not, what do I need to do to make it better?

7. Take action based on timelines and priorities. Questions to ask are: Am I moving in the right direction and at a brisk, steady pace? Have I activated my strongest

motivators to stay focused on reaching my goal for making my mission a reality? If I am close to reaching my goal, have I developed new goals to keep my momentum going?

*A SWOT analysis involves identifying your strengths, weaknesses, opportunities, and threats. It is important that you know the differences between each of these elements. Take time, if necessary, right now to sort out in your mind the differences among each of the SWOT elements. Consult the dictionary, if needed. Also, enter into an introspective discussion with other individuals as to what SWOT really means. Such discussions will help you distinguish among the SWOT elements and will help you tremendously when you put the SWOT analysis into practice (that is, when you actively begin turning your weaknesses into strengths and your threats into opportunities). You will also be able to expand your perspective of what a SWOT analysis can do for you—and discern the subtleties that lead you to a thorough and accurate analysis of yourself.

## A FOUNDATION OF CONCRETE

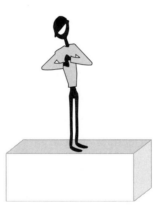

Obviously developing a motivational business plan is not a single day's activity, but it is one that needs nurturing over time. If your plan is built on a solid foundation, you will make an important investment in your future. You are also more likely to devote more time to a well thought-out plan. Thus, your initial investment is critical and you'll want to give some time (even 10 to 15 minutes) every single day to the development of your plan to assure you get it done.

A good way to be sure you'll pay some daily attention to the development of your plan is to put a note on your bathroom mirror or in some other visible place. Your note might read: "At (time of day) today, I will spend (amount of time) on my personal plan." Or set up a file for your vision, mission, and goals that you can and will access frequently. Your file should be in a prominent place (by your telephone, on a breakfast table, etc.) so you nearly stumble over it every day. That is, if your plan (or materials you need to develop it) is in a place that cannot be avoided by your frequent attention, you will be more apt to develop it quickly and keep it in focus. Your Card also can be a reminder to keep your plan activated.

A grid is provided here to assist you in developing a plan based on the previous steps. It is suggested that you make several copies of the grid before completing it so you can have easy access to a blank grid each time you identify a new goal you wish to define and evaluate. Once you have completed grids for two or more of your goals, you may want to prioritize the grids. That is, if one goal is more important and immediate than another, you can organize each of the grid goals in your file for quick access.

If you develop several goals, you may even benefit from color coding the files for your goals. A green file, for example, may remind you to be devising ways you can put aside more savings for certain goals. A red file may alert you to looking at a goal or project more frequently because of its urgency (suggestion: develop a checklist where you'll check off items to give you satisfaction—motivation—you are making progress). A yellow file may serve as your vision and mission statement file. Place your vision and mission statements (or vision/mission file) first in the sequence of your files so you can frequently review these important statements—remember, they should provide motivation for you because you are excited about them. Develop other files or reminders about the importance of both your plan and following your plan. Never lose the perspective of how important your Card is to reach your goals.

---

**Value-Added Motivator** | **MY PRIORITY GOALS**

### Critical Goals for My Personal Plan

Name _____ Date _____ Priority _____

To be accomplished from (date) _____ to (date) _____.

1. A goal I want to reach is _____
   _____
   _____

   Questions: What are my vision and mission? Is my goal aimed at achieving my vision and mission? Are my expectations realistic, yet challenging, and reachable with effort?

2. My SWOT (strengths, weaknesses, opportunities, threats) analysis pertaining to my goal, mission, or vision is:
   A. Strengths _____
   _____
   _____

   Questions: What are my strengths? How can I maximize them?
   B. Weaknesses _____
   _____
   _____

Questions: What are my weaknesses? How can I minimize them or change them into strengths?

C. Opportunities _____

_____

_____

Questions: What are my opportunities? How I can take advantage of or capitalize on them?

D. Threats _____

_____

_____

Questions: What threats or potential threats stand in my way? How can I avoid, circumvent, or challenge them to reach my goal?

3. The strategic elements and the basic steps to meet my goal are (number each one for ease of reference):

_____

_____

_____

_____

_____

_____

_____

_____

_____

_____

Questions: What are the critical elements needed to achieve my goal? What steps can I take (or motivators can I employ) to assure I will stay headed (and will make progress) in the right direction?

4. The strategic elements I should evaluate to reach my goal are (tie each to the items in number 3 for ease of reference):

_____

_____

_____

_____

_____

_____

_____

_____

_____

Questions: What are the value, need, and timing of each of the critical elements of my goal? What alternatives are available to me when challenges enter the picture? (Challenges may be factors within your control—internal; or factors outside your control—external.) What measurements can I make and what quality measures can I put in place to assess each element to assure I will be taking the right course of action toward my goal? What resources will I need for each element to accomplish my goal?

5. The time, place, and emphasis needed to reach my goal satisfactorily are:

_____

_____

_____

_____

_____

Questions: What is the most conducive environment or my options for implementing my goal to my greatest satisfaction? How much effort am I willing to give to make my goal a reality? How will I "market" (implement) my goal?

6. The elements or steps I need to revisit (or place special emphasis on) are (again, number each according to the items in number 4 for ease of reference):

_____

_____

_____

_____

_____

Questions: Do I need to reevaluate my choices? What alternatives may be open to me if I recycle, revamp, or take another approach to the elements and steps in my plan? Is this the best plan I can develop? If not, what do I need to do to make it better?

7. The action I need to take (when and how often) is:

_____

_____

_____

_____

_____

Questions: Am I moving in the right direction and at a brisk, steady pace? Have I activated my strongest motivators to stay focused on reaching my goal for making my mission a reality? If I am close to reaching my goal, have I developed new goals to keep my momentum going?

Notes and comments:

_____

_____

_____

_____

_____

_____

The success for reaching your mission via your goals depends upon your seriousness to implement the necessary steps for action. That is, if you commit to planning, organizing, evaluating, and acting on your goals, you will be successful—success, as you know, is usually attained more readily by those who work toward it. Revisiting and completing the goals grid periodically will help you stay on track. At first you may need to ask yourself if your actions contribute to your goals. If they don't, it is important to be honest with yourself and try to get back on track as soon as possible. Take out your personal Motivational ATM Card. Read the statements on the back of your Card and tell yourself how important the statements are for helping you work toward and reach your goals.

So how often should you reevaluate your goals? As often as it is necessary for you to stay motivated. As stated earlier, a starting point should be to develop your vision and mission statements and at least one long-term goal that contributes to your vision. Also, as noted earlier, it is wise to review your plan daily (at least initially), preferably at the end of the day so you can reflect on what you did to further your goal(s). By rereading the five statements on the back of your Card, you can ask yourself what you have done and need to do to spur you to action or continue momentum. An end-of-the-day review will help you determine what you need to do tomorrow (possibly to determine how components of your goal should be modified, changed, or be given more or less emphasis). Associating the five statements on your Card with what direction you will take tomorrow also will renew your commitment to move ahead.

## A MOTIVATIONAL ASSESSMENT ROUTINE

Once you find a routine for addressing your goals and implementing the plan reflecting each goal, a good rule of thumb is to review your total plan (which represents all of your goals) at the end of each month. An end-of-month review is similar to an end-of-day review: You can begin anew each month not only to meet new challenges, but also to improve on the weaknesses you experienced in the previous month. Keep in mind that for some people, a monthly reassessment may never be frequent enough. Thus, do your reassessment as often as necessary—each week or, as needed, continue it on a daily basis. Again, rely on your Card to give you the motivational push to move you on to higher levels of accomplishment.

Because the frequency of your assessment depends on how well you can stay on track, the key to your success definitely depends on how motivated you are to continue each activity toward your major goal. Only you can determine how motivated you are to continue working toward your important goals when immediate needs get in the way to sidetrack your long-term accomplishments. As you get better and better at goal setting for long-term planning, you will find it easier and easier to be focused on the important things. If you have made a strong commitment to your Card and how vital it is to the process, your success will follow in the same strength. You determine the outcome.

Before we move on to other important elements associated with your plan, consider Bret's options.

# Who's Motivated?

Bret, a cosmetics sales trainer, believes he finally has a long-term career goal (even though he had said that many times before in most of his other careers). Bret has held several jobs and made some dramatic career changes. He's been a grocery clerk, a machinist, an administrative assistant, a weight trainer, a food service supervisor, an accounting specialist, a quality control inspector, and a central receiving agent—for all types and sizes of firms over the past 10 years. Most of Bret's jobs have offered him several career paths, but he never really planned out a specific path he wanted to take. Thus, he just kept changing jobs when he saw a more interesting opportunity. Taking advantages of the opportunities was what Bret thought he had to do to develop a career. He's done quite well and has enjoyed the many jobs he's had, but he doesn't see a direction to his career. Most of his jobs have had challenging elements as well as lots of lateral and upward mobility, but he doesn't seem to really know what is in store for him and his family.

Bret believes he knows what most of his motivators are, but until now he has never before considered developing a career plan. A colleague of Bret suggested that the only way to really know what direction he wants to take, and be able to stay on track to get there, is to develop a plan. Bret thinks he wants to become his own boss—he wants to start his own consulting business in training (based on his confidence in his potential as a trainer for cosmetics sales). He believes he can reach this goal because he has experienced success in all his varied careers. He does, however, wonder if his ambition to be self-employed is a good move in providing for the future of his family (he has a wife and three children). He's not sure what he can expect to gain (or lose) from taking such a giant career leap.

1. Why do you think it is important for Bret to consider what he wants to be doing 5, 10, or 20 years from now? What resources will he need to do so?

2. If Bret wants to become self-employed, what questions should he ask himself? How should he weigh each of the questions? For example, what importance should he give to family needs and goals as well as to health and life insurance, schooling, savings, and retirement, versus his desire to become self-employed?

3. What will Bret gain (or lose) by doing a SWOT analysis?

4. Insofar as possible, apply each of the seven steps of project management to Bret's goal. Specifically, identify what questions he should ask to assure he is developing a good plan for himself. How should he evaluate the success of his plan?

5. What role do Bret's positive attitude and motivation play in helping him be successful in his quest for a new career?

If you can work with a group or at least two other people in responding to the scenario about Bret, it will be very beneficial for expanding your ideas about developing your own plan. You should come up with lots of questions Bret should ask. And, believe it or not, it will be easier for you to assess your own goals than those of Bret or others mainly because you know yourself better than you know anyone else. Thus, if you find there are many unanswered questions Bret should consider, that's good. The more questions you can ask about his situation, the more alternatives you may find will work for you. There is always more than one way to achieve a goal; there is always more than one alternative for solving a problem and meeting a challenge that lies ahead. The more consideration you give to your questions, the more you will broaden your horizons to find ways to achieve your goals.

## IS YOUR MOTIVATIONAL HORIZON WITHIN REACH?

You can now see how important it is to identify the components that provide the steps to successful, ongoing motivation. If you write out your expectations and targets, you force yourself to verbalize what is important to your own satisfaction. You then set goals (or reevaluate the ones you have already identified), plan how you will reach those goals via objectives, and focus on how to make things happen. By keeping your ATM Card healthy and prosperous throughout the process, your goals are clearly in sight. Further, if you take timely action toward your goals, your progress can be significant. Thus, the adaptation of a business plan and project management guidelines to your own life has taken on new meaning.

A word to the wise: Keep in mind that when a major goal is too much to handle as a single unit, the only way to keep moving toward your goal usually is to micro-focus on the smaller steps along the way. You may not think the small steps are important, but each one adds to another to reach the plateaus that contribute to the larger picture. While many people try to bypass the small steps of an activity, most people quickly find they cannot accomplish anything significant without paying keen attention to what seem to be small or insignificant steps. It is a major mistake for anyone who views the smaller steps as insignificant and tries to take shortcuts to the larger, more glamorous horizon. A few shortcuts may work part of the time, but they can quickly get you into trouble over the long haul and thwart your progress to keep you focused on your real mission.

## MOTIVATION BEYOND A MICROWAVE MINUTE

As just suggested, shortcuts may be good for a quick fix to an immediate challenge. However, to be truly effective for successful achievement or accomplishment (the end result as well as milestones of your personal plan, for example), each situation needs to be weighed for its overall value. If there is a price to pay in the end, a quick fix may be costly, yet in other situations, getting the job done quickly is essential to success. A motivational quick fix may be just the thing you need to get you going—to start a project, to give your attitude a boost, or to explore a new goal toward your vision.

Keep in mind that frequently a minute in a microwave can be just as valuable as an hour in an oven to achieve a quality result. That is, you need to determine what is most appropriate for what you want to accomplish. If you compare popcorn and pot roast, remember that each needs a different application. Each needs different attention and provides different rewards. However, each may contribute to a goal which, if successful, will promote further satisfaction. In a somewhat similar manner, sustained motivation is what is needed for things you consider important in your personal plan because you are aimed at long-term gratification. Along the way, short-term motivation and bursts of motivation are always good because you can frequently get the next burst of momentum from the last one. No doubt a combination of all types of motivation will be to your advantage since reaching your goal will depend upon how positive you can be while you are working toward it. And you know that you cannot overlook using all the motivators you can find to contribute to your positive attitude, because you can never be too positive.

## SEVENTY PERCENT OF THE MOTIVATIONAL ICEBERG IS BELOW THE SURFACE

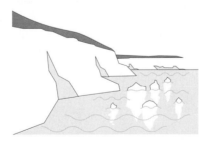

It probably goes without repeating that you should continue to identify motivators that you can use today, tomorrow, and for the longer term. It is for the longer term, as you develop and implement your personal plan, where motivators really come into play and become important. What is critical at this point is that you have a variety of strong motivators that can be applied to all aspects of your personal plan—especially because you know that most challenges, like an iceberg, come without too much warning. It is the under-the-surface challenge of which you are uncertain that may cause you to consider deviating from your plan. You know that your personal plan is a long-term endeavor, that it will take a lifetime to accomplish, and that you will need to give your best concerted efforts.

Your plan, however, can be realized if you are dedicated and motivated to stay on track. As you pursue each of your goals, there will be lots of times along the way that icebergs will appear and your motivation may wane. No doubt you'll need your Card to remind you of the ultimate reward you can attain if you don't deviate from your plan. Thus, continually look for ways that will keep you sufficiently motivated to stay focused on your vision. As you exert the effort to inject bursts of motivation along the way, you can smile to yourself because you know that sustaining those bursts of energy is what gets the job done.

## WINNING THE GOLD, SILVER, OR BRONZE

Your degree of success in life is based on what choices you make and how you meet the challenges along the way. In the long run, your attention to your own personal project management will determine the importance of developing and following a quality personal business plan aimed at realizing your expectations. If you don't start with a quality plan, you probably will be disappointed long before you arrive at your determined destination. You, too, are the only one who can evaluate how rewarding you find the journey along the way. Your positive attitude—to enjoy the journey—is truly up to you.

Also you know that you need motivation to keep you headed in the right direction. Motivation not only keeps you from becoming discouraged, it is what tells you to keep going to reach a greater reward beyond the present. Since you and you alone control your attitude and motivation, you determine what value you give to your life and your life's mission. Why not go for the gold?

## CHAPTER 10: MOTIVATIONAL REINFORCEMENT

Reinforce your understanding of the chapter by responding to the following items.

1. Discuss some of the benefits of having the right goals and motivators.

2. What is meant by "project management," and how can it help an individual?

3. What are some of the benefits of developing a personal plan?

4. Describe the differences among vision, mission, and goals.

5. What are the basic components of a strategic plan and why are they important?

6. Discuss the seven steps for developing your "motivational business plan."

7. Explain the differences and importance of the SWOT elements.

8. What are some of the questions you should answer about your motivational plan?

9. How does a commitment to your Card help you implement your "motivational business plan"?

10. Suggest what can happen if you skip small steps that contribute to your goals.

11. What is meant by and how does one attack under-the-surface challenges?

# SECTION IV

# Maximizing Strategies for Motivation

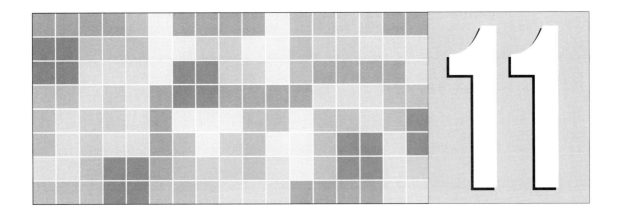

# Bullish on Success: Your Diversified Portfolio

## THE COMFORT OF SUCCESS

Have you ever thought of what your life would be like if you didn't have any challenges? If you didn't have any problems to solve? If you didn't have to think about your next move? Or if you could just relax and picture yourself on a warm sunny beach with no cares or worries? Sure, you may have wished at times for some of these things. And you've probably said to yourself you wished you didn't have to start (or finish) the day, make a hard decision, or even get out of bed some mornings. No doubt you can think of some instances where you may have been somewhat hesitant to step out and take a risk regardless of the magnitude of the issue. It is possible, too, you may have found yourself avoiding or pushing aside some challenges facing you.

Why do these things happen? Because making hard decisions and taking risks usually put you outside your comfort zone. You are uncomfortable because you are uncertain of the outcome or potential outcomes. You are not sure if the challenge is too big for you to handle at that particular time. Your confidence is a little shaky if you haven't experienced a similar situation or you may be a bit gun shy because of a past failure. The bottom line really comes down to this: You want to be successful so you hesitate because you fear making an irreversible mistake.

# MAXIMIZING YOUR STRATEGIES FOR SUCCESS

What do you think about when you are faced with a challenge, especially a risky challenge? Let's say, for example, there's a biotechnology stock that you believe you should buy. Athough the stock has been only inching its way up in price, its potential is quite exciting. You're not sure what to do, but you know you'll kick yourself if you don't add the stock to your portfolio and your hunch turns out to be right. After all, you have done a lot of homework on this stock and everything points to good profits for investors. The question confronting you is: Is your goal to minimize failure or is it to maximize success? Answer that question below and give some rationale for your answer:

_____

_____

Probably you answered the dual question with the rationale that you need to consider both sides of the issue. Obviously you are right and it is the safest way to evaluate a potential outcome. Looking at both sides—buying the stock or not buying it—helps you identify where you may be vulnerable and where you have a distinct advantage. It's a good strategy.

However, if you focused your answer on how to capitalize on assuring success, you probably looked at the more positive side of the same issue—why you should buy or why you should not buy the stock. You projected what positive outcomes are possible if you took different positive approaches. You weighed the negatives of the situation by focusing on the positives. That is, you were positive as you strategized your position.

On the other hand, you may have answered the question by stating several not-so-positive things that might have happened if you had taken the risk. By looking at the question in a negative manner, you try to find all the things that could go wrong before proceeding. Your negative approach to buying the stock (only looking at reasons not to buy the stock), probably was so compelling you would not consider the risk under any circumstances.

There are no absolute right or wrong ways to approach most situations. However, if you capitalize on a positive approach to challenges, your solutions will probably be broader in scope, more creative and innovative, farther reaching, and even more workable than if a negative approach is taken. This is not to say that the risk will be minimized, but the exploration of the factors associated with the risk will contribute to giving you a better handle on the potential outcomes associated with the risk. In actuality what you have done by looking at the problem with a positive outlook is to maximize your strategy for meeting the challenge. You have given yourself the advantage for success because you want to be successful, you think success, you plan for success, and you achieve success.

## YOUR SURGE PROTECTOR STRATEGY

Planning your strategies, with a positive attitude, for meeting challenges can be one of the greatest assets you can have for achieving success. You know that the more positive your attitude is, the better chance you have in achieving a positive outcome. In a way your positive attitude is like having a surge protector on your computer. Consider Ramie's rationale for installing a surge protector.

### Who's Motivated?

When Ramie purchased his computer, he immediately installed a surge protector. He wanted the assurance his computer was protected from an electrical power surge since he knew this could be a costly risk. He didn't anticipate having a problem, but he didn't want to have to act under adverse conditions if a power surge affected his computer at a critical time. He considered the small investment in a surge protector (with a minimal amount of time expended before the fact) well worth it. Why? Because the projects he needed to complete had tight timelines and he needed to send them electronically to his suppliers. He also considered how important it would be for him to avoid a loss of data, be able to continue working during a critical time, and not have to consider costly computer repairs if something did happen. In essence, he felt he was protecting himself against a potential crisis with a small investment while giving himself the peace of mind that he was taking a positive approach to a potentially negative result.

1. Do you believe Ramie took a positive approach regarding his purchase? Why or why not?

2. What were Ramie's advantages associated with his purchase?

3. What were Ramie's disadvantages associated with his purchase?

4. Could Ramie have taken a different approach to the situation? If so, tell why the alternative approach(es) may be positive or negative.

While there may be differing opinions as to Ramie's approach to purchasing a surge protector, he identified a potential problem area and met it head-on before having to deal with the problem at a more critical time. If you make a comparison of Ramie's scenario to applying a "surge protector" to your own life, you may be able to see a good analogy in the comparison. That is, by anticipating potential risks (which do not necessarily need to be viewed as negative) in your personal and professional life, you can avoid negative situations, and possibly disaster, if you take some precautions ahead of time. Similarly, you can also consider potential outcomes for projects. If there are potential risks that could get out of hand (and maybe become devastating to you or others), consider installing a surge protector to help you avoid a potential crisis.

As you consider the potential risks, you'll probably also consider what changes would be particularly beneficial to meet those challenges. Your creativity usually is greater when your thinking is positive (versus being creative in a negative situation). Also, by activating your creative thinking, you maximize your ability to solve future problems. Practicing this approach for meeting challenges is another strategy from which you can yield considerable benefit in both your personal and professional life. This strategy, like so many others, is also a motivator. Obviously, the more strategies you have for maximizing your motivation, the more successful you will be in motivating yourself. You can now consider your Card in yet another way for giving you motivation—it is a strategic motivator. Because your Card appreciates in value, frequent use of your Card can increase your motivational strategies. There are not many things in life that work that way!

Let's look at several other strategies for expanding the value of your Card.

## EXPLORING THE MOTIVATIONAL INTERNET

Each time you practice good habits you know those habits are reinforced. The same holds true, unfortunately, for bad habits. A strategy that should engulf nearly everything you do is to look for positive ways of doing things. While you may have read that statement by placing emphasis on "positive ways of doing things," there's not better advice anywhere. When you look for those positive ways, you are employing yet another strategy to become successful. You skew the advantages in your direction by finding resources that give you the competitive edge. You are always on alert to new ways of doing things and open to new avenues for future endeavors.

When you look for positive things, your creativity is heightened and you are more receptive to change. That is, your motivational internet is limited only by how adept you are at using it. When you seek out opportunities, you'll find them. Even if you see the door closed, look for a wee crack, an open window, or an alternative opening. Your Card should help you to stay motivated, to be so positive you don't give up. The ultimate and best strategy you can have is to stay positive while seeking out opportunities. To persevere with a vengeance is a strategy of many investors in the financial markets. Why not be just as bullish on your quests and expand your horizons in the process?

## THE SAND IN THE HOUR GLASS IS SLIPPING AWAY

Managing your time wisely as you seek out opportunities is another strategy that can be extremely beneficial to your success. Time has become so precious to most people that any strategy to save time is well worth considering. For example, technology has improved many things to help people work easier and smarter, frequently speeding up the processes to maximize efficiency and time.

Technology also has opened up so many resources to the world that most everything we need or do is readily available at our fingertips. E-commerce and e-business are the way of doing business—for nearly every type and manner of business. Faster, better, more efficiently, and less costly are commonly shared elements of e-business. Yet, most people still have considerable challenges with time. While most everyone applauds the availability of the vast resources that are at our fingertips, the increased accessibility of information has created the need for people to employ good time management strategies. Strategies for managing time are probably the most needed and wanted commodities in today's society.

Can you relate to the last time you had to sort or wade through a technology menu (maybe on the Internet or on the phone)—a menu you had to encounter before you found an answer to a question or completed a task? Do technology gadgets sometimes complicate their significance? Do you get better or expanded services with advanced technology options? Has technology actually contributed to your being able to accomplish more (or being expected to do so) in less time? Do you have added stress because time always seems to be staring you in the face? Do you take more and more shortcuts, yet rarely find that they save you effort or time?

## IT'S ONLY TIME THAT KEEPS TIME MANAGEMENT FROM WORKING

Taking shortcuts to save time may be a real paradox. That is, many shortcuts frequently end up being very costly—some in subtle ways and others on a grandiose scale. For example, significant time may be saved producing a product, yielding a savings in both time and money. But if the quality of the product is compromised, the lack of strong customer satisfaction may result in fewer products being purchased or more products being returned. Or let's say a product can be produced more cost effectively if production is slowed or shut down while waiting on less expensive, yet quality materials. But, let's say that the materials end up arriving too late for the product to be marketed before the product is needed by customers. Timing was everything. Numerous examples of diminishing returns abound—for example, consider a hurricane that is threatening beach residents. Providing the necessary supplies to hurricane victims when they need them most is an important consideration.

There are also many examples of how timing shortcuts have become time wasters. Sometimes what appears to be a time saver in the short term can actually become a significant waste of time in the long term. That is, you know that some things cannot be rushed. Others must be done immediately to be effective. The importance of time and timing to your goals depends upon how well you are able to evaluate what actions need to be taken and when. That is, your plan is more apt to proceed without major incident if you carefully identify and evaluate the elements that contribute to the intermediate milestones that are critical to the end result.

You know, too, that time and timing have become such important factors in our modern technological society that nearly everyone must be cognizant of the clock. Practicing good time management has become a necessity for nearly everyone because the time factor touches everyone's life in some form or manner. How do you manage your time? Does your time management contribute to or hinder your daily activities? Are you good at meeting deadlines? How does your timing affect those around you?

Complete the following exercise to give you an idea of how you can approach time management. If you haven't done an assessment of how you use your time, you may find you can readily improve your management of time with a few simple practices. You may be able to improve your productivity—and that in itself can be a motivator.

| **Value-Added Motivator** | **MY BACK BURNER PROJECT** |
| --- | --- |

Describe a work (or at-home) project you have been thinking about doing for some time and would like to complete, but—for whatever reason—you just haven't been able to get it started or completed:

_____

_____

Assuming you can assign a critical importance factor to this project as to your need to complete it, how would you rate the project in terms of it getting it done? That is, on a scale of 1 to 10 (1 being the most critical importance), how would you rate the critical importance of this project? Rating: ____; Why did you rate the critical importance of the project as you did?

_____

_____

If you gave your project a 1-5 critical importance rating, give at least one reason why you are not getting your project started/completed.

_____

_____

You may have indicated that the importance of the project is really based on timing—that the project needs to be done now (or at a specified time). If you did, go back and ask yourself why the project is important without considering the timing. Readjust your rating without the timing issue being considered.

Now that you've determined why the project is important, consider the timing of getting the project done. Again, using a scale of 1 to 10 (1 being the most critical timing), how would you rate the critical timing of this project? Rating: _____; What is your rationale for the rating you gave to the critical timing of this project?

_____

_____

Draw some conclusions about the critical importance and critical timing of the project you described:

_____

_____

_____

If you were to break up the project into smaller units or tasks, would you rate the importance and timing of the project higher? Why or why not?

_____

Describe how you might split the project into smaller units:

_____

_____

Identify one of the smaller tasks of the project that you believe you can complete within a specified (realistic) time frame:

_____

_____

If you can break up or segment the entire project into smaller units or tasks, list the tasks or segments to be completed:

1. _____

2. _____

3. _____

4. _____

5. _____

6. _____

Now, prioritize each of the tasks as to their importance. If the tasks must be ordered in a particular way, determine the first task that must be done and/or the one that has the highest priority. Once all tasks have been ordered, set a timeline for completing the first task you need to do. If you can realistically assign a timeline to all tasks, do it now.

Can you get to work on your first task right now? If not, why not? Do you need to reassess the reality of your project and/or each of the tasks? If so, identify the *real* reason(s) why you may not be getting the project done. Write the reason(s) here:

_____

_____

If there is even a slight hint that your interest level in the project is rather low, your lack of motivation may be standing in the way of your project. Consider what would motivate you to action if the project included some of the rewards you consider as motivators. Since it is quite possible the main reason you haven't completed the project is because you do not have the right motivators to spur you into action, set the activity aside briefly until you identify the right motivators. While setting the activity aside is a dangerous action (or inaction), do not view your present assessment or postponement at this point as a failure if *the postponement is brief.* That is, if you cannot get your project or the tasks and mini-goals started, it will be to your advantage to identify (as quickly as possible) what it will take to get you to want to do the project and tasks. The following discussion provides some of the elements that may help you to get started on the project just described (or to get started on any project for that matter).

## WEIGHING YOUR SATISFACTION

Finding the right balance of motivators can be accomplished in much the same manner as you determine how to do your work tasks. That is, you have a certain amount of work to be done. Some of it is extremely important and needs to be done immediately. Other parts of your work may be less important, but if these tasks aren't addressed immediately they may affect other more important work projects. Still other aspects of your daily routine may be so interesting you may give priority to these tasks. And, similarly, just the opposite may be true about your job: Some of your work is relatively unimportant, can wait forever, and is totally uninteresting. Here's an example of the interest component and how it can get in the way of projects and tasks that need your attention:

### Who's Motivated?

Ingrid really enjoys reading and responding to her e-mail. And she processes it several times a day. Her e-mail routine, while she does not view it as that, has become a recurring ritual. Ingrid enjoys accessing her e-mail because it is interesting and stimulating even though she is quite aware that much of it is not that important, let alone urgent. Ingrid is proud of the fact she is always on top of things (e-mail gives her an "edge"), and frequently forwards information to coworkers. The problem that most of her coworkers see that Ingrid's other work projects and tasks are being slighted. Ingrid, herself, is quite stressed because she is not accomplishing as much as her manager has asked her to do and some of her partially completed projects have had to be reassigned.

1. Do you think Ingrid sees the real problem? Why or why not?

2. Assuming Ingrid's manager is not as aware as you are of her working habits, what could you do to help both Ingrid and her manager?

3. How could Ingrid turn her e-mail into a motivator to help her get more of her other work done and possibly enjoy her e-mail even more?

4. What concrete suggestions can you offer to Ingrid?

An excellent way to complete work tasks is to maximize your work-related motivators through an assessment of critical importance and critical timing along with a third factor—your motivational interest level, or how interesting the tasks may be to you. That is, maximizing your motivators is most successful by categorizing your daily tasks as to their a) critical importance, b) critical timing, and c) motivational interest. Here's how this three-level assessment works.

| Value-Added Motivator | MY WORK TASKS |
|---|---|

Identify up to 15 specific work tasks (and other "to do" tasks as appropriate) you plan to do tomorrow (or in the next two or three days, if needed):

1. _____
2. _____
3. _____
4. _____
5. _____
6. _____
7. _____
8. _____
9. _____
10. _____
11. _____
12. _____
13. _____
14. _____
15. _____

Look at each of the tasks and determine the best way to group them into five categories (three tasks for each category is ideal; however, each category should have no less than two tasks nor more than four tasks). For example, you may group the tasks according to how similar or related they may be to each other, such as: tasks needed to complete a specific project, tasks to start your day, tasks to do prior to a meeting, tasks to complete when your office traffic is heavy (or light), or tasks that require assistance.

Now, assign a label to each of the five categories or groupings using the letters A, B, C, D, and E. (Later, if you wish, you can do this same activity for activities that represent a week, month, or other time period.) Transfer each of the tasks into the following grid cells representing the five categories. An explanation of the formulas within and below each of the category cells is provided later.

| Category A | Category B | Category C | Category D | Category E |
|---|---|---|---|---|
| 1 2 3 4 5 × _ = _ | 1 2 3 4 5 × _ = _ | 1 2 3 4 5 × _ = _ | 1 2 3 4 5 × _ = _ | 1 2 3 4 5 × _ = _ |
| __-I/T__ | __-I/T__ | __-I/T__ | __-I/T__ | __-I/T__ |

Look at the combined tasks in each of the cells representing each of the five categories. What is the importance of the combined tasks for each cell? Which cell represents the most important tasks you need to do? It may be difficult to identify a specific cell as to its importance; however, force yourself to do so. If it is helpful to you, compare two cells to determine which one is more important than another until you have determined the most important cell and so on to the least important cell. As you rank each of the combined cells (from one to five) in terms of critical importance for the combined tasks in a cell, do not consider critical timing in your ranking. That is, without considering critical timing, which cell represents the tasks that are of the highest critical importance? Circle the number 1 in the cell which represents the combined tasks with the greatest critical importance of all the cells. Then circle a 2 in the cell which represents the tasks having the next highest critical importance. Continue with 3, 4, and 5 with a 5 representing the cell with the tasks that have the least critical importance. If the critical importance of two cells is equal, force a rank order decision.

In the same way you indicated the critical importance for each of the categories, evaluate the critical timing for each of the categories. That is, identify which cell of combined tasks has the most urgency and place a 1 on the blank line after the x in that cell. Place a 2 after the x in the cell that is next in urgency; continue with 3, 4, and 5 in each of the remaining cells that represent a decreasing order of how urgent you feel it is to complete the combined category of tasks. Lastly, for each category, multiple together the two identified numbers in each cell (multiply the circled importance number by the urgency number you added). Record the resulting product for each cell after the equal sign on the line in each respective cell. Now compare the products for each of the categories.

Which category has the lowest product? Note the category with the lowest product and add an A next to -I/T on the line under each cell. The A-I/T category is the cell with combined tasks that are most critical in terms of combined importance (I) and timing (T). Label each of the other four cells with

B-I/T, C-I/T, D-I/T, and E-I/T, respectively, to indicate the next lowest product, and so on. Thus, the cell with the largest product will be labeled E-I/T. What you have done is indicated a new rank order for each of the categories. That is, the tasks in the category cell labeled A-I/T represents the combined tasks you feel are most critical for both importance/timing. The category E-I/T represents the least critical for importance/timing.

Now, draw five large boxes on a separate sheet of paper (see sample below). Transfer all of the tasks of your A-I/T, B-I/T, C-I/T, D-I/T, and E-I/T categories into their respective boxes or cells. The top cell, A-I/T, represents the grouping of tasks that you feel deserves the most critical importance/timing. The cell, E-I/T, represents the grouping of tasks that you feel deserves the least critical importance/timing.

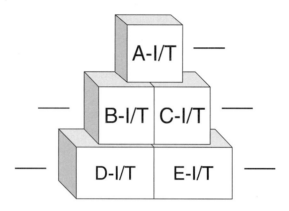

Before you draw any conclusions about this exercise, estimate the approximate amount of time out of your day it will take to complete the combined tasks in each cell. If the job cannot be completed in a day, determine the total amount of time you plan to devote to the job during any one day, for example, the time you can devote to the combined tasks tomorrow. In the sample pyramid above, note the lines associated with the outside of each category cell. On the respective cell lines, write the amount of time you can devote to the combined tasks in each category cell. If you haven't assigned the greatest amount of time to the highest critical importance/timing tasks (cell A-I/T), it is probably a very wise decision to consider doing so.

Finally, take another look at the stack of tasks. Is there a category of tasks that you believe you would enjoy doing more than another group of tasks? If so, add an asterisk to the category cell that you think you would enjoy doing the most. Continue to rank order your interest level for each category in a similar manner as you rank ordered your critical importance/timing for each cell. That is, add one asterisk, to the category which interests you the most, two asterisks, to the next most interesting, etc. Then, on the lines below, explain your rankings—doing so may not be easy, but force yourself to find explanations. That is, why did the task group represented by one asterisk interest you? Or why did the one-asterisk task grouping get a higher rating than the two-asterisk group and so on?

\* _____

\*\* _____

\*\*\* _____

\*\*\*\* _____

\*\*\*\*\* _____

Questioning yourself about what interests you and why it interests you gives you a better understanding of your motivators. Thus, look at the responses you provided. Is there some rationale, common thread, or similarity that suggests why you have more interest in some things and less in others? If so, what is it that interests you? Can you translate your answer into a similar or related interest (e.g., description of another motivator)? If you can identify a related or even more interesting activity that is not represented, but is one that motivates you to take action, write that activity on the line below. Can you use this motivator to good advantage in accomplishing some of your work tasks?

_____

If your A group of tasks (critical important/timing list) is also your top interest (one asterisk) tasks, you have a good chance of completing the tasks. However, if your A group is your lowest interest (five asterisks), you will need to work at finding motivators to raise your interest level. How can you raise your interest level? You know you must either a) find motivators to increase your interest in completing these critical important/timing tasks, or b) work on these tasks first and use your motivators as a reward for doing so.

So what does this rather complicated multifaceted exercise really mean? You, most likely, realize that when you identify a task or group of tasks that has a high importance/timing, that task or group is the one you probably should attack with speed. If the task is not interesting to you, you must call on your motivators to keep you on track. For many important and time-dependent tasks, you may need to further identify motivators that mesh or fit the various tasks. In any event, don't be shy about relying on your Card to find the motivators you need in critical times. And don't be shy—lean on your Card to spur you to action to complete these important and time-sensitive tasks.

Your Card can help you avoid procrastination if you make a strong commitment to your Card. Procrastination can be your worst enemy—to your motivation, to your positive attitude, to getting things done, and to damaging good relationships. Procrastination usually adds more stress to your life because you probably think and worry about what you really need to do (the "head game") while things continue to pile up. If you use your Card as frequently as needed to remind you of the rewards you can receive from progress or accomplishment, your Card will help you become more and more bullish on success.

## STRATEGIZING THE CHALLENGES OF PROJECT MANAGEMENT

The critical importance/timing exercise, with interest activities added, should give you a fairly clear picture of what you feel is important versus what you actually do during your day. In addition, you may have identified other insights about how you can add interest to your workday; for example, your motives or desires that activate motivators to complete the tasks you need to do. Also, you probably found several challenges in completing this exercise. It is difficult to identify specific tasks and the time it takes to complete them (categorizing is yet another matter); realizing that your time isn't your own (including meetings scheduled by others); that interruptions are inevitable; that there isn't enough time in the day to do what is expected of you; and that there is no place for your interest (fun work) activities during the day.

While it is nearly impossible to pigeonhole most of your daily activities (especially in groupings that give equal weight to importance, timing, and interest), the exercise should provide an assessment strategy along with some insights about your daily chores and tasks. Thus, in the following spaces, draw some conclusions about this exercise in relation to what you believe you should be doing during the day (and possibly why you should be doing it).

1. _____

2. _____

3. _____

4. _____

Look at your conclusions. If any of them are negative, determine how you might turn them into positives—especially positive actions. That is, can you take any action to change your workday destiny? How might you integrate your interests into your daily activities? If you can identify ways to be in more control of your own work environment, especially by adding your interest motivators, you may find your job more satisfying while you strive to reach the goals that are important to you.

Keep in mind that whenever you can prioritize your activities according to their importance and timing *and* add an interesting and enjoyable activity (motivator) at various intervals, you will get more satisfaction from working (or from whatever you are doing). As your satisfaction levels increase, you will be happier with your accomplishments and your stress levels usually will decrease. Your accomplishments will provide a degree of closure to your activities—another contributor to satisfaction and motivation. Furthermore, others around you will benefit, too, from your more positive attitude.

It is now time to go back to the previous activity, "My Back Burner Project," and determine how you can get started *now* to complete it. Probably you will need to find an interesting work activity to use as a motivator to reward yourself for embarking on the project—do it. Devise a clear, concise plan of action and get started immediately. Refer to your Card and make a commitment that you will not let your back burner project simmer—it may already be more than a little burned. Let your Card give you the confidence, desire, and drive to change and take steps to try something new. Get that back burner project completed. Consider ways you may be able to use the project as a motivator to embark on a new project that is waiting in the wings. The new project also will be more enjoyable if you have completed your albatross. As you become successful in practicing this piggyback strategy, you can maximize your motivation through a very valuable strategy.

## LIKING WHAT YOU DO AND DOING WHAT YOU LIKE

Frequently if you accomplish some small tasks, the success of accomplishment will be a motivator that will spur you on to greater satisfaction to tackle more tasks—big and small. If you prioritize your activities by their importance/timing—and add interest elements—you'll reduce your stress by avoiding delays that just happen or that may be attributed to procrastination. When you find closure and accomplishment, you will be more likely to really like what you have done. You'll get self-satisfaction (intrinsic satisfaction that is a reward for your effort). You begin to view tasks that you previously saw as boring and tedious as tasks that now are challenging and interesting. Your positive attitude is reflected in your accomplishments. Your motivation is increased. Before you know it, you are not only liking what you do, but you're also doing what you like.

When your daily activities combine both of these elements, you become a winner of your environment. You become a practitioner of motivational project management because you take control of your life and your environment. You find an all-important balance in your life because you understand what is critical and what is not. And you determine how and when to turn up your motivation. Others may view your motivation as Las Vegas-style motivation because your increased motivational effort has increased your propensity for luck. The result of your more positive outlook is that you become a master of your positive attitude and your motivation. It really doesn't make a difference if you're in a bear market or a bull market because you are bullish on your motivation! Who could possibly ask for a more satisfying reward or accomplishment?

## WHEN BANANA TREES PRODUCE FRUIT (BUT THE BANANAS DON'T RIPEN)

But . . . you also know that discouragement is inevitable, especially in a bear market. Keeping a positive outlook through discouragement means that wallowing in negativism and self-pity serves no value in your life. No one wants to be around a negative person. You may find someone who wants to help you over a slump, but staying in the doldrums of unhappiness will not yield lasting, healthy friendships (and may totally disintegrate your support system). So how do you keep a positive outlook when you expect the bananas to ripen and they don't? Basically, by staying focused on the big picture.

You know that frequently it's the small stuff that drags you down—the boss makes a snide remark or a colleague ridicules something you've worked hard to achieve. Or possibly you're rushed for time and someone is ahead of you at the copy machine. What is suggested here is not meant, in any way, to diminish the importance of these events. Nor is it meant to downplay the significance of more critical emotional events that touch your life. However, you can probably think of something negative that happened a year or two ago—something you felt was quite devastating. Today, however, you have adjusted to the hurt and may even feel quite different about the situation or event because time has healed your tender wound or started to soothe your bruised ego. You've let your positive attitude rise above the situation.

At the time of discouragement, it may seem that the sky will fall—or has fallen and pulled you under a huge barrier that is impossible to move. The barrier may be weighted in cruelty and be so crushing that you believe you cannot be rescued or, at best, will never see recovery. It may also be a barrier that is unfair. Usually, however, as time goes by, the event becomes less painful because you have the will to overcome the tragedy or what appeared to be a tragedy. Life, it is said, is what happens to you when you make plans—the roadblocks, the pitfalls, the twists and turns all take their toll. But in the overall scheme of things, you have two options: You can be negative, give up, and let the world get you down. Or you can force yourself to take a positive outlook and pull yourself up to find enjoyment in your surroundings. It's your choice.

## THE "WOULD'VE BEEN, SHOULD'VE BEEN" SYNDROME

Taking a positive outlook to life includes reflection, but not to the point of turning it into the crutch called hindsight. Hindsight, as you know, would be worth a fortune if it could somehow be turned into foresight. The truth is, the only real value of hindsight is learning from the experience to avoid future mistakes. Making mistakes will happen and can actually be good for you if you can learn something from them. Repeating the same mistakes over and over, however, can be unforgivable. This is not to say that once you've made a mistake (or even repeated it), you should avoid further action. Inaction, at best, produces nothing. Since nothing comes from nothing, it doesn't take too much reflection to evaluate the merits of inaction. If you reflect on the past for the right purpose, however, it can be useful guiding your future action. That is, the reflection should be long enough to give understanding to the present or future, but not long enough that you set up housekeeping in past events!

Living in the past is reflection that becomes continuous and sometimes obsessive. Such reflection can be detrimental to any type of action, both positive and negative. When reflection or hindsight is verbalized, it may be translated as the "would've been, should've been" syndrome. Most people who fall into this syndrome usually are not even aware that it is their own inaction (or wrong action) that needs to be changed. All too often, people refer to the would've been, should've been syndrome as action of others versus their own. The reference may be simple reflection, but it also may become serious criticism. Can you relate to some of the following would've been, should've been statements?

---

**THE PERFECT WOULD'VE BEEN AND SHOULD'VE BEEN**

**The Perfect Golf Shot:**

If the green had been cut properly, that golf shot Would've Been a ringer. My putt was so good it Should've Been a birdie—I was robbed.

**The Perfect Crepes:**

The crepes Should've Been lighter using that recipe. If the heat had been just a little higher, they Would've Been perfect.

**The Perfect Date:**

My date Should've Been a little more considerate of my feelings. If he (she) had treated me just a little better, I Would've Been a lot nicer to him (her).

**The Perfect Boss:**

My boss Should've Been more accepting of the creative ideas I used to bring to the table. That promotion really Should've Been mine based on my past record.

**The Perfect Vacation:**

Going on a vacation with relatives Should've Been lots of fun. It Would've Been if the kids hadn't wanted to sleep late every morning.

The would've been, should've been syndrome works well if everything and everyone is perfect. Perfection is something to strive for, but it is not often achieved or maintained. For example, consider how many wanna-bes and hopefuls actually make it to the Olympics. Fewer get a medal and it's a rare occasion when an athlete gets a perfect score. However, just because perfection is hard to achieve, it should not be abandoned as a goal. Neither should it become an end all to end all. Taken too literally, seeking perfection, especially if it is based on hindsight, can create a would've been, should've been syndrome.

If you feel you have the would've been, should've been syndrome, it's time to do a reality check. The place to start is by taking ownership of your own actions (and avoid taking ownership of others). If there are obstacles that stand in your way, and usually there are (real or perceived), begin to view them as potential challenges. If they become real challenges to you, you can rely on your positive attitude and the motivation of your Card to help you approach the obstacles that you will enjoy tackling.

Turning obstacles into challenges is possible by taking a proactive stature, keeping a positive attitude, and practicing a can-do approach. It is very encouraging to know that assuming a can-do posture is totally up to you. While the choice seems easy, it really isn't. But it can be easier with your Card in hand. Your Card can remind you that staying positive is absolutely necessary even though it may be extremely difficult with so much negative stimuli all around you. Keeping a bright perspective will help you prevent or diminish discouragement, and will be somewhat easier if you use your Card to help you stay focused. Your Card can also help you recognize the need for realigning your priorities and strategies if you don't appear to be making progress. If you can identify the elements and motivators that open the door to your success channel, you can keep your efforts headed in the right direction.

## YOUR PORTFOLIO OF SUCCESSES

Selecting the right motivators to get a job done in a timely manner may be one of the hardest things you will ever have to do. But having a wide range and large number of motivators at your disposal always make the process a little easier. Suc-

cess happens when you look for it. Success comes from identifying, developing, and using your motivators to help you manage your time and stay on task. You can always count on your ever-growing diversified portfolio of motivational strategies to be a value-added commodity to boost your successes.

Are you bullish on success? Of course you are! But if you aren't convinced of your success, look back at your accomplishments, big and small. Consider the motivators you've identified and used on a daily basis, especially those motivators you activated when you needed that little push to get you over a plateau. Also, think of how your commitment to your Card has contributed to your developing a diversified portfolio of motivators. When you evaluate your whole portfolio, there can be little doubt that your motivation is a significant player in the strides you've made toward being successful. Your collective accomplishments add up to one important conclusion: Your accomplishments certainly make success look easy!

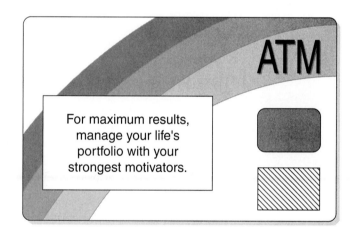

For maximum results, manage your life's portfolio with your strongest motivators.

# CHAPTER 11: MOTIVATIONAL REINFORCEMENT

Reinforce your understanding of the chapter by responding to the following items.

1. What makes a person comfortable or uncomfortable making decisions and taking risks?

2. Explain what usually happens when you take a positive approach to things.

3. Why is it advantageous to plan your strategies to meet your challenges?

4. Contrast what happens to creativity in a negative versus a positive environment.

5. When you practice good habits, what usually happens?

6. Why have time management strategies become so important to nearly everyone?

7. Contrast the critical importance factor with the critical timing factor.

8. Describe how you can categorize work tasks to manage your time.

9. Discuss procrastination and its pitfalls.

10. How does one address the small stuff that frequently drags a person down?

11. How can you turn obstacles into challenges?

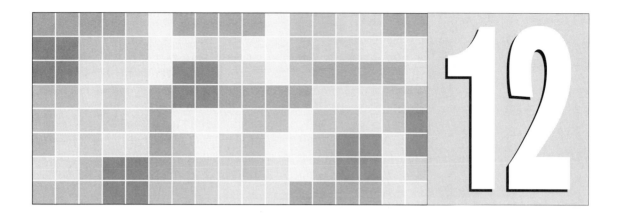

# Forever Motivated

## PUTTING IT ALL TOGETHER

So what will it take to be forever motivated? It begins with a single positive thought. It can extend forever and become continuous if you add one positive thought to another and take one positive action after another. Motivation plays a significant role in assuring that the elements and components that contribute to your well-being are maximized. By drawing on and activating your cache of motivators, you can accomplish great things; you can be successful in getting the most out of everything you do. Your goal, aimed at success, is to maintain your motivation over time and through whatever challenges come your way. Without a doubt, it is motivation, continuous and sustained, that will move you closer to your vision.

Because your personal Motivational ATM Card is the icon that represents motivation, you carry the Card and you believe in its power. The power of your Card is determined by you—power that you, and you alone, give to your Card by your use, care, and protection of your Card. In turn, it is the power or value you place on your Card that gives you the desire to be motivated and sustains the duration and intensity of your attitude). You act accordingly because you've made your Card the reminder that helps you know you must turn up your positivism when you need motivation the most—in times of discouragement, stress, mental or emotional exhaustion, or when you are physically tired. It is your Card that you rely on to give you hope and encouragement to get you through the tough situations. You know your Card is reliable because you have used your Card over and over again with satisfaction and success.

## Who's Motivated?

Wanda carries her Card with her everywhere she goes because she knows it works for her. She shares the value of her Card with everyone with whom she comes in contact. She sees a lot of people since she operates a fish, bait, tackle, rods, grocery, and boat rental general store at a popular year-round resort. Her store has actually grown to include "fishy" gifts and a coffee shop. The coffee shop has become a popular gathering place for resort guests and Wanda usually can be found there mingling with vacationers and spreading her positive attitude. The general store's reputation is evidenced by early morning customers who are frequently found waiting for the store to open. The store always closes late because people just don't want to leave. Wanda knows she and her employees are walking images of motivation—and she is delighted!

1. What makes Wanda know that her Card works for her?

2. Make a list of some of the Card's values Wanda shares with her customers.

3. What appears to make Wanda's coffee shop so popular?

4. Why is it likely that the coffee shop contributes to other business in her store?

5. Give your opinions why Wanda knows she and her employees are walking images of motivation.

Your Card, of course, should continuously remind you that your most prized possession is your positive attitude. Your positive actions are vitally important at those times when you need a boost—just a little more positivism and motivation. Your motivation, via a positive attitude, gives you the push and interest to help spur you to action when you know you must get something done. Your motivation gives you the assurance that you'll find a more satisfying outcome if you keep a positive attitude as you are faced with a negative or potentially adverse situation. Your motivation also helps you weigh a situation to determine the best course of action, even if it's to get some much-needed rest or sleep when your physical needs overshadow others. Your motivation, in essence, is the driving force (when you activate it) to put it all together.

## MOTIVATIONAL CONNECTIVITY

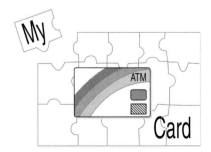

Integrating all the components of your life is not easy. But integration is easier when motivation is present. You and everyone around you have some degree of motivational desire to be successful. Motivation may or may not necessarily be ingrained in your innate abilities; but, either way, motivation is activated with practice. You have found that motivation can be learned and enhanced with practice. And as you practice it, you like the results. You expand your abilities because of your increased motivation.

It is through a desire to maximize your abilities that you want to learn more and more about yourself, to understand your personality and personal style, and to identify what motivates you. As you do, you continue to expand and enhance your abilities in an effort to become a good decision maker, be in control, and gain more confidence. You develop an exciting vision and mission that you want to follow; and you expand your vision into meaningful long- and short-term goals that focus on important things—important things you value and treasure. You employ project management to find the best alternatives for achieving your goals, and you develop a personal business plan to help you become more focused on success. You are more aware of the important/timing activities and rely on your motivators, with the use of your Card, to accomplish everyday tasks. All in all, you acquire a command of many individual and connected components associated with your environment. You expand your sphere to include other people, and you learn about their needs and desires. You are more cognizant of their individual personalities and what motivates them. You become more and more confident in your interactions with them. And, as a result, you are further motivated, which contributes to your gaining even more control of your life.

Most people need motivation every day of their life. That means most people need a wide range of motivators to draw on at various times each day. Motivators come in all shapes and sizes, and some require more effort than others. The significance of your motivators is what is important—you call on whatever motivator will meet your needs in a particular situation. Frequently motivation comes from doing simple things. Here are a few of the easiest motivators that can give you motivation seven days a week, every day of the year:

---

### MY 24/7 MOTIVATION

#### AN EVERY DAY, SEVEN-DAY-A-WEEK PLAN

Just for today, I will

- wake up happy, smile at myself, and think about having a great day.
- try hard to control my emotions or cool them quickly if they heat up.
- make my positive attitude radiate by giving a smile or kind word to someone.
- do something nice for someone or help someone who could use a helping hand.
- think positive thoughts (and quickly turn negative thoughts into positive ones).
- look for something nice about my environment.
- do something just for me that I really enjoy.

The seven motivators in "My 24/7 Motivation" are accessible to everyone, easy to practice, and powerful. Motivation happens when you make it happen, and a commitment to 24/7 motivation is a commitment to your mission. Your commitment says, "I will spend time on my mission." When you make such a commitment, you are more apt to be truly dedicated to achieve your mission. For example, if you need motivation that takes a concerted and conscious effort, you can use the 24/7 motivators to help you activate a more powerful motivator. When practiced frequently each day, these motivators will become as automatic for you as other things you do on a routine basis. They will contribute to your long-term motivation and lead you to a more rewarding life.

Motivation becomes an automatic response and an integrated part of your life as you understand what it is and what it can do for you. You practice the components of motivation by placing emphasis on the components where and when motivation is needed. When motivation becomes part of your daily regimen, it becomes so important to you that you integrate it into everything you do. That is, you maximize your motivation by creating an integrated package of the various elements related to your own motivation.

In a way, your motivation can be likened to an analog signal—it is continuous and available to you as long as you are connected to the power source. The power source controls the fluctuations and gives constancy to the signal. To be connected really means you are in control of the signal. And when you are in control of the signal, you have the desire to take on challenges. You have the confidence and commitment to move ahead.

## CLOSING ON A RECORD HIGH FOR THE DAY

Self-confidence and dedicated commitment to any endeavor will yield results. While you can't predict the future, you can experience record highs as you strive to maximize profits (successes) and minimize losses (failures). There are always plenty of challenges and risks involved in everyone's life; however, your investment in motivation will keep you headed in the right direction.

Your investment can be very lucrative if your vision, mission, and goals are focused on your business plan. Your commitment to and investment in your plan are directly proportional to the end result. There are no absolute guarantees, but you cannot help but find success if you are convinced you have developed the best plan for your life. Of course, you must do your homework so you are prepared and motivated to meet the everyday challenges. And, if you follow your plan without whimsical detours, you'll find more and more motivation leading to record highs that you never would have imagined possible.

Although you have already completed several exercises to identify your motivators, it is possible that you may have found certain motivators that help you stay focused. Powerful motivators are those that sustain you in the most critical times. And you know that powerful motivators don't necessarily need to be complicated or grandiose.

| **Value-Added Motivator** | MY MOST POWERFUL MOTIVATORS |

List below what you believe are your 10 strongest motivators that you call on most frequently. Of the 10 motivators you include in your list, try to identify at least five easy or quick motivators—ones that you can activate every day. Keep in mind, too, a motivator may be an end result. That is, if you believe you need to do something and the only way you can seem to force yourself to do it is to focus on how nice it will be to have it done, then list the end result as the motivator. You may want to refer to earlier chapters (especially to activities in Chapter 2) to review the top 20 most popular motivators and the primary motivators you have already identified.

My most powerful motivators are:

1. _____

2. _____

3. _____

4. _____

5. _____

6. _____

7. _____

8. _____

9. _____

10. _____

Carefully read over your list and determine which of the 10 motivators you could practice or call on a little (or a lot) more often than you do now. In the following space, develop a commitment statement (i.e., make a covenant to yourself) based on your motivators that will help you focus on and work at becoming forever motivated.

_____

_____

_____

_____

Keep your covenant prominently ingrained in your mind so you will strive to be the very best you can be every day—one day at a time. Because it is your commitment to yourself, it is a commitment that you and you alone can break or keep. Honor your commitment with your motivators. The ultimate power, confidence, and control to act on your commitment are in your hands.

## YOU ARE YOUR OWN (LIMITED?) LIABILITY

Your commitment, or lack thereof, to your positive attitude, motivation, and success is a choice that you make. If it is superficial and approached halfheartedly, you cannot expect more than minimal success. You cannot hope to act one way and expect an opposite return on your investment. While it may seem trite, there is considerable merit in "practicing what you preach" and in working hard to improve your luck.

Are you a liability to yourself and to others? What commitments have you made to yourself or to others? Are those commitments realistic? Are they honest? No matter what type of commitment you make to yourself or to others, it must begin with being honest. If you aren't honest, skepticism or even negativism can quickly grab your positive attitude. Skepticism can act like a vapor that permeates everything as it spreads without warning. Skepticism, which is frequently based on negativism, can have such uncanny speed and encompassing effects, it should be avoided at all costs so as not to destroy your values and goals as well as the interpersonal relationships and commitments that are important to you.

Your honesty, trust, sincerity, and integrity determine the value of your commitments—to yourself and to others. Strong, healthy commitments will, in turn, yield friendships and help build a support system that can move you toward your goals faster than you could get to them by yourself. Seeking out and surrounding yourself with people who are positive influences should be a worthy goal you value throughout life. Such a goal will bolster your confidence, contribute to your motivation, foster positive interpersonal relationships, and provide many value-added experiences for all concerned.

## CHALLENGES CAN BE FOUND IN ALL THE RIGHT PLACES

The confidence you have to take on challenges creates or stymies an atmosphere of motivation for growth. Not only is your own motivation heightened when you take an "I can" approach, but others notice your confidence and self-assurance. They see your independence and strength. If you show an interest in them (their interests, needs, ideas, and contributions), they probably will want to be associated with you. You contribute to their desire to join projects and endeavors in which you are involved. They make a commitment to a project and take action. They, similarly to you, are motivated to action.

As your positive attitude and motivation rub off on others, so to speak, you make a contribution to their lives. The extent to which others want to and actually become involved in an activity obviously is up to them; however, you have provided the impetus for them to activate their motivators. The activity levels for everyone involved will likely increase, often by manyfold. The output from the combined efforts of you and your colleagues may be so significant that the end result can be highly synergistic. That is, when all the individual efforts are combined and work together, the whole is greater than the sum of each of the individual actions.

## MOTIVATIONAL SYNERGISM

A good example of synergy is forming a cohesive group of independent thinkers and good decision makers. Individually, each has a significant contribution to make because each person offers ideas to the challenge at hand. The alternatives, however, may be expanded by group interaction due to the additional ideas that may be generated from a team approach. By pooling their team's collective thinking, the group comes up with better alternatives and makes better decisions than could be generated from the same number of individuals working independently.

Because each person on the team contributes to the thinking of others in the group, the final result generated by the team effort is enhanced. The result is better than it might have been if merely the individual efforts had been collected. Why? Because each person is more apt to think beyond the box or outside her comfort zone. One person's idea frequently triggers another person to think about the situation in a slightly different way than the original line of thought. The idea mill becomes expanded from each person adding to his own as well as others' ideas. Not only are more solutions found to meet the challenge head-on, but everyone has a stake in the decision by contributing to the effort to ensure its success.

## HARNESSING THE INDIVIDUAL SPIRIT OF THE TEAM

The individual who is confident, independent, and focused already has mastered several elements of a good motivational strategy. In addition, she can be a strong leader if she has good decision-making ability, good interpersonal and communication skills, and integrity. Good leaders solicit others to get interested in projects and activities. Good leaders empower followers and create effective teams. Leaders who can get teams to expand their synergy focus on the strengths, interests, and abilities of team members. They help individuals find ways their specific needs can be met. They help others identify and turn their weaknesses into strengths and their threats into opportunities. The goal of a good leader is to make her team successful and, insofar as possible, to capitalize on the best strategies that will benefit everyone.

To bring the team concept full circle, frequently the efforts of a team also contribute to improving the confidence and decision making of each of the individuals on the team. Generally, it is indecision and uncertainty that cause most people to doubt their abilities. When success is achieved through team spirit and enthusiasm, your individual contribution to the effort is a boost to your confidence level. Confidence contributes to your positive attitude and motivation and vice versa. You enjoy the fact you have contributed to the team's accomplishment. Your self-worth continues to move up one notch at a time with each success.

Your contribution as well as your team involvement and collaborative experience have not taken away from your independence. In fact you feel more compelled to share your ideas (greater independence) and to be a more significant contributor. You want the team to harness all its resources (especially the good thinking of each of its members) to come up with the best decision for the situation. You are motivated and confident enough to reach out for the next challenge. You give more and expect less. In turn, you receive more—your intrinsic, and possibly even extrinsic, satisfaction and rewards grow. You are good for the team and the team is good for you; everyone benefits and everyone is rewarded.

## GOOD STRATEGIES DEPEND ON GOOD IMPLEMENTATION

So now you are motivated and you are committed to staying motivated. You're no longer a bystander to motivation. You've committed yourself to being a full-time employee of motivation. You have identified and implemented multitudes of motivators to stay on target. Your mission will be reached because you have the goals to move in the right direction. There is no way you can lose because you know your strengths and you are working on improving your weaknesses.

You are already feeling the rewards of having a vision and you're progressing at a brisk pace toward your intended mission. Your return on investment is looking very good. You're confident in your strategies. Above all, you have a positive attitude. You want to share it with everyone.

## SPREADING THE MOTIVATIONAL VIRUS

Because you want others to experience the same satisfaction and rewards you get from being motivated, you look for ways to share your motivation. You know you can't really motivate anyone except yourself, but your positive attitude and motivation does show. People like to be around positive, motivated people. And you know the more positive you are, the more your motivation shows. Certainly you can influence others if you are determined to make your motivation contagious! So you go about being positive—thinking positive thoughts, doing positive things, and making positive choices.

As others see what your positive attitude and motivation do for you, in reality, you share and spread the motivational virus. You want the virus to become an epidemic because of what it does for you and what you know it can do for others. You think of the impact your motivation can have in precipitating change, and you are more determined than ever to start a motivational epidemic. As you go about sharing your motivation, you know the motivational virus offers many avenues for you and others to be forever motivated. No doubt, you want everyone to catch the motivational virus and help spread it. Consider how Richard may contribute to a motivational epidemic.

## Who's Motivated?

Richard, a day-care worker, has so many opportunities to practice his motivation it is nearly impossible for him to ever think he will lack ideas for staying positive and motivated. He really likes his job and finds new and interesting challenges each day. Sure, some of the children can, at times, wear on his patience, but Richard knows that patience is a virtue that has many rewards. He hopes to have children of his own someday and already knows how he would like to have his kids behave. He knows, too, that he has a significant influence on the kids with whom he works—and he views that as an awesome responsibility. Richard is obviously very good at what he does. The parents of many of the children in Richard's care frequently comment on his gentle, caring approach he shows. Their evaluations of Richard include such comments as "Richard's positive attitude is a real asset to helping my child develop self-control" or "Richard is a kind person who has the talent of balancing concern and compassion with respect and firmness." In fact, most everyone feels Richard's motivation is automatic because he was born a happy, positive person.

1. What makes Richard so sure he can always be positive and motivated?

2. How does Richard's view of patience contribute to his motivation?

3. What are some of the ways Richard's actions might start a motivational epidemic?

4. Discuss why Richard's attitude is more than just being born with happy, positive genes.

## SHUNNING THE EASY WAY OUT

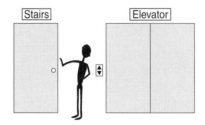

The more positive you are, the more you are motivated to positive actions. It may be easy to fall into negativism, but you're on a positive roll. You don't have time to be negative because you know negativism and the absence of motivation can contribute to a severe liability. Sure, it takes work to be motivated, and it takes effort to be positive. However, while it may be easy to be negative, you know the adventures of life are too precious to miss or to be thwarted by negativism. Your target is too important to let the easy way become your mode of operation.

As long as you keep your eye on each of the elements for implementing your plan of action, you'll be able to stay on target. So you'll focus your thoughts and emotions on positive things, but you'll be aware of pitfalls that can cause you to deviate. You'll try not to sacrifice some things at the cost of others because you know growth and prosperity require attention. You'll give consistent and regular upkeep to strengthen your weak areas because you know your future depends on it. Of course you know you can't stay totally positive all of the time, but you'll try hard to do it. If your attitude gets stepped on, you'll be determined to pick yourself up quickly and move on to avoid any permanent damage.

You're glad you have your own personal Motivational ATM Card to help you stay focused. Your Card tells you the pot of gold at the end of the rainbow is within reach and you also can enjoy the journey you've mapped out to reach it. You'll avoid the easy road and taking shortcuts because you know your luck is directly proportional to how hard you work. You'll be aware that the grass is always greener over the compost heap, so you'll be sure to nurture and broaden your skills and talents. Your Card serves as your reminder that you want something more than instant gratification. And each time you renew your commitment to your Card and what it stands for, you are reenergized to be positive and motivated to action.

## IN THE BEGINNING WAS MOTIVATION

You know that to be positive and motivated to action, you can maximize your progress with considerable effort and a wide variety of motivators. Knowing you must or need to do something, you call on the motivators that either help you achieve the action, help you focus on the end result, or get you well beyond completing the task to give you more time for more interesting activities. Your desire to be forever motivated helps you to get started meeting each of the challenges of your life. You take one day at a time, and each action you take has a beginning and an end. To be forever motivated, there must be a starting point with incremental, continuous steps that move you to a goal. In a way, the scenario may go something like this:

| MOTIVATION |
| --- |
| In the beginning was motivation. And motivation was found to be stimulating and satisfying. It was good. |
|     Motivation was found to be a part of what you saw to be essential to your well-being. And you found your well-being to be influenced by your thoughts, emotions, and actions. |
|     You found there were many ways to channel your thoughts to be positive and productive. |
|     You found your emotions to be strongly influenced by your thoughts. |
|     You found your actions to be directly linked to your thoughts. And the basis of your actions was motivation. And it was good. |

You found motivation to be contingent upon a positive attitude. And you found your positive attitude to be a dominant factor that was desired in an ideal personality.

You found your personality could be enhanced by learning about your strengths and weaknesses.

You found there were many types of personalities that made up the world of humankind.

You found humanity with a keen desire to achieve goals.

You found it highly acceptable to possess a goal-oriented value system aimed at success. And the way to achieve success was through motivation. And it was good.

You found that a positive attitude was paramount to maximizing your motivation.

You found you could reflect your positive attitude in everything you do.

You found your attitude to be your most coveted possession. And you began to value your positive attitude highly. As you did, you found your negativism being suppressed.

You found others wanting to be associated with you.

You found pleasure in being positive. And your positive attitude provided many different kinds of motivation for you.

You found your motivators were very plentiful.

You found your motivation to be a significant part of your way of life. And your motivation was maximized. And it was declared to be good.

Can you remember back when you began to focus on motivation and your positive attitude? Even if you can't, you probably have come to an important conclusion that "In the beginning was motivation . . . and motivation was found to be good."

## YOUR PORTFOLIO OF LIFE

A positive attitude coupled with motivation may be the most powerful duo of all time. It is a marriage that, when focused on a mission, makes the mission not only possible, but highly successful. As you determine the direction you will take from the decisions and choices you make, you develop patterns that predict your behavior. Can you identify some of your patterns? What do your patterns say about you? How will your future be influenced by the patterns you've already established?

As you answer these questions, you will see your life's portfolio unfolding. Your life is a work in progress. You will see how, by selecting certain things and actions over others, your likes and dislikes are quite evident. Your value system shows. If you like what you see, you can enhance your portfolio by consciously reinforcing your choices over and over again to mold them into your behavioral patterns. Alternatively, if you don't like the direction you are taking, you have the choice to change it.

You can predict your motivational horoscope by the behavior you practice. That is, do you want to be a negative or a positive person? People who think negative thoughts look for negative things. They look for the weeds rather than the flowers in the garden. They find reasons why things can't be done. They look for the stop signs. Frequently, they want people to feel sorry for them.

On the other hand, positive people look for things that are right and will always find something good in any situation. A positive person takes a compliment gracefully and responds with a sincere thank you (versus the apologetic person who finds something wrong or responds in a negative manner). While both positive and negative persons can have equally strong beliefs and values, positive people look for opportunities and challenges. Because they do, positive people can maximize motivation toward successful achievement.

Positive people can scale the face of Mount Impossible. This doesn't mean they will always see sunny skies, but they can meet hurdles of disappointment because they have a positive attitude toward expecting the unexpected. They know the consequences associated with "trespassing" and "no entry." They know the merits of being cautious through stressful and difficult situations. The positive person's portfolio is definitely one to be desired. Are you that person who is focused on reinforcing positive behaviors to maximize your motivational patterns? Are you establishing an enviable portfolio?

## MAINTAINING YOUR MOTIVATIONAL SURVIVAL KIT

Your portfolio can be a powerful tool that contributes to your motivational survival. Because motivational survival is dependent on a positive attitude, you entrench yourself in positive thoughts, gestures, and actions. You may even give hugs (figuratively or literally) to people and help others erase or minimize their mistakes. You think like a winner; you are a winner; and you help others to be winners.

The power of your motivation is unbeatable. You know it is your motivational power that makes you a survivor. And you know the more positive you are, the more your mind opens up to positive things. You also know that to maintain your motivational survival, you will continually draw from all the resources you can find. Your kit of resources has many motivators and it will continue to grow as you use your Card. As you further expand your resources, you find success all along the way. You practice the motto: "Success is thinking I am successful."

| Value-Added Motivator | MY MOTIVATIONAL PORTFOLIO |
|---|---|

Because your future success depends, to a certain degree, upon what you believe you can do, you also draw on past experiences that will give you wisdom to be successful. Some of the experiences you've had may be categorized as "lessons learned." Others may be "rewards earned" or "precious moments."

Describe some (at least four) of the experiences, especially successes you've experienced (big and small), of which you are particularly appreciative or proud. Many of your experiences are probably the result of a number of important elements, factors, events, and people—include them in your description.

1. _____

_____

2. _____

_____

3. _____

_____

4. _____

_____

Because you'll probably need more space to list and describe your experiences, start a notebook that you label, "My Motivational Portfolio." Take time to describe your experiences and write out your philosophy of success (which, by now, should include motivation). Also, include exhibits of things you treasure and other items that are important to you. Continue to add to your portfolio and frequently look at it to give you motivational rewards. Ask yourself, "What does my portfolio say about me?" As you answer that question, your portfolio should be a good reason for you to want to keep a clear focus on the goals that represent your beliefs and aspirations. Your portfolio should also help you to keep a positive attitude. It should be one more motivational element that helps point your actions, present and future, toward the successes you desire—to be forever motivated.

## A MISSION POSSIBLE

Being forever motivated is definitely a mission that is reachable. It is attainable because your positive attitude helps you follow an important dictum that says "Attitude Is What Attitude Does." You do something nice for someone because you want to and you feel good about it. You give unselfishly because you know there are greater rewards than are possible with any other alternatives. Yet you also know that you cannot help others unless you have your feet firmly grounded and your emotions under control. You know your actions must be heartfelt; you're not a robot who is devoid of emotions. You may need to turn up the volume to be a positive force, but each time you do, you know it will be easier the next time because your attitude reflects your emotions, thoughts, actions, and motivation. Thus, it's important you inspire yourself first because your positive attitude can be inspiring to others.

Continue to make recommitments to your Card. Stop and reread your Card frequently. It reads, "I, (your name), control my destiny. It is up to me to enjoy life and help others do the same. By understanding myself and learning why others do as they do, I can assist them to make the most out of their lives and, in turn, I will find more enjoyment and satisfaction for myself."

Forever motivated? A mission worth pursuing? Of course it is! What possibly could be better than being forever motivated? What possibly could be more important than offering your contribution to make the world a better place? What possibly could be more exciting than enjoying your life's journey with your Motivational ATM Card?

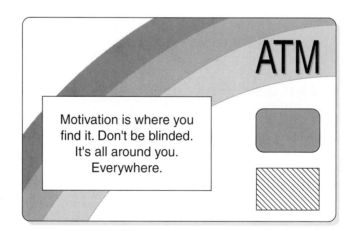

## CHAPTER 12: MOTIVATIONAL REINFORCEMENT

Reinforce your understanding of the chapter by responding to the following items.

1. Explain why a positive attitude must be the basis of being forever motivated.

2. Why can you always depend on your Card to be reliable?

3. What does practice have to do with increasing motivation?

4. Describe the 24/7 motivational plan.

5. How can motivation become automatic and continuous, similar to an analog signal?

6. Why should you continue to identify your motivators, especially the powerful ones?

7. Discuss why it is critical for you to be honest with yourself.

8. What is motivational synergism, and how does it work?

9. Discuss what is meant by "becoming a full-time employee" of motivation.

10. Suggest several ways your Card can help you stay focused.

11. What are the two elements that constitute a "marriage focused on a mission?"

12. What is meant by a positive portfolio, and how do you get one?

# Suggested Responses to "Who's Motivated?"

## CHAPTER 1

### Valerie

Making a change, especially a job or career change, is motivating to most people. When advancement and other long-term factors are taken into consideration, a strong value system can enhance personal skills and attributes. Defining the important things in life and making decisions based on those values will contribute to your lifelong learning and will give benefits to those around you. Valerie and her parents probably could benefit from talking about Valerie's long-term goals for career growth—an important element for mutual reciprocity.

### Bob

A commitment to whatever you do is important to success. Bob's apparent lack of interest in his students may be a contributing factor to his class responding in a similar manner. Enthusiasm is catching. There is good wisdom in the saying, "Be careful what you ask for because you might get it." Bob may do well in considering how reciprocity can occur if he provides the example and sets the stage for his students' successes.

## CHAPTER 2

### Jack and Charlie

What motivates one person does not necessarily motivate another. Jack's perception of what his children really enjoy may not be as broad as it could be. Charlie knows that Jack wants to please his children, yet Jack doesn't seem to be aware of how he can be fulfilled by contributing to their happiness. Once Jack begins to broaden his perspective (beyond pleasing himself), he will see the merit in pleasing his children; that is, motivation can be significantly enhanced by contributing to the happiness of others.

### Marshall

Marshall may need to be honest with himself on several fronts. What really motivates him? Is he hiding behind inaction, or does he have a choice to pursue his dream, if it really is a dream? Marshall's motivation may come from ignoring reality—there is a price to pay for not following society's rules. For him to envy something he can or cannot have should not be an excuse for inaction. Marshall would do well to take stock and find the motivators that make him happy, to identify realistic goals, and to take action toward reaching his goals.

### Jason and Peter

Satisfaction is greatest when it comes from knowing you have given your best toward achieving a goal. Although some people believe money is a strong motivator, happiness is not frequently associated with monetary rewards unless there is considerable effort and commitment to achieve whatever yielded the reward. Similarly, knowing you have contributed to a cause or outcome in which you believe can be the best motivator one can have. While competition can contribute to one's motivation, Jason and Peter may find their conversation very useful in determining their own views as well as in appreciating each other's views.

# CHAPTER 3

### Fred and Stephen

Motivation is not usually automatic. A positive attitude contributes to motivation and motivation requires effort and commitment. Individuals who are not honest with themselves may possibly get by with many things in life, but they will not truly be motivated by finding excuses for the lack of accomplishment. Motivation is not given to you; you motivate yourself. Others can help you enable your motivators, but motivation is personal. Your motivation is as strong as you want it to be and it may need many small reinforcing steps to become long term, and valued.

### Carrie

Carrie's "can-do" attitude probably is her greatest attribute. Her approach to life appears to include a balance of activities along with her high energy and interest levels. Her energy and balance are aimed at staying fit, enjoying her children, assuring her own well-being, pursuing lifelong learning, and valuing other elements that point to her strong internal or intrinsic motivation.

# CHAPTER 4

### Jose, Olivia, and Kate

It appears Jose has not taken inventory of his life and does not have a very good self-image. He appears to want to blame others rather than himself for his fate. His negative perceptions have overtaken his ability to take responsibility for his own actions. Although Olivia and Kate are helping him solve his situation, they may be able to help him further by encouraging him to improve his attitude. If he is creative and skilled, he will be more successful with a positive attitude when he looks for ways to improve himself and his future happiness.

### Mark, Peg, and Henry

Often it is all too easy to blurt out a response to a situation that is irritating rather than find ways to improve it for yourself and others. Mark's reply that he was sorry did not imply that he was wrong, but that it was unfortunate that Peg and Henry felt the way they did. Mark did not want to start an argument that all of them would regret. Paving the way to avoid conflict can be an important influence on others' behavior, and it can give you a boost. Finding the good in every situation may not be possible, but it is usually a better approach than any other alternative.

### Trish

People who are or desire to be in the limelight usually face more emotional pressures, such as being accepted, rejected, or ignored, than ordinary people. When your life is under a microscope, it may be harder to stay motivated at critical times. You may lose your focus and your positive attitude if others are critical of you. If you don't measure up to your own standards or if you have your dreams shattered or distorted, it can give you wide mood swings. When this happens, a positive attitude and finding the important things in life become critical. A strong value system with a cache of motivators will be the best arsenal to keep you going toward the values that bring you success.

# CHAPTER 5

### Trevor, Jamie

A lot of people don't know what they really want or seek things they only think they want. Sometimes people want unrealistic things or want them for the wrong reason; then, if disappointment comes, it can be a hard blow. On the other hand, wanting a reward, such as a car, is not an unrealistic goal. Working toward materialistic goals can be extremely motivational; however, one must keep a perspective that life is not totally predictable. If wanting a car overshadows everything else—as well as jeopardizes relationships or long-term success—one may need to reconsider what is important toward reaching more lasting and rewarding goals.

### Tony

Each year billions of dollars are spent in marketing efforts to encourage people to buy products and services. For many people, marketing is what it takes to get them to spend their money. For others, such as chronic shoppers, marketing can be a detriment because they have such an addiction to shopping and spending that they find themselves in financial woes—and frequently denying it. A person's ability to sort out what is essential (and what is not) or what may be a reward (and what is a burden) is a good exercise for the person who lacks balance in motivation. Taking stock of one's habits is not an easy task because we often don't see our own patterns. It may take friends and associates to provide a little help to see the out-of-balance perspective that is contributing to a person's imbalance.

### Rosa and Darla

Depending upon your idea of who has the better value system, you may discover what values are of importance to you. You may also find the values that you hold dear are not necessarily the ones you value in others. The choices you make may make you feel good, but the choices may not be acceptable to others or reflect the image you desire. Your motivation is directly related to your desire and action toward achieving your goals. If your value system is focused on success, you will strive to make others happy. You will seek out admirable traits and values, as well as pay attention to building an image that gives you motivation to meet your everyday challenges.

# CHAPTER 6

### Ulga and Geraldo

Life doesn't always turn out the way we plan it or the way our family, teachers, employers, or friends envision it. Our environment, our attitude, our motivation, and our perspectives are formed from the experiences we have (or don't have). Perceptions are not facts, but perceptions are formed every day. You perceive a situation the way you view it. You perceive a person's behavior because of your past experiences and choose whether or not you accept or reject that behavior. Others do the same about you; thus, the choices you make are based on how positive you are and how much you want to accept or reject a person or situation.

### Gary

People often form opinions about others without any type of exchange; perceptions about others are based on what you believe to be true. When you judge a situation without knowing all of the facts, the outcome can be very different than if you had a better understanding of a situation. To understand yourself better is to understand others better, too. Similarly, when you see the other person's point of view, you get a better perspective of their behavior. As you gain a better understanding of the people around you, behaviors can be explained and tolerated. If you are aware that some of your behaviors are irritating to others, try to change them. You can help others do the same. Improved interactions will undoubtedly result.

### Paul

When you cannot do something about a situation, it can be frustrating. However, if you can do something and don't, you may be hurting yourself as well as the people around you. A person's positive attitude can easily turn negative in such a situation. Usually no one benefits from a repeated story, especially if it is negative. A repeated negative event does nothing to resolve it, but may affect how others interact with you. Putting the event behind you or taking some positive action to correct it is the best way to get on with your life. Seeking to be positive and to be motivated should be one's goal for negotiating the challenges in life.

### Rita

Frequently a strong-willed person may unduly influence others to the point that they retaliate by not responding or by responding in a negative way. Heavy-handedness is not a trait that many people like, especially if a person rules on issues that could be resolved amicably with the input of a team. When others' opinions are discounted or not counted at all, people have less incentive and desire to participate. Also, being right at the expense of others will not win you any support. Your own motivation and that of others can be enhanced through an introspection of how your behavior is affecting others. Make a good assessment of what is important to you and those around you.

## CHAPTER 7

### Michelle

The real value of inner satisfaction is that it is usually a powerful motivator. An accomplishment, especially based on a job well done, is a confidence booster. Although external rewards can add to inner satisfaction, they don't usually spur you to move ahead or help you to be more creative or productive. Michelle's strong work ethic and understanding of satisfaction should result in providing rewards that she and her staff value. In turn, a stronger team effort should result. Michelle may become more creative and adventuresome in her menu and more successful in her business endeavors as long as she knows that accolades never take the place of quality, service, and excellence.

### Martin and Candice

Martin may have been robbed of an extrinsic honor, but it appears he has not let it stand in the way of being successful. If he knows he has given his best and continues to strive for excellence with a positive attitude, he will have won the ultimate prize. On the other hand, if he lets negative feelings get in the way, he may diminish his talent and actually defeat himself by his nonproductive thinking and actions. Most everyone has hoped for some reward that didn't materialize, but sulking over it will not make it or the future better. Martin should be thrilled by Candice's unsolicited gestures; they attest to his contributions and stature in his field.

# CHAPTER 8

### Alicia

Fortunately Alicia saw the value of a positive attitude and how it could be used to her benefit. She also was able to see that it takes effort to change. Although many things in life are not predictable, success is not something that happens without nurturing. Alicia's determination to better herself brought her rewards. Her "luck" was based on hard work to channel her energies into positive things. She, no doubt, has had many (and will have more) challenges in her lifetime, but it appears she knows she is on the right track because her positive personality change and newfound ambitions are working to her benefit. They are motivators that have become critical to her well-being.

### Lijun

Frequently, change requires facing the unknown. It may not be comfortable, but Lijun's positive attitude may be her greatest asset in capitalizing on the challenges that lay ahead. She may not know what the future holds, but she is looking for the positive side of things. Although Lijun may be sad for good reason, she had an enjoyable family visit and is determined not to let her sadness turn into negative emotions and actions. She has accomplished much and has a bright future. She will be open to change and convey her positive attitude—her season's greetings. Because people like to be around positive people, her new friends and associates probably will admire her and try to emulate the way she shares the true meaning of life.

# CHAPTER 9

### Kylie

Kylie's education, ambition, energy, and positive attitude are all in her favor. Also her success with diverse teams will be an asset for managing, but she will probably face many challenges. She may be at a disadvantage by not having formal managerial training and experience. In addition, being a female in a traditionally male-dominated field may present obstacles. Of all the challenges she may encounter, she feels she can meet them head-on with her positive attitude and confidence in her abilities. She, no doubt, will find ways to turn her weaknesses into strengths. Because she is goal oriented, is focused, and does realistic self-analysis, she will find solutions that work for her and for the good of others.

### Glen

Glen has a healthy mix of all the styles, with great ability to work with people and achieve positive outcomes. He is keenly aware of his own motivators, attributes, and capabilities. Because he understands how his strong and weak characteristics affect his ability to work with others, he is very attuned to the needs and styles of others. He focuses on what works, takes positive action to encourage maximum results, and practices what he preaches. Glen's positive attitude is an underlying factor why people want to be around him as well as to please him. Glen's motivation is fueled by others' accomplishments. He takes genuine pride in promoting and encouraging others to do their best and, as growth milestones are reached, he enjoys inner satisfaction.

# CHAPTER 10

### Lydia and Bradley

It is difficult for Lydia and Bradley to see each other's point of view because they are focused on their own needs, desires, and perspectives of happiness. It is possible they might be able to identify together why they don't see eye to eye, but it may be better for each of them to develop individual personal plans. (Refer to the text for elements and steps most businesses find important for project management and the development of strategic business plans.) If, however, Lydia and Bradley honestly discuss their views in light of what they want from life; what motivates them; and what their likes, dislikes, strengths, and weaknesses are, they may be able to develop a shared personal plan so they can work toward a common goal.

### Bret

Bret is in need of a reality check, even though he has been quite successful in the many careers he has pursued. His family deserves more than Bret's "belief" that he can be successful in yet another career. Bret would do himself and his family a favor by doing a SWOT analysis to identify and assess his goals (and include his family or others in evaluating his assessment). He needs to know what motivates him and which motivators are best for the situations he finds himself facing. Thus, if Bret can identify his expectations and goals, he will be more apt to reach them than if he just took a shotgun approach to a career.

# CHAPTER 11

### Ramie

To identify an outcome or result that can help you find a solution to prevent going awry is a healthy thing to do. Most people would agree that Ramie did the logical thing in buying a surge protector. His very small investment was a fairly easy decision considering how costly it could be for him to experience a potential loss of information at a critical time. Risks, however, give meaning and interest to life; risks prompt change and innovation. Although most risks do not have simple remedies for predicting outcomes, planning for risks is important. The person with a positive attitude, strong motivators, and multiple strategies for addressing risks and unanticipated challenges, of course, has the best chance of being successful.

### Ingrid

Offering suggestions to Ingrid's problem may be relatively easy, but to be helpful to Ingrid, she first must be able to see that she has a problem. Ingrid probably doesn't believe a real problem exists because she has turned her e-mail into her most important work task—a task that comes before other more critical projects her coworkers and supervisors have identified. Ingrid could benefit from identifying her work tasks and determining how important and critical each one is. She may find her priorities are somewhat skewed in terms of her job responsibilities. Her e-mail, however, could become an important motivator to reward herself for taking care of some of her other more important and critical work tasks.

# CHAPTER 12

### Wanda

Wanda has made her positive attitude her most important asset in developing her business and in conducting her everyday life. Her positive attitude and all the characteristics associated with it are her most prized possessions. Her customers want to be around her because she is motivated, vibrant, and enjoys what she does. She makes each one of them feel special and has built a good business on her good value system, which is based on her positive attitude. Although opinions will vary, there is no substitute for the motivators that contribute to a positive attitude. More than likely, Wanda is always finding new motivators that keep her attitude positive and rejuvenated.

### Richard

Richard's job appears easy, but it isn't. His success is not by accident. Richard devotes energy, enthusiasm, and positive creativity to his job—a job he loves because the rewards are so great! Richard is always looking for new ways to enrich the lives of the children in his care. His patience with the children and parents enhances what he does and contributes to his motivation as well as to those around him. The voluntary involvement Richard gets from children and their parents creates a caring, happy environment that extends well beyond the day-care center. Richard may have the propensity to be kind and happy, but, like everyone else, he chooses to be positive and works at it every day.

# Index